The Price of Fish

A New Approach to
Wicked Economics
and Better Decisions

Michael Mainelli
& Ian Harris

nb

NICHOLAS BREALEY
PUBLISHING

London · Boston

First published by
Nicholas Brealey Publishing in 2011

3–5 Spafield Street
Clerkenwell, London
EC1R 4QB, UK
Tel: +44 (0)20 7239 0360
Fax: +44 (0)20 7239 0370

20 Park Plaza, Suite 1115a
Boston
MA 02116, USA
Tel: (888) BREALEY
Fax: (617) 523 3708

www.nicholasbrealey.com
www.priceoffish.info

ISBN 978-1-85788-571-2

Library of Congress Cataloging-in-Publication Data

Mainelli, Michael.
  The price of fish / [Michael Mainelli, Ian Harris].
    p. cm.
  Includes bibliographical references and index.
  ISBN 978-1-85788-571-2
  1. Economics. 2. Commerce--Social aspects. 3. Fishery products--Case
studies. I. Harris, Ian, 1962- II. Title.
  HB171.M319 2011
  381--dc23

                                                        2011022262

British Library Cataloguing in Publication Data
A catalogue record for this book is available from the
British Library.

Origami koi created and photographed by Won Park.
Illustrations by Jacob Blandy.

FSC
Mixed Sources
Product group from well-managed
forests and other controlled sources

Cert no. SGS - COC - 2061
www.fsc.org
© 1996 Forest Stewardship Council

Printed in the UK by Clays Ltd, St Ives plc

CONTENTS

ABOUT THE AUTHORS

Both of us have spent large chunks of our working lives trying to help people make better long-term decisions. In Michael's case, that working life has often involved scientific innovation. After aerospace research, Michael conceived and produced the first complete digital map of the world, Mundocart, the "Google Earth" of the 1980s. Michael then moved into finance, becoming a partner at an accountancy firm running global projects, where he met Ian. After studying law and economics, Ian had qualified as an accountant and worked with numerous clients, but found himself drawn to the problems of long-term thinking in charities and other nongovernmental organizations.

We have worked together for over 20 years in the City of London, one of the world's leading global financial centers, with financial, technological, governmental, social, and commercial clients. In 1994 we founded the commercial think tank Z/Yen, in order to promote societal advance through better finance and technology.

Among many projects at Z/Yen, Michael has served as Corporate Development Director of Europe's largest R&D organization (the UK Ministry of Defence's Defence Evaluation and Research Agency, DERA), created the Global Financial Centres Index, and built award-winning statistical systems. Meanwhile, Ian helped to conceive and launch the ground-breaking joint venture Charityshare, guided the Marine Stewardship Council toward a Best Practice award for strategic planning and governance, and became Chair of BCS The Chartered Institute for IT's Ethics Group.

We tend to work with organizations that need to make commercial choices in complex circumstances. Such is commerce in the real world, yet rarely could we find a book for staff or friends that provided a foundation or guide to analyzing and making choices in line with our experiences. In 2005 Michael became Professor of Commerce at Gresham College, which has provided free lectures in the City of London since 1597 and founded the Royal Society. Michael calls Gresham College a "Tudor Open University." His lecture theme was "Society's Commercial Choice—Risks and Rewards of Markets." Naturally, Michael borrowed heavily from Ian's work (as well as his own), so we both recognized the potential to turn the lecture series into a book that explains how we feel the world really works.

This story doesn't end here. Z/Yen's work with Gresham College and others has led to several new initiatives. Perhaps the most relevant initiative for readers of this book is long finance, where our community explores the vital question: When would we know our financial system is working?

1 | MAKING SENSE OF THE WAY
THE WORLD REALLY WORKS

There is an old financial markets story about fish trading. Back in the early 1900s, on rumors that sardines had disappeared from their traditional waters in Monterey, California, commodity traders started to bid up the price of tinned sardines. A vibrant market ensued and the price of a tin of sardines soared—a classic bubble. This fervent trading went on for some time. One day, after some particularly successful trading, a trader chose to treat himself to an expensive snack: he actually opened a tin and ate some of the sardines he'd been exchanging. They tasted awful and made him feel ill, so the buyer called the seller and told him the sardines were no good. For the buyer's enlightenment, the seller explained, "You don't understand. Those are not eating sardines, they are trading sardines."[1]

Ultimately, sardines off California were fished out by the 1950s.

What this story demonstrates is that we don't really know the price of fish. Had we really known the price of fish over space and time, we wouldn't have overfished the North Sea, the Grand Banks of Newfoundland, and other fishing stocks, including Monterey's. Society still lacks a complete set of tools, or conceptual frameworks, that let us understand what is happening in the supply and demand for fish, the wider politics of fishing communities, and the even wider global market pressures on fishing industries. In our experience, economics alone is not sufficient for this purpose. Humanity needs a collection of ideas beyond economics—in essence, theories about how the world really works, to help us make better long-term decisions.

Wicked problems is a phrase popularized in the 1970s by Horst Rittel and Melvin Webber,[2] and we could use it to describe overfishing. Wicked problems are not the comparatively tame problems most decision theorists love, for example chess, game theory, or puzzle solving. The real world is messy, circular, and aggressive. Wheels within wheels lead to bigger messes and unintended consequences. According to Laurence J Peter of *The Peter Principle* fame, "Some problems are so complex that you have to be highly intelligent and well informed just to be undecided about them."

Wicked problems involve what we call "real commerce." The term commerce is often applied to simple money or transactional exchanges—buying and selling—but commerce actually means much more. *Real commerce* is what people do with each other every day. It includes the complex ways in which individuals, organizations, and societies communicate and deal with one another; and the ways in which complex interactions adapt and change over time. Real commerce drives society, politics, the economy, and our future. To bait the hook, real commerce, indeed the aim of this book, is about making sense of the way the world really works. Or, to rephrase our goal, what do people need to know in order to know everything that has to do with the price of fish?

THE FOUR STREAMS

While there is as yet no grand unified theory of commerce, and may never be, we can still embark on a journey to explore the tools and ideas that can help us make better decisions about how to live successfully with each other on a shrinking planet. This book's journey covers four basic areas of knowledge, or *four streams*, that we believe need to be included and integrated:

- *Choice*: understanding how people develop knowledge and biases and how these perceptions affect behavior. We explore decision-making theories, the perils of too much choice, and how real-world observations of choice often differ from theory. Normative aspects of choice such as fairness, trust, and ethics feature in this stream.
- *Economics*: pondering existing models of exchange between people and expanding the debate about the role of government and social institutions. We discuss the ways in which taxation can affect markets and consider whether network economics is new economics.
- *Systems*: in the world of commercial and political economics, systems thinking encourages us to break down complex systems into subsystems with interlinked information loops of feedforward and feedback. We consider the roles of chance and imperfect information to understand why markets misbehave. Ideas such as volatility, liquidity, commercial diversity, fads, and fashions feature in this stream.
- *Evolution*: in particular, innovation and competitive selection. This stream highlights problems that are extremely difficult to solve, such as climate change and economic sustainability.

In combination, the four streams of knowledge can improve both understanding and decision making.

We can examine the sardine story from the point of view of any one of the four streams:

- *Choice*: the behavior of sardine buyers, sellers, and traders.
- *Economics*: supply and demand for tinned sardines.
- *Systems*: for fishing, canning, distributing, trading, consuming, and not-nurturing-too-well sardines.
- *Evolution*: the competitive evolution of commodity trading in sardines.

Despite its simplicity, we miss the essence of the sardine story unless we think about the richness of all four streams. The traders had lost sight of the very nature of the commodity they were trading. Trading sardines had become a game. Real sardines only have intrinsic value if they are eating sardines. Real commerce in sardines has little place for trading sardines. Isolated views of money or economics can thus hinder the process of making good decisions over time. Moreover, scientists find that the natural cycles of sardines and the California current form such a complex system that overfishing may have been the primary, but not the sole (sic), cause for the disappearances of fish.

As another example, we worked with the Marine Stewardship Council (MSC) in its formative years. The MSC was established in 1996 through a joint initiative by the environmental group WWF and the consumer products multinational Unilever. They sought to find ways of creating real economic incentives for the improved management of fish resources. The result was an environmental standard and independent certification program for sustainable fishing and seafood traceability. Products from compliant fisheries can display the MSC label and consumers can choose to obtain their fish from certified sustainable sources. Indeed, environmental, ethical, and social standards such as the MSC have become highly influential in large segments of the world economy, including forestry, agriculture, and domestic appliances, as well as fisheries. Consumer choice is not the only form of choice involved. If such standards programs are to succeed, decision makers within the industry must choose to participate. In the early days of the MSC it seemed easier to encourage consumers to choose sustainable fish than it was to encourage fisheries to participate.

In 2000 the MSC asked us to help it grapple with the question: Is it possible to prove the value of certification to the fisheries, who ultimately have to pay for the certification process and meet the cost of implementing any changes required in order to become certified? We examined the potential financial impact of the reduced volatility in stocks that might arise from sustainable fisheries practice, in order to prove the financial case for industry participation in the scheme. Apart from learning more about Alaskan salmon than we expect you want to know, our study did prove that there should be substantial economic benefit through price stability when fisheries engage in sustainable fishing practices, regardless of any additional benefit that might accrue through consumer choice. That substantial benefit should more than outweigh the costs of certification. Subsequently, MSC standards have increasingly been deployed in major fisheries worldwide. Much of the fishing industry has evolved to adopt the standards.

This example illustrates how the four streams of choice, economics, systems, and evolution are intertwined. The MSC harnessed the power of consumer choice for positive change. Economics, both practical and theoretical, helped with decisions on costing, pricing, and calculating value. The fishing system was improved by distinguishing eating fish from exploited fish. Finally, the entire standards system was designed to evolve, using competition to improve specifications and certification firms, as well as to have fishermen keep each other in check. Depletion of the world's fish stocks remains a wicked problem. Wicked problems do not have right or wrong answers, but you can make better or worse decisions toward solving those problems.

A POTTED HISTORY OF THE PRICE OF FISH

Back in the mists of time, life (and language) was quite plain for most people. We mostly foraged, caught, or tended our own produce for our immediate needs. There was some exchange, mainly in the form of gifts within a local community and perhaps some barter with outsiders. Then we realized that our surplus of a good could be traded for other people's surpluses of different goods, or used as credit in a future shortage. Formal exchange, such as regular market meetings, may have begun just over 5,000 years ago. Economies underpinned by legal and political systems emerged in the Middle East around 1,000 years after that and soon the world became more complex. We increasingly sought to store wealth over time as well as transact, and exchange really kicked off when the Lydians invented coinage around 600 BC. Diverse financial instruments emerged, both for exchange and for storing value, including derivative financial products similar to today's.

Societies also adopted more complex forms of markets, organization, and control. City states and nation states emerged. Today, economic activity takes place over increasing amounts of space, both international and global. Consider the relative poverty of the developing world or the complex chains by which we often satisfy apparently frivolous desires. Increasing activity also has a huge and disparate impact over time—there are looming disasters in the environment, from climate change to overfishing, or funding pensions and healthcare.

The actual price of fish has, similarly, become more complex since ancient times. Until relatively recently, almost all edible fish was either caught and eaten domestically or traded in a local market. Ancient preservation techniques—drying, smoking, and salting fish—allowed slightly more protracted trading. Seaside towns have, of course, had fish markets for thousands of years, but by Roman times people were extensively trading everything across the empire from oysters to garum (fermented fish sauce seems to emerge in all great piscine markets). The advent of canning, freezing, and refrigeration in the nineteenth and twentieth centuries accelerated and widened fish trading enormously. Today, global fish prices represent the hopes and dreams of fishermen, their families, marine rescue services, lighthouse-keepers, trawlermen, cannery owners, freezing facilities, transportation firms, food companies, retailers, restaurants, and consumers.

The price of fish both affects and is affected by all of these people. A tin of tuna from the Pacific Ocean might at first glance seem to be a simple sandwich filling, but it is also an economic marvel, delivered across half the world through a complex supply chain involving many thousands of people. At Billingsgate fish market in London, we might buy fresh fish from a local supplier as near as Dover or perhaps frozen fish from a global seller as far away as Chile. Fish constitutes the main source of protein for over one billion people, a sixth of the world's population. It is regarded as one of the great traded commodities and constitutes a significant chunk of global commerce, estimated at a few hundred billion dollars per annum.

However, fishing is not a real commerce success story. Overfishing has depleted many important fish stocks to dangerously low levels. More than half the world's fish stocks are over-exploited and the demise of most fisheries is predicted by the middle of the twenty-first century. The sudden and unexpected collapse of cod stocks in the Canadian Grand Banks of Newfoundland in 1992 was one high-profile example of a phenomenon many experts on overfishing had been warning about for some years. Some 40,000 jobs were lost and the fisheries remain closed at the time of writing, with attempts to help rebuild stocks so far unsuccessful. Much like the sardine story, all four streams of knowledge are involved, but no single one of the four streams completely explains the collapse.

Choice alone cannot explain why politicians and fishermen failed, in the face of many years' evidence of stock depletion, to make difficult but necessary choices that should have staved off the collapse. Classical economics alone would say that as the price of cod rises due to expectations of depleted stocks, fewer people would buy cod at those higher prices, less cod would be fished for some time, and cod stocks would rise again. Systems thinking has yet to produce a model that can explain why the cod stocks on the Grand Banks of Newfoundland collapsed, possibly irrecoverably, nor can systems predict with reasonable certainty what needs to be done to prevent similar collapses elsewhere. And evolution alone cannot explain why the Newfoundland cod supply chain failed to evolve toward a stable and sustainable state.

WHAT'S IN IT FOR YOU?

The diverse topics covered in this book affect everyone profoundly, as individuals, as organizations, and as a society. It is all too easy to fall into the traps of the Monterey sardine traders or the Newfoundland fisheries—to lose sight of the real purpose of commerce. When focusing on the individual topics in isolation, it can be hard to get a detailed grip on the big picture. In this book we've tried to explore the many topics of real commerce as we go along and to get those topics to flow together by the end.

The commercial and financial world is replete with wicked problems of sustainability or long-term viability, from natural resource destruction to pollution to poor infrastructure to financial crises. Creating stable, enduring value has consistently been elusive. We believe that understanding and integrating the four streams of real commerce can enable better understanding of these vital matters, and therefore better decision making. If a grand unified theory of commerce ever does emerge, we are confident that these four streams will feature strongly within it.

STREAM A | Choice

2 | HOW DECISIONS GET MADE WHEN YOU HAVE TOO MUCH CHOICE

We start our journey down the four streams of knowledge by thinking about how we can make better decisions, as individuals and as groups. People like to think that they are rational, but you have to look well beyond economic rationality to explain many of the decisions people make. Does modern society sometimes present us with too much choice and is that choice sometimes merely pseudo-choice rather than genuine choice? Procurement processes for businesses and governments can easily become "tender traps," so that it is difficult to make wise choices. This chapter describes these phenomena and explains how decisions get made in our choice-laden world.

Consider the following two scenarios, each requiring a choice between two possible decisions.

Scenario One: A large coastal fishery with three fish-processing factories has recently been hit with a number of commercial setbacks and should cut back its workforce drastically. The finance director has developed two alternative rescue plans:

- Plan A: Certainly saves one factory and 200 staff.
- Plan B: Has a one-third probability of saving all three factories and all 600 jobs, but a two-thirds probability of saving no factories and no jobs.

Would you implement Plan A or Plan B?

Now try a slightly different scenario.

Scenario Two: A large coastal fishery with three fish-processing factories has recently been hit with a number of commercial setbacks, but may be able to rescue matters. The finance director has developed two alternative rescue plans:

- Plan Y: Certainly loses two factories and sheds 400 staff.
- Plan Z: Has a two-thirds probability of losing all three factories and all 600 jobs, but a one-third probability of losing no factories and no jobs.

Would you implement Plan Y or Plan Z?

Most people (more than 80 percent in experiments) would decide to implement Plan A in Scenario One and Plan Z in Scenario Two. We are risk avoiding when we feel that we are ahead, risk seeking when we feel that we are behind. Plans A/Y and B/Z are identical in expected outcomes, but people tend to favor one or the other depending on the wording.

RATIONAL DECISION MAKING

Examining the differences between actual decisions and ideal decisions is one of the hottest areas in economics. The fact that we have freedom of choice leads to the capability for irrationality, the ability to make inconsistent decisions. In our view, understanding of these behavioral aspects of economic decision making underpins real commerce.

Thinking about economic rationality is a good place to begin to understand how irrational the idea of economic rationality really is. Rational decision making is a model that assumes that decision makers define the problem, identify and weigh criteria according to their preferences, know and assess all relevant alternatives, and accurately calculate and choose the alternative with the highest perceived value. While many problem-solving systems eschew the notion of a best solution, decision theorists can be dogmatic about the definition of a rational choice. "By the logical law of contradiction, reasoning processes based on the same evidence that reach contradictory conclusions are irrational," say Hastie and Dawes in *Rational Choice in an Uncertain World*.[1] For example, scenario planning exercises may use the same evidence to reach contradictory conclusions, so it is unlikely that strategic planning systems would qualify as rational under a strict application of the definition of rational choice.

The Nobel laureate Herbert Simon moved most economists toward the idea of *bounded rationality* in his prize-winning work in the late 1950s.[2] Bounded rationality takes into account the limitations of both knowledge and cognitive capacity. It forces us to look at actual decision making and to relax one or more assumptions of standard expected utility theory. Decision makers tend to lack some of the essential information that is required to define problems, weigh up all the criteria, and choose the optimal solution. Even when a plethora of information is available, most decision makers cannot retain and/or calculate optima from all that information. Economists, and other social scientists with an interest in decision making, have found that the difference between the rational model (how decisions ought to be made) and the real world (what decisions are made in practice) is so significant that their rational models can be of little use. Increasingly, they are trying to take into account empirical work on decision making in the real world.

Nevertheless, standard economic teaching still promotes rationality: we are expected to make decisions based on their expected utility and with all the information to hand. To quote 1992 Nobel prize winner Gary Becker, "[a]ll human behavior can be viewed as involving participants who maximize their utility from a stable set of preferences and accumulate an optimal amount of information and other inputs in a variety of markets."[3]

In short, decision making can be studied from two contrasting perspectives:

- 🐟 A prescriptive perspective, following Becker and many others, prescribing models for optimal decision making.
- 🐟 A descriptive perspective, following Simon and others, looking at the ways in which decisions are actually made and trying to understand why they are made that way.

Although we see merit and value in both, the next few sections are primarily concerned with the descriptive perspective.

HEURISTICS, BIASES, AND PROSPECT THEORY

Daniel Kahneman and the late Amos Tversky undertook seminal work in the 1960s and 1970s looking at the relationships between psychology and economics. Their prospect theory attempts to describe why individuals make decisions that deviate from rational decision making.[4] Where Herbert Simon had explained *why* we bound our rationality, Kahneman and Tversky examined *how* we do so. To cope with the constraints of limited information, time, effort, and processing ability, we simplify our decision-making strategies by applying "rules of thumb." Of course, you don't win Nobel prizes for theories about rules of thumb, so Kahneman and Tversky described these strategies as *heuristics*. Heuristics are not bad things: if you cannot assimilate and use all the information available to you, you need to deploy heuristics in order to make decisions. The problem is that people tend to make certain systematic errors when deploying heuristics. Kahneman and Tversky described these errors as *biases*.

We use various heuristics to help make decisions, some very specific to the decisions required for our jobs or other activities.

Max Bazerman, in his book *Judgment in Managerial Decision Making*,[5] helpfully reduces the heuristics for prospect theory down to three generic ones:

- *Availability heuristic*: we normally use examples that are readily available in our memories to assess the likelihood and/or potential causes of an uncertain event. However, our memories tend to retain evocative examples more readily than bland examples, and to make those evocative examples available when we are making decisions, regardless of how frequently they occur and/or their direct applicability to the uncertain event about which the decision is being made. In today's information-overload society, this heuristic can be useful and can often help us reach valid decisions. However, it often leads to overestimating the likelihood of a high-profile risk, such as a plane crash, while underestimating the likelihood of a less dramatic risk, such as a car crash. We tend to bias our thinking toward information that is more easily recalled and/or retrieved. We also tend to overestimate the probability of multiple events coinciding if we can identify with examples of such coincidences.
- *Representativeness heuristic*: we tend to categorize and assess factors (such as the potential impact and likelihood of an event occurring) by stereotyping such new factors in terms of previous, seemingly similar occurrences. This heuristic can lead to discriminatory practices, for example when deployed for an organization's recruitment decision making. People seem keen to rely on heuristics of this kind in all sorts of decision-making situations, even sometimes when more useful information is available. We tend to bias judgment toward descriptive information, even if it is not directly relevant. We also tend to expect an appearance of randomness even when that is not a logical expectation, and conversely can ignore

the fact that extreme events tend to regress to the mean in subsequent instances.

- *Anchoring and adjustment heuristic*: we often start assessments using an initial value, frequently a historical value, and adjust from that anchoring value to reach a decision value. A common example in business is to determine budgets by taking the current year's budget and adjusting by a percentage to determine next year's. Anchoring can be observed in a variety of situations (domestic and organizational), yet rarely leads to optimal decisions. Biases arise because the anchor is inappropriate and/or the adjustments from the anchor are inadequate for the purpose. We also tend to be overconfident in our ability to estimate.

Several other biases arising from these heuristics will emerge in this and the next two chapters. A couple of other biases are worth highlighting at this stage. First, we tend to bias searches for information in favor of information that will confirm our views rather than information that might challenge our views. Karl Popper believed that scientific progress depends on seeking information that falsifies or contradicts our hypotheses. We also, with the benefit of hindsight, tend to overestimate the extent to which we would have predicted an outcome correctly, while also tending to ignore the fact that we might possess information that others do not have when trying to predict the behavior of those others.

Tversky and Kahneman sought to explain how "people underweight outcomes that are merely probable in comparison with outcomes that are obtained with certainty. This tendency, called the certainty effect, contributes to risk aversion in choices involving sure gains and to risk seeking in choices involving sure losses... Overweighting of low probabilities may contribute to the attractiveness of both insurance and gambling." The concept of "framing" is crucial to these ideas: on average, we prefer risk when we feel "behind" and prefer safety when we feel "ahead." The way we frame the question has a significant impact on the decision maker's propensity to prefer riskier or less risky decisions.

In relation to framing, prospect theory proposes the following:

- We evaluate rewards and losses relative to a neutral reference point—if we change the frame of the reference point, our decisions might change.
- We adopt risk-averse behavior concerning gains—we value initial gains more than subsequent gains.
- We adopt risk-seeking behavior over losses—we forgo higher degrees of certainty over loss to seek choices that reduce the loss more markedly.
- Our response to loss is greater than our response to gain— the pain associated with losing £100 is greater than the pleasure of winning £100.
- We tend to give too much emphasis to low-probability events—we overweight low-probability events while underweighting medium- and high-probability events.

Framing affects many decisions. Think back to the fish-processing example at the beginning of the chapter. You might well have realized that both scenarios are effectively the same and that both sets of decisions are equal in terms of expected value. If so, you will have consistently chosen A/Y or B/Z. However, if you're the finance director, it might not feel that way. You might be willing to take that one-third chance just to have the opportunity to avoid making anyone redundant. You might want to say that you exhausted every avenue. Of course, you might also like to say that you were conservative and chose to cut back prudently. Changing the description of the outcome from "saved" to "lost" is sufficient to make people favor certainty or take a gamble on uncertainty. In Scenario One, most people, because of the framing, interpret the decision based on preserving or saving what they have, so they feel risk averse. In Scenario Two, most interpret the decision based on framing that suggests they are already in a losing position, so they feel that they might as well take a chance.

Richard Thaler and Eric Johnson describe a simple experiment that they conducted to illustrate the importance of perceived reference points.[6] They made a subtly different proposal to each of two classes. In Class A, they said that each student had won $30. They offered students an optional gamble, a coin flip where the individual won $9 on heads and lost $9 on tails. Alternatively, they could simply keep the $30. The result was that 70 percent of Class A students selected the coin flip.

Thaler and Johnson then offered Class B the following options:

- A coin flip where the individual won $39 on heads and $21 on tails.
- $30 for certain.

Only 43 percent of Class B students selected the coin flip. Both games are absolutely identical in terms of expected outcomes, but, crucially, the reference point for Class A students, who mostly took the gamble, was that the $30 was framed as "previous winnings"; they felt ahead anyway. Class B students perceived the coin toss as an unnecessary risk in a game in which they were able to win $30 for sure. In *Against the Gods*, Peter Bernstein describes this discrepancy in simple terms: "people who start out with money in their pockets will choose to gamble, while people who start out with empty pockets will reject the gamble."[7]

There are thus some simple messages in prospect theory for people who are trying to persuade decision makers. If you want to drive decision makers toward a riskier decision, convince them that they are already losing—"Don't get left behind in the information society; buy our all-singing all-dancing new gadget today!" If you want to drive decision makers toward a risk-averse decision, convince them that they are ahead and stand to lose quite a bit—"Life sometimes throws nasty surprises at us; don't get caught out, buy our comprehensive insurance today!"

CHOICE OF CHOICES

Is there a surfeit of choice today? Before the days of supermarkets, we bought groceries in shops where assistants gathered products for customers and the choice in all but the very largest grocers was a few hundred different products. Today, even a small, local supermarket will be offering self-service choices running to several thousand different products. Are you going to buy haddock, salmon, plaice, cod, mackerel, sole, pollock, trout, sea bass, or tuna, and will that be as fillets, steaks, loins, and with or without skin?

We believe that you cannot separate the idea of evolving consumer choice from the forces of competition. Consider Shiv Mathur's model from *How Firms Compete*.[8] The model sets out generic competitive strategies and explains how commercial choices evolve by concentrating on the interface between an organization's offerings and its customers.

Figure 2.1, adapted from Mathur, shows four competitive strategies: commodity, product, service, and system. The four types of strategy are dictated by the amount of "hard" merchandise and by the amount of "support" needed. If you look at the information technology industry, for example, you can see all four strategies in action. Large-scale warehouses sell boxes of personal computers as a commodity. Some suppliers try to brand their products so that we care about the label, for example an

How decisions get made when you have too much choice

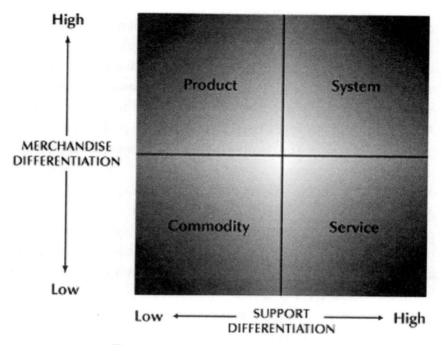

Figure 2.1 Four competitive strategies

Apple computer. Some local firms that hold your hands for a new computer network are service oriented, while some of the biggest firms compete in the outsourcing market trying to provide a complete system solution.

New offerings normally start off in the top right box as *systems*. The first computers, the first automobiles, and the first aircraft were all offerings that couldn't simply be bought. They needed people who understood precisely how they had been made, people who could repair them at short notice, people who would work with the new owners on improvements. As competition intensifies, standards emerge, mass production becomes the norm, we are clearer about what we want. Customers want to buy *services* and *products* as cheaply as possible. The flow in this diagram is from the top-right system box where new complex products emerge to the bottom-left *commodity* box. How do you know you are in the commodity box? To us, you know you are selling a commodity when buyers don't care who you are.

Strangely, advertising is a strong sign that people are trying to swim against the tide flowing down the commoditization plug-hole, by emphasizing the choices we face, whether real or illusory. At the same time, we get bored with making obvious decisions. "I just want: a car that gets me from A to B… a piece of software that does what it says… a simple fish finger." The evolution of choice is part of the evolution of industries. Advertising in a competitive, innovative market is healthy and shouldn't get out of control, because competition will ensure that ineffective advertisers, or those who advertise too much at the expense of profit, will go bust. This surfeit of advertised choice is not a sign of market failure; rather, it is a sign of uncertainty about the future choices people may want to make and an effort by firms in competition to evolve to new sets of choices.

We are not always able to grasp choice when it's offered. When television competition heated up a couple of decades ago with new cable and satellite entrants, there was talk of opera channels and art channels and science channels. Once technology unleashed micro-broadcasting, apparently there was going to be an explosion of interest in self-improvement. Two decades on these channels do exist, scraping by, while the majority of people watch mass-media reality television or sports events. On the other hand, the micro-broadcasting vision has partially arrived and flourishes in some new media, such as social networks and blogs.

Businesspeople have been talking for a few years about Chris Anderson's idea of the "long tail" of the statistical distribution of interest.[9] The idea is that the internet allows firms, for example Amazon, to make money by supplying people with a full book-shop of rare, infrequently ordered books. A traditional bookseller would go broke on space cost alone stocking such low-frequency items, but an online bookseller can turn lots of smaller pieces of inventory into significant market share. Again, there is a fantastic range of choice. So why is it that such a huge chunk of market share goes to a handful of books written by an even smaller number of bestselling authors?

Just because there is a tremendous amount of consumer choice compared with the past doesn't necessarily mean that we have "too much" choice, only "more" choice. Indeed, one indicator of available choice is advertising, albeit an imperfect one. Some of the most annoying advertising comprises little jingles from near-monopolistic operating systems suppliers or government-sponsored advertising. Monopolists can clog up the airways without giving us any options—the advertising without the choice, or offering illusory choices. On the other hand, there is a danger of looking at commercial advertisers striving to inject biases directly into consumers' minds and concluding that those advertisers are also out of control. Instead, advertising may be a sign that we have sufficient choice in certain areas, without implying that there is too much. When there is a dearth of advertising, perhaps that indicates scarcity or monopoly control. But even if we welcome advertising and agree that people do have increasing consumer choice, how might we measure a surfeit? At what point would we say, "Enough choice! Stop here!"?

In *The Paradox of Choice*, Barry Schwartz refers back to prospect theory on this question of too much choice, using the example of replacing a car.[10] Bombarded with so many makes and models to choose from, together with so many sources of information on those products' comparative merits and snags, mere mortals tend to fall back on heuristics. In this type of situation, it is availability heuristics, which tends to mean "listening to what friends and neighbors say" and perhaps giving disproportionate weight to a couple of anecdotes ahead of a consumer report with feedback from 100,000 car owners.

Too much choice can also disadvantage the seller, by confusing the potential buyer, who then might defer the buying decision rather than make a more complex choice, especially if that more complex choice includes tradeoffs. In the car-buying example, the tradeoff might be between safety and price, which is a highly significant matter. But even less significant tradeoffs, such as the functions and features of music equipment, tend to unsettle potential buyers into deferring decisions.

One experiment by Tversky and Shafir showed several examples of subjects choosing whether or not to buy discounted CD players.[11] When there was just one bargain offer, a mid-range Sony for $99, 66 percent chose to buy, 34 percent chose to defer. When an additional, conflicting choice was added (a top-end Aiwa for $169), 27 percent chose the Sony, 27 percent opted for the Aiwa, and 46 percent deferred their decision. However, if the main (Sony) bargain offer was "framed" by an additional but less good offer (an inferior Aiwa for $105), 73 percent chose the Sony (described by Tversky and Shafir as a dominating offer), 3 percent made the contrarian choice of the inferior Aiwa, and only 24 percent chose to defer the decision.

Of course, bargain offers of this kind, usually designed by the seller to encourage impulse buying, form only one type of choice. However, the principle that we tend to defer decisions if faced with too much and/or conflicting choice seems to apply to most of the commercial choices we make in our lives.

SHOPPING AND BUYING

Another way of looking at these conundrums of choice is to think about procurement as a mixture of both buying and shopping. We could harp on about bizarre bazaar stories, suggesting that "buying is from Mars and shopping is from Venus," but there are far too many stereotypical pitfalls in that line of argument. Table 2.1 takes a (mostly) considered view on the characteristics of buying and shopping.

Table 2.1 Buying and shopping compared

BUYING	SHOPPING
Preconditioned	See possibilities
Often decided in advance	Often exploratory
Compare prices	Compare features
One-off process	Learning process
Quick process	Iterative process
Hunt down purchase	Tease out purchase

Straightforward buying is quite possibly all we need when choosing between highly commoditized products, but almost anything else we procure (most purchases and all the most important purchases) benefit from elements of shopping as well as buying.

Let us return to the example of buying a car. Sorry, shopping for a car. When you go shopping for a car, you learn. You learn about prices, back seats, financing deals, safety, speed, colors. You can honestly go shopping for a sports car and come home with a sensible family vehicle, even without falling out with your partner; or indeed vice versa. Sometimes you learn, and as a result change your mind. Such shoppers are perhaps better economists in the mold of John Maynard Keynes, who reportedly said: "When the facts change, I change my mind. What do you do, sir?"

Herbert Simon's notion of bounded rationality explains how mere mortals attempt to be rational despite their limitations, both in terms of the information available to assist with decisions and the cognitive ability to process that information rationally. Simon also coined the term "satisficing," to describe the strategies people often deploy to identify adequate (i.e., satisfactory and/or sufficient) rather than optimal economic decisions.[12] This thinking underpins behavioral economics and was a precursor to prospect theory.

Barry Schwartz, looking at these ideas more from a psychological than an economic perspective, considers that people fall into two main categories: maximizers and satisficers. *Maximizers* try to find optimal solutions; they are not content to choose until they feel they have evaluated all the options using all the available information. *Satisficers*, on the other hand, are more likely to reach a rapid conclusion, by deploying heuristics and choosing a solution that they believe is sufficiently close to maximal in satisfying their needs. Naturally, the maximizer–satisficer axis is a continuum rather than two absolutes, but equally naturally, there are psychological tests that can position people neatly in one camp or the other. Most of us drift between the two for certain choices. Using ourselves as examples, both authors are primarily satisficers for choices of consumer goods such as clothes, gadgets, and motor vehicles. Yet we are both primarily maximizers, on behalf of ourselves and our respective families, when choosing our homes or making choices about health and education.

Returning to the notion of buying and shopping, we can now propose a better rule of thumb than "buying is from Mars, shopping is from Venus." Despite pitfalls of its own, "buying is for satisficers, shopping is for maximizers" is hopefully a helpful slogan.

INDUSTRIAL-SCALE PURCHASING

Large organizations are quite capable of turning buying and shopping into intense organizational schizophrenia. Large companies and government departments centralize their purchasing, supposedly to achieve economies of scale. This is normally done in aid of making sure that the really important decisions are made by professionals. Sometimes these really important decisions include things like all hiring, for example a central personnel or human resources team does all of the hiring; at other times they are about travel or car fleets or stationery. Sometimes these central units work well, particularly in relation to commodities bought in bulk and choices that are static. Many times these central units fail, however, as they cannot satisfy local needs from central buying. How can HQ choose some country manager's personal assistant better than he or she can? Central buying does not permit local shopping and without shopping there is no learning. We call the resulting problems "tender traps."

A good example is software purchasing by central government departments. Rather than going shopping, to learn what is achievable, and then redesigning their requests for tender, government departments set out "requirements specifications" just about as soon as they can. Most requirements specifications might as well read: "We know what we want and don't need to learn what might be available because we're so important and too busy to shop." Bureaucrats hand these requirements specifications to people who know next to nothing about how the software will be used nor much about software in general; they are purchasing experts. These experts do know how to drive suppliers to meet the specification exactly. So, even if the requirements specification is accurate, suppliers wind up creating something at great expense, and late, and using older technology, to meet a requirement that might easily have been met with off-the-shelf software had a little flexibility been involved. Buying can evolve, but only through shopping.

There are also substantial pitfalls for sellers. Putting to one side the obvious point that most bidders in competitive tendering processes do not win the business, even the "winning" organization often finds itself losing, due to an affliction known as the *winner's curse*. The principle of the winner's curse is that in a competitive tendering situation, where the competitors have incomplete information about the exact costs and/or value involved, the "winning" competitor nearly always underprices its bid and is eventually disappointed. The disappointment might not be actual losses (although in many cases on a full-costing basis it does result in real losses), but there is a lower than expected return. One intriguing and somewhat counter-intuitive element of the winner's curse, highlighted by Richard Thaler in his eponymous book, is that the larger the number of participants in the competition, the more pronounced the winner's curse effect.[13]

While economic theory suggests that rational contestants should price "known unknowns" into their bids, experimental situations demonstrate that participants can be familiar with the phenomenon of the winner's curse, yet repeatedly make the same mistakes in subsequent experiments. In the real world, you often see the same contestants caught out by the winner's curse in fields such as mergers and acquisitions (they rarely add value) and auctions of scarce resources (for example broadcasting spectrum auctions). It is easy to tut-tut at corporate executives' excessive competitiveness, hubris, or anomalous decision-making behavior, but in many ways the phenomenon is even worse when experienced by NGOs, especially charities.[14] In the UK, where increasingly public services are being contracted out to charities and/or commercial care providers, this is a significant problem. Charities (perhaps unwittingly) frequently disguise their winner's curse losses through hidden subsidies from donated funds on contracts that are supposed to be fully funded, often hidden in overheads or infrastructure costs.

Buyer–User–Shopper–Chooser is a phrase we started to use in the firm we both worked at in the late 1980s. The four words have always resonated with us, as has the acronym BUSCK (adding the notion of Key decision maker to the mix), and we have found the model most useful over the years. We are unsure whether we came up with it or someone brought it in; we have

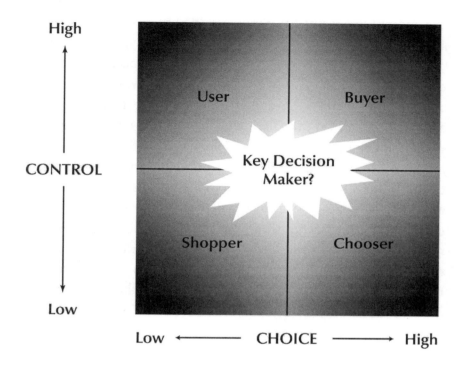

Figure 2.2 Who is the key decision maker?

searched earnestly for a reference to the model without success, so we apologize to anyone if we have failed to credit them.

In Figure 2.2 there are two axes, the degree of choice and the degree of control. In theory, a *buyer* has a great deal of control over the purchasing process and can spread the procurement net widely or narrowly. A *shopper*, on the other hand, might make on-the-spot decisions but is probably not controlling the procurement process and is likely only looking at choices within the constraints of the options presented to them. A *chooser* is often a professional procurement person (sometimes an external consultant) who might ensure that the appropriate range of choices is presented, but might have little control over decision making beyond that. On the other hand, a *user* is the person or people who might have a great deal of control over the procurement process, perhaps substantial input into writing the specification, but little input to the choices that are eventually made.

Of course, in many cases one individual fulfills more than one of those four roles. If one person occupies several of the roles, you might well have identified your *key decision maker*. However, when the roles are well spread between several individuals, it can be very difficult to work out who the key decision maker is. Only occasionally does the decision really get made collectively by a selection panel; more frequently than you might realize there is a key decision maker who ultimately makes the decision. If you are speaking that person's language you are more likely to win, so it is extremely helpful for the seller at least to try to identify who that person is and what will motivate them to select you. It is therefore important when selling to form your BUSCK assessment as early in the procurement process as possible.

Thinking back to Shiv Mathur's model of strategy illustrated in Figure 2.1, the Buyer–User–Shopper–Chooser model is most distinct when decisions are most complicated; that is, in the system box. For instance when you need a medical procedure, the buyer might be your physician; you are the user. The hospital and the doctors, and your insurance firm, are choosers and shoppers for all sorts of tests, treatments, and items.

Once you think about procurement this way, you realize that for many decisions these four roles are done by four different people or organizations. When you buy a house on mortgage, to some degree the bank is a buyer with you, your family is the user, the estate agent might be the shopper, and your partner might be the chooser. You can form your own view on who the key decision maker is in that situation. In contrast, for commodities the Buyer–User–Shopper–Chooser model might collapse into a single person. When you go out and buy a newspaper, you are almost certainly buyer/user/shopper/ chooser and therefore key decision maker.

In large-scale public procurement, very often the buyer is the Treasury, the user is the government department, the shopper is the procurement unit, and the chooser is a specialist panel, often involving technical consultants. This plethora of experts frequently leads to overcomplex specifications and processes, as discussed above, even if the exercise started out with the best of intentions. With those complications come increased risks, which are not for the faint hearted. You only have to look at what happened when the UK's Department of Health opted to outsource its logistics division. The original £715 million ($114 billion) contract, advertised in the *Official Journal of the European Union*, turned out to be worth a cool £3.7 billion ($6 billion) annually. The way in which the apparent and actual deal value was presented to hopeful suppliers left the procurement process open to challenge from unsuccessful bidders. This put at risk the bid fees incurred by all parties over the two years it took to bring the deal to life, not to mention the opportunity costs.

OPPORTUNITY GUILT

After opportunity cost comes *opportunity guilt*. Take an organization that has just finished an extensive strategic planning exercise. The moment it is finished, an opportunity presents itself that was not foreseen in the strategic plan. If the organization takes the opportunity, was the plan wrong for not including the possibility, and was the exercise a waste of time and resource? If the organization forgoes the opportunity, is it slavishly following a plan oblivious to changing circumstances?

For example, a chain of retail fishmongers finishes its strategic planning exercise assuming that no acquisitions are available because the only desirable acquisition has an exorbitantly high price/earnings ratio or is "takeover proof." The plan focuses on organic growth. Suddenly, the founder of a venerable competitive chain of retail fishmongers dies and his heirs wish to sell immediately. When confronted with this sudden, unexpected acquisition opportunity, people in the first chain of fishmongers are going to feel regret, either about a decision to proceed on the acquisition or about a decision to stick to the organic growth plan. Because of all the hard work on the strategic plan, they can take the opportunity, yet feel guilty that the strategy work was wasted. Or they can stick to their strategic plan, despite the opportunity, yet also feel guilty about what they might have missed.

In *The Paradox of Choice*, Barry Schwartz notes that opportunity guilt can be preceded by choice guilt. He talks about conflicts between personal responsibility and a profusion of alternatives being exacerbated by the availability of choice:

> When there are no options, what can you do? Disappointment, maybe; regret, no. When you have only a few options, you do the best you can, but the world may simply not allow you to do as well as you would like. When there are many options, the chances increase that there is a really good one out there, and you feel that you ought to be able to find it.

Schwartz goes on to note, "there comes a point at which opportunities become so numerous that we feel overwhelmed. Instead of feeling in control, we feel unable to cope." Furthermore, when confronted with difficult choices in pressured situations, many people do not want to make their own choices, even if they think in advance that they would want to do so. A classic example is cancer treatment. When surveyed, most people state that they would want to choose their mode of treatment if they got cancer, but when you ask those who actually have cancer, on balance most prefer that the professionals choose the mode of treatment.

CHOICE ARCHITECTURE

With choice comes responsibility for our own decisions, but we do not always want to face that responsibility. Alternatively, we might want our choices framed in a way that helps us to make decisions. In recent years, a political philosophy has emerged that recognizes this conflict between choice and responsibility: soft paternalism, also known as libertarian paternalism or asymmetrical paternalism. Despite sounding like a contradiction in terms, the idea does straddle both the libertarian and paternalistic camps. The form of paternalism involved does not constrain individual freedom, it merely points people in one direction through the way in which the choice is framed.

A famous example is organ donation. Some societies have an "opt-in" system, where people have to make a conscious choice to consent to donating their organs for medical use after their death, otherwise there is a presumption of no consent. In other societies there is an "opt-out" system, where people have to make a conscious choice to withdraw their presumed consent. In France, where the system theoretically works on an opt-out basis, survivors are allowed to veto the deceased's consent and very often do so when that consent is implicit rather than explicit. Richard Thaler and Cass Sunstein, leading proponents of libertarian paternalism and authors of *Nudge*, advocate obtaining enforceable, explicit consent wherever possible.[15] In Illinois, you cannot get a driving license without explicitly opting in or opting out of the organ-donation program. Thaler and Sunstein believe that this approach would provide more donor organs than other schemes.

Note that the individuals' liberty need not be constrained in any material way. Someone who does not want to donate their organs can choose to live (and die) by those decisions. Note also that this form of paternalistic policy is asymmetric in several ways. It helps those whose rationality is "strongly bounded"; and, indeed, those who tend to behave irrationally to reach the "right" decision (the one that is aligned with public policy and the perceived best interests of the decision maker). Such policies also allow those who wish to make a considered, rational choice of their own to do so with minimal additional effort if their choice is something other than the default.

This kind of policy is also asymmetric, in that it does not matter whether you believe that we tend to make such choices rationally or not, the policy should still be acceptable. If you believe that people are basically rational in respect of the matter to be chosen, then they would migrate to their genuine preference regardless of the default. If you believe that people are basically irrational in respect of the matter, then you would accept that the default choice might as well be aligned with public policy. You might not agree with that particular public policy, but that is another, entirely political matter.

Thaler and Sunstein also describe this phenomenon as *choice architecture*, which is perhaps the most helpful description of it for our purposes. Many of us indulge in choice architecture without thinking about it in those terms. If you were to design a menu for an eatery (perhaps an exclusive new fish restaurant located near a university faculty where they do lots of behavioral experiments offering fancy fish suppers as one of the choices), all the decisions you make about the layout of that menu constitute its choice architecture. If you envisage the restaurant as a traditional "three-course meal" sort of place, you will probably have sections for starters, main courses, and desserts. If you want people to focus on particular types of food, you might split the menu into fish, meat, and vegetable sections, perhaps leading with fish if your reputation is fishy. If yours is a very informal eatery, perhaps you will set out all of the choices in price sequence. If you are well known for a handful of specialty dishes, you might well start your menu with those. All such menu layouts are a form of choice architecture, trying to guide the reader of the menu to the choices that will be the most satisfying for them and hopefully also lucrative for you as a restaurateur.

To quote Thaler from his 2008 lecture at The Edge Masterclass: "[t]here is no such thing as neutral choice architecture any more than there is neutral architecture… Given that we cannot avoid meddling, let's meddle in a good way."[16]

IMMORTAL MARKETS OR ANCIENT DEMOCRACY?

Despite our valid concerns about too much choice and helpful guidance to those offering choices, we are nevertheless advocates of choice. Promoting the importance of choice and markets is an unenviable position today; it is far trendier to talk about "third ways" or "total inclusion." In some ways, the importance of choice and markets is a return to basic themes of individual liberty, liberal markets, and the importance of competition. Still, enhancing choice and making choice manageable involve at least three subthemes:

- *Better information*. Choice without adequate information is no choice at all. New technology and networks are increasing the potential for improving markets simply through the provision of better information. While a surfeit of information can equally reduce choice by drowning information in noise, it is probably best to get the information out first and then to worry about techniques for editing and managing it.
- *Promotion of market-based solutions and true competition*. In numerous cases, markets are easier and more effective than politics or regulation so long as they are competitive, but, paradoxically, they require leadership and faith more than technical analysis. Society also needs vigilance against

regulatory capture or industry capture, through which choices often become limited or even pseudo-choices.

- *Proper measures.* Society frequently views markets a bit like "sorcerer's apprentices": they start off okay but then suddenly seem to function all too well. However, closer examination often reveals that society was never too sure how it would evaluate a market's success, for instance carbon markets in the early twenty-first century. Yet while markets do what they do rather well (share information and arrive at sensible resource allocations), they do have to be sensibly targeted with the right resource information toward appropriate decisions.

We return to these themes in Chapter 7, when we look in more detail at markets, measures, and forecasting. Building on questions of rational decision making, Chapter 3 explores choices involving multiple parties, repeated interactions, and longer-term effects.

3 | BEYOND PRICE: TRUST AND ETHICS

When you need to make a decision, particularly when the choice involves multiple parties, how do you know whom to trust? The choices relating to trust and ethics raised in this chapter go beyond price—indeed beyond economics—and we start the chapter with a topic much loved by many mathematically inclined decision makers: game theory.

FAIR GAMES

Game theory is an interdisciplinary branch of applied mathematics that is used by economists, biologists, engineers, political scientists, computer scientists, and philosophers. It uses mathematics, for example logic or probability, to model strategic situations in which an individual's success at decision making depends on the decisions of others. Game theory started with zero-sum games (those in which one party's gain is necessarily offset by an equivalent loss by one or more other parties), such as poker, but rapidly encompassed non-zero-sum games, where cooperation can increase the overall winnings, to the benefit of many or even all players.

There are particular points in many games called equilibria. At an equilibrium, each player follows a strategy that he or she is unlikely to change. Mathematician John Nash identified game theory solutions that are now known as Nash equilibria. These are solutions where two or more players know the equilibrium strategies of the other players, and no player can benefit by changing their strategy while the other players remain unmoved.

However, a Nash equilibrium does not mean that the best cumulative payoff has been achieved. A classic example might be businesspeople competing under traditional economic assumptions. They could move beyond a Nash equilibrium and alter the rules of the game by forming a cartel. Then they would achieve a higher payoff through cooperation, though perhaps to the detriment of other players.

Choices about whether to cooperate and/or trust one another come to the fore in non-zero-sum and cooperation games. Perceptions of fairness have a significant impact on our behavior.

One simple and well-known two-player game is known as the Ultimatum Game. The two players have to choose how to divide a sum of money, say 100 one-pound coins, between them. Player A has to make a proposal to Player B on how those coins should be split. Player B can accept or reject the proposal. If Player B accepts, the money is split between the two players in accordance with the proposal. If Player B rejects Player A's proposal, both players get nothing. The game is played once and once only, anonymously.

In a Nash equilibrium world, the solution to this game is simple. Player A proposes a 99/1 split in favor of Player A. Player B, being logical, rational, and theoretical, accepts this offer on the basis that £1 is better than nothing. Because it is entirely logical and rational that Player B will do this, Player A will always make the minimum non-zero offer possible, in this case £1, keeping the rest of the spoils.

In practice, real Player As very rarely make a derisory offer and on the rare occasions that this does happen, real Player Bs nearly always reject them. Results vary from culture to culture (and there have even been experiments that look at the impact of hormone levels such as oxytocin and serotonin on this game[1]), but an 80/20 split seems to be quite a common minimum-level offer that tends to be accepted more often than not. The average offer tends to be around 70/30 in western cultures, but offering to split the money 50/50 is remarkably common. The size of the prize doesn't seem to affect the behavior much (although perhaps it would change at very high levels, say a million pounds in £10,000 units).

The key point is that principles of fairness, justice, and equity come into consideration here. Often, Player B would sooner go without and bring Player A down with them than accept a derisory offer. The nonrational element of Player B's behavior is basically a moral stance. Player A recognizes this risk and to some extent formulates strategies to minimize the chance of falling foul of it. Player A does also seem to want to perceive their offer as having been fair in the circumstances.

In the Ultimatum Game, the Nash equilibrium solution is the prescriptive result (theoretical optimum) and the way in which people actually tend to behave is the descriptive result. However, ideas such as fairness, cooperation, and trustworthiness bring a third perspective into play, a normative perspective: How *should* we behave? What choices *should* we make in these circumstances?

One interesting variant of the Ultimatum Game, known as the Dictator Game, gives Player B no choice in the matter. Player A simply decides how to split the spoils and Player B gets whatever Player A offers, if anything. The Nash equilibrium in this situation (technically not a game, as Player B is entirely passive) is for Player A to take 100 percent of the money and offer Player B nothing at all. In practice, only about one in three Player As go for this decision, the remainder offering something to the powerless Player Bs. This shows that some element of fairness and justice comes into Player A's reckoning.

Another interesting variant of the Ultimatum Game, sometimes described as the Competitive Ultimatum Game, has many proposers but only one responder, who can only accept one offer. Rejected proposers go home empty-handed. If the number of proposers exceeds three, in practice this game nearly always results in its Nash equilibrium: the winning proposer offers just under 100 percent of the spoils in order to secure the position of winning proposer. Thus in this simple variation, Player A is transformed from a position where most of the spoils normally remain with them, to a position where almost nothing can be gained by them. We described the idea of the winner's curse in a competitive procurement situation in the previous chapter; this variant of the Ultimatum Game illustrates an important aspect of why the winner's curse so regularly occurs in competitive situations, especially when many parties are involved in the competition.

PRINCIPAL–AGENT PROBLEMS AND PROCUREMENT

It is timely to return to questions of competitive procurement in this context, as games, trust, and ethics all play a part in the choices we make as buyers and sellers in procurement situations.

Other than the simplest buying and selling, procurement is subject to the principal–agent problem. In short, this stems from two issues that subsist in such transactions: the interests of the principal and the agent are not wholly aligned, and there are usually significant information asymmetries between the parties, leading to substantial uncertainty and risk. Figure 3.1 illustrates the principal–agent problem.

In the procurement situation, the buyer is the principal and the seller is the agent, although principal–agent problems do not only arise in such a situation. Indeed, this form of analysis, sometimes known as agency theory, came to the fore when examining the principal–agent relationship in employment. Other practical applications of this theory include performance-related pay, stock option models, and corporate governance frameworks.

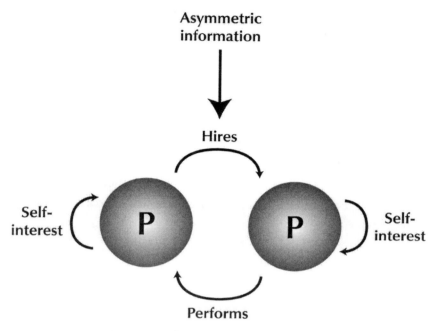

Figure 3.1 The principal–agent problem

Source: http://en.wikipedia.org/wiki/Principal-agent_problem

Principal–agent problems tend to be especially complex in circumstances where a large organization is making a substantial procurement. There are several principal–agent relationships in play, including those between the buying organization and the selling organization, plus that between the buying organization and its own staff who are undertaking the procurement. For example, the buying organization often worries about the risk of corruption between its staff and the selling organization. As a result, it might bring in a specialist third party to manage the procurement process for it—hey presto, another principal–agent relationship to manage. The selling organization also might have multiple principal–agent relationships involved, such as the use of a third party to help prepare the competitive tender. There is a great deal of room for information asymmetry, uncertainty, risk, mistrust, and foul play in these circumstances.

In fact, large-scale procurement situations are rich with potential ethical problems as well as potential malfeasance. There are ethical issues for both parties. For the buyer, there is the opportunity to squeeze every last drop out of the negotiation, especially if the buyer knows that the seller is desperate to sell. That stance might not be wise from a purely practical or commercial point of view; decent outcomes from squeezed suppliers are rare. Longer-term benefits may accompany a supplier with more freedom to maneuver. Ethical quandaries about whether that is the right way to behave in such circumstances are akin to Player A's fairness considerations in the Ultimatum Game. Is a hard bargain on the part of the buyer nevertheless fair in the circumstances? Does the buyer have an ethical obligation to attempt to prevent the winner from suffering from the winner's curse?

The seller also has ethical issues. There is an ethical imperative to tell the truth, yet the seller often knows that being wholly truthful will disadvantage their chances of success. Nevertheless, the seller might profoundly believe that their product or service is the most suitable. Can you be too truthful when selling in such circumstances? And where do you determine the lines between too truthful, appropriately truthful, and not truthful enough?

In his seminal 1968 essay "Is Business Bluffing Ethical?" Albert Carr draws an analogy between poker and business:

> Poker's own brand of ethics is different from the ethical ideals of civilised human relationships. The game calls for distrust of the other fellow... No one thinks any the worse of poker on that account. And no one should think any the worse of the game of business because its standards of right and wrong differ from the prevailing traditions of morality in our society.[2]

We return to ethical choices later in the chapter.

IN GAMES WE TRUST

An absence of trust in the game of poker is all very well, but many commercial "games" would struggle to get started at all without a smattering of cooperation and trust.

Here is a little thought experiment about trust and commercial rationality. Imagine that you meet a fish merchant who knows you love to eat fish every Friday and promises to leave a hermetically sealed platter of your favorite seafood by a tree in the woods each Friday morning. She says that you should leave £5 in exchange for the platter. The first Friday morning in the woods, to your delight, you see the platter next to the tree, leave the £5, take the platter home, and enjoy a delicious seafood lunch.

This goes on every Friday, but at some point you start to worry about this arrangement. After all, one day you might get home and discover that today's fish was bad, in which case you will have spent £5 on bad fish and won't want to return. In any case, even if she never leaves you bad fish, at some point she will probably stop coming. One Friday you'll turn up and there'll be no seafood lunch waiting for you. You'll have wasted your time and in fact spent £5 the previous week that you could, with the benefit of hindsight, have kept. If you knew the date of the last Friday she was going to turn up, there would be no reason for you to leave £5 that time, as it wouldn't be any good as an incentive for the following week. In those circumstances, you could have the last seafood platter for free. But if the fish merchant also knows which will be the last Friday of this arrangement, there's no reason for her to leave the seafood platter because she knows you have no rational reason to leave the money.

The same argument goes for the penultimate Friday. Since you know the fish merchant won't bring the platter on the second-to-last Friday, it makes no sense to leave money on the previous

Friday as incentive. The fish merchant knows this and so won't bring the seafood platter on the second-to-last Friday, or the third-to-last. In short, this fishy deal can never get started with rational people. The Nash equilibrium of this simple commercial transaction is for neither party to initiate the commerce.

There is a variant of the Dictator Game (discussed above) known as the Trust Game, which explores this problem and has been heavily tested in practice. It is quite a simple game; the players are anonymous and expect to play the game only once. Player A is endowed with a sum of money, say $10, and told that they can choose to send all, some, or none of this money to Player B as an "investment." Any money sent to Player B gains substantial "interest" in Player B's hands. Most practical experiments triple the value of the investment. Player B can then choose to send any sum of money (or none) back to Player A. This second part resembles the Dictator Game, except that Player A has trusted Player B with money that Player B would not have otherwise received.

The Nash equilibrium of this game is a nonstarter. Player A would expect nothing back from Player B, so why would Player A send anything to Player B? Player A would simply retain the $10 and nothing else would happen. Yet, with cooperation, there is $30 available to be shared between Player A and Player B. It is a game requiring cooperation but with no recourse to collaboration. In other words, it relies entirely on trust for cooperation to occur and thus for commercial activity to take place, much like the Friday fish platter thought experiment. In practice, Player As tend to send most or all of their endowment to Player Bs and Player Bs tend to reciprocate by returning a reasonably fair share of the increased spoils.

Trust is not a simple concept, nor is it necessarily an unmitigated good. Of course, trust is about much more than just money; it is about human relationships, obligations, experiences, and anticipating what other people will do. Indeed, it is about a great many things that we have so far in this book been saying comprise real commerce, as opposed to classical economics.

A cursory review of the etymology and definitions of the word "trust" throws up many contexts. The Old English *trēowe* and Old Norse *traust* are both about faithfulness. Trust as a noun is defined as "a relationship of reliance," but also as a dependence on some future contingency, credit (buying something on trust), holding property on behalf of another, as well as a charge or duty, for example a child committed to your trust. Furthermore, as a noun it often means a legal or business structure for third-party beneficiaries, but equally a cartel to reduce competition, for instance antitrust laws. As a verb, trust means relying on someone or something, but also to entrust into care, believe someone, or extend credit. And then there are the adjectival forms of trust. In short, reliance establishes the relationship of trust.

Trust is more subtle than cooperation. Cooperation is when people agree to work together for mutual benefit. Without cooperation society could not function at all, at least not in any meaningful sense of the word "society." You can have cooperation without trust; indeed, some simple commercial activities depend on cooperation but do not require trust. Robert Axelrod, in *The Evolution of Cooperation*, suggests that cooperation depends on something he calls "the shadow of the future," the expectation that you will have future interactions with the people you deal with and that your previous interactions might come back to haunt you if you don't play fair.[3] Reputation is extremely important to both individuals and organizations. It is established through multiple rounds of interactions and it is entirely rational to behave cooperatively to enhance and maintain your reputation.

However, as we illustrated in the two examples above, you wouldn't get started with the seafood platter trading or indulge in the investment activity without trust. The reason trading and commercial activity take place is illustrated in the Ultimatum Game and the Dictator Game, outlined earlier. In the real world, it is reasonable to anticipate that people will be somewhat fair toward you, even in situations where they don't have to be; extensive experiments done with these games demonstrate conclusively that most people behave that way. This is not a new observation, not even to classical economists. In his 1759 book *The Theory of Moral Sentiments*, Adam Smith said:

> how selfish soever man may be supposed, there are evidently some principles in his nature, which interest him in the fortune of others, and render their happiness necessary to him, though he derives nothing from it, except the pleasure of seeing it.[4]

Beginning under the assumption of trust may not be strictly rational or theoretically sensible, but it is reasonable to anticipate fair treatment and therefore cooperation from the other party in these situations, purely on the basis of trust. Trust occurs when we leverage on a history of relationships to extend credit and the benefit of the doubt to someone. In most situations we encounter, there is heuristic evidence to help form trust—the results of previous encounters with that person, the reputation of that individual or organization, or the knowledge that there are likely to be future transactions that will encourage the other party to get this transaction right. Even in one-off, anonymous situations, people tend to leverage on a generic history of relationships. Most of us intuitively know that most strangers will be trustworthy and that we ourselves will be trustworthy. Trust benefits society as a common good that helps commerce flourish. Trust, perhaps more than free trade, leads a person "by an invisible hand to promote an end which was no part of his intention," to paraphrase Smith in his subsequent and better-known book, *The Wealth of Nations*.

SOME TIPPING POINTS

Axelrod's "shadow of the future" is very relevant to multiple-round games and indeed to most real-world situations where people transact. The point we are making here is that it is not sufficient to explain why people play fair and anticipate fair play and trust in one-off situations.

An area of commercial activity that can illustrate both one-off and multiple-round behavior is tipping. We tip in a variety of situations. We may be far from home, where the chances of encountering the same service person again are negligible, yet most people still tip. We usually take the trouble to ascertain the tipping norm for the place we are visiting; travel guidebooks normally take the trouble to spell out such matters. Having anchored the potential tip around the recommended guidebook rate, as adjusted for your perception of the quality of the service you have just received, also taking into account how much local currency you have about your person, and perhaps factoring in more whimsical criteria such as your general prevailing mood and that of your loved ones, you present your service provider with a tip.

Very few people abstain from tipping in such one-off circumstances, although the rational chain of thought would be that the service provider has already delivered the service. The chance of you ever encountering that person and requiring their services again is also nearly zero. Indeed, the entirely rational nontipping person would reason that, as the service provider must know that you are about to leave town never to return, his or her chances of receiving a tip would be miniscule. It would be irrational of the service provider to expect a tip in this theoretical, rational world. Yet, as with our earlier seafood platter, Trust Game, and Dictator Game examples, the human psyche is such that we mostly want to do the right thing, therefore most people tip in most such circumstances.

When you visit somewhere frequently, such as a favorite local restaurant or a hotel you stay at regularly on business, tipping becomes a more understandable matter in terms of purely rational analysis and the "shadow of the future" argument. You tip, perhaps generously, as part of an ongoing relationship between customer and service provider. Tipping in those circumstances can also be a way of ensuring that you get a premium service. Perhaps your generous tip is a reward to the maître d' who always ensures that your reservation secures your favorite table, or the waiter who knows that you are pre-theater regulars and ensures that you get rapid service, or indeed the waiter who lets you linger over your after-dinner drinks, knowing that you like to do that.

We discussed principal–agent dilemmas in the context of large-scale procurement earlier in this chapter. The principal–agent relationship exists in an environment of information asymmetry, uncertainty, and risk. In that context, consider tipping in a top-notch fish restaurant, and in this case the principal–agent relationship between the restaurant owner and the waiter. The restaurant owner is the principal. The principal wants the agents (waiters) to provide a good service. The principal's goals are slightly unclear: making a profit on customers, having happy customers, portion control, and/or rapid throughput to maximize the use of tables, all need balancing. The differential cost to the agent, the waiter, can be high. There is a big difference in effort between moving a few plates of fish from the kitchen to the tables, and providing high-quality, attentive service. There is moral hazard: the waiting staff don't bear the cost of losing customers. There is adverse selection: most principals don't know whether a waiter is any good until they try them. Finally, the costs of evaluating the elements of agent performance are high. Does the principal want to hold a job appraisal after every table is served? The principal often decides that performance evaluation is best left to customers to provide in the form of a "bonus," a tip. Tips also help reduce the moral hazard of losing customers to bad service and the risk of adverse selection because, with bonuses available, the principal doesn't feel obliged to pay agents so much. Some customers might disagree: just pay your staff properly to do good work and let's consign this tipping business to the irrational dustbin where it belongs.

Indeed, some cultures feel strongly that tipping is immoral. In China, outside of the tourist areas, tipping is rude and has whiffs of corruption and special favor. Inside tourist areas, tipping has led to newspaper and online discussions of a move to a more dissolute society due to Western influences. If the waiter or waitress provides a differential service in aid of a tip, tipping fulfills Transparency International's definition of corruption, "the misuse of entrusted power for private gain," albeit on a small scale. If the customer considers anything other than always giving a tip of standard size or percentage, then the customer is gauging how to entice the misuse of the entrusted power of the waiter or waitress for private gain in the form of a better than average meal.

So next time you're in a restaurant wondering how much to tip, not only should you think about anchoring (what is the normal level of tip for this place) and fairness in what might be a one-off or many-round variant of the Trust Game, you also should deploy your ethical radar to ensure that neither you nor the waiter is being unethical or even corrupt. Enjoy your meal!

TRUST AND CORRUPTION

The tipping example raises an issue that has intrigued us for many years: the relationship between trust and corruption. You can look on the widespread practice of tipping both as a real-world example of the Trust Game and as an example of low-level corruption, or at least an environment ripe for such.

Tipping is not the only sphere of commercial life where trust and corruption interact. In *The Wisdom of Crowds*, James Surowiecki discusses some of the social history of commercial trust (and protection from breaches of trust), using examples as diverse as the Quakers for British and transatlantic trading, the Maghribi traders across the Mediterranean, and guilds such as the German Hanseatic League.[5] But, as he points out, "social benefits of trust and co-operation... do create a problem; the more people trust, the easier they are for others to exploit." He uses the stock market bubble of the late 1990s and the Tyco scandal to illustrate his point, although there are many periods and examples that could be used to the same effect. After gently pointing out that Arthur Andersen was auditing a remarkable number of the troublesome examples at that time, not least WorldCom and Enron, Surowiecki advises: "in a world in which not all capitalists are Quakers, 'trust but verify' remains a useful byword." The more entrusted power there is, the more private gain might be obtained, and therefore the more likely it is that someone will try to misuse that trust.

So should we want a high-trust or a low-trust society? This question has been tackled by many commentators. The general consensus is that a high-trust society is a preferable place to live and is probably more efficient and effective. However, that does not mean that trust is an unmitigated good, nor costless, nor that we should not retain some mistrust. In a mythical "no fraud" country, we can imagine corrupt tourists skipping out of restaurants without paying or fear of being caught, while gullible locals wonder at unpaid bills. A low level of fraud might be analogous to a low level of viruses that help a host keep up its defenses. Ideally you want rising levels of trust without losing basic levels of suspicion. In a high-trust society there might not be enough incentive for competitive checking, not enough suspicion, too much confidence. In a high-trust society, competition may not work effectively at keeping self-interest in check. In a low-trust society, continual checking wastes resources, for example because people are being ripped off by one another. This reminds us of an anecdote our friend Malcolm Cooper likes to tell of a journey in a taxi in Washington, DC with a Nigerian taxi driver. Malcolm asked the driver how he found the US compared with Nigeria. The driver replied: "What I like about this country is that it has a nice level of corruption." This is a telling point: most people agree that you can have too much corruption, but perhaps you can have too little.

Commerce is about people and trust, not only money. Low-trust and high-value transactions are almost wholly consigned to the criminal backwaters of society. Equally, there will always be large numbers of low-trust and low-value transactions, ranging from street stalls to chance encounters. When society functions well there are large numbers of high-trust and low-value transactions being conducted efficiently, such as buying books or filling medical prescriptions. When times are good there are quite a few high-trust and high-value transactions, such as long-term construction contracts, that are precisely the transactions to suffer most when society as a whole is leaking trust.

In "The Bulging Pocket and the Rule of Law," Eric Uslaner says, "corruption, of course, depends upon trust—or honor among thieves."[6] In other words, that same, seemingly inherent human characteristic we observe when people play the Ultimatum Game and the Trust Game—trust and be trustworthy—is a prerequisite for corruption as well as a prerequisite for many forms of beneficial commercial activity. Al Capone famously described capitalism as "the legitimate racket of the ruling class"; perhaps he had this paradox in mind.

Dan Ariely considers the innate dishonest elements of the human character in *Predictably Irrational*, reporting on several fascinating experiments into dishonest behaviors.[7] Using Harvard Business School as a source of subjects, students were asked to fill in multiple-choice tests and then transpose their answers from a working sheet onto a form for submission; the latter form would then be used to award the students money for each correct answer. Some students were shown the correct answers on the second form, affording them the opportunity to change their answers; in other words, to cheat. Ariely has tried variants of this experiment, including versions where the students were told to shred their initial working sheet (thus destroying any evidence of wrongdoing) and another where the students were simply told to take their "winnings" out of a money jar without reporting in any paperwork at all.

Large numbers of students have participated in this experiment and it probably doesn't surprise you to learn that all the evidence points toward some cheating, albeit relatively low levels of around 10 percent mark inflation. Strangely, the variants that afforded students additional opportunities to conceal their fiddling had no discernable effect on the overall results. Furthermore, Ariely was able to learn (by analyzing the results of the "cheating without shredding" group) that most people cheated a little bit. This was not results being skewed by a small minority of flagrant cheats.

In a variant of the above experiment, prior to the "cheat test" Ariely asked the students, at UCLA this time, to do a recollection test. Half the group were asked to recall the names of ten books they had read at school, the other half were asked to recall as many of the ten commandments as possible. As it happens, most of the students weren't terribly good at recalling the ten commandments, but the group who were asked to recall those (rather than book titles) were far less likely to cheat in the subsequent cheat test. In a similar variant conducted at MIT, some students were asked to sign a statement on their answer sheet, "I understand that this study falls under the MIT honor system." There is no such system in reality, but those who signed that statement were, much like the ten commandment recollection group, much less likely to cheat than the other group. It seems that merely thinking about ethical matters—indeed, just about the abstract notion of ethics—prior to the cheating opportunity significantly reduces instances of dishonesty.

A similar experiment at Newcastle University in the UK shows how easy it is to change people's perception of the context for honesty.[8] The university canteen operated on an honesty box basis. There was no one to supervise the canteen, so people were expected to help themselves to drinks and snacks, paying for them by putting the money into an honesty box. The researchers changed the picture above the honesty box on alternating weeks: one week a picture of flowers, the next week a rather crude black-and-white photocopied picture of eyes (presumably looking as if they might be overlooking the honesty box and the canteen user). The canteen takings were 2.76 percent higher when the "crude eyes" poster was used. It seems that it takes very little to change our perception of whether a situation requires us to be cooperative and honest.

Another factor that seems to affect our perception is whether or not real money is involved. Here is just one more of the many variants of the Ariely experiment, again at MIT, involving a simple distinction between two groups within the "test cheating opportunity" community. One group went to see the experimenter to collect their cash for correct questions (as had occurred in other variants). Members of the other group were sent to an intermediary to claim tokens for correct questions; they then walked a few yards to a cashier, who would trade those tokens for cash. Despite the fact that the tokens were a very small, transitory step toward exactly the same result (real money), those who were in the "tokens followed by cash for questions" group cheated at more than double the rate of the "direct cash for questions" group.

Other experiments giving people the opportunity to be dishonest for money, compared with the opportunity to be dishonest for goods or proxies for money, bear out a baffling distinction between "real money" and "proxy money." People place an element of trust or honesty moderation on cash that they perhaps don't place on proxies for cash. Would you take a pencil (value 20 cents) from work and give it to your child for their homework? Alternatively, would you take 20 cents from the petty cash tin at work so that you could go and buy your child a pencil for their homework? Most people would, perhaps with a slight squirm, admit having done (or being prepared to do) the first of these petty offenses. Most would not be prepared to do the second.

There are significant implications of the innate honesty distinction between money and proxies for money, as our society becomes far less oriented toward the former and more toward the latter, in the form of electronic transactions and the pseudo-money we increasingly use in online commerce. Perhaps our perception of tokens compared with real money will change and converge, or perhaps society is inadvertently opening the doors to unprecedented types and levels of small-scale crime in our brave new online world.

ETHICAL CHOICES

One theme that has run through this chapter's discussions on fairness, cooperation, and trust is the distinction between our theoretical expectation of rational behavior and what happens in practice. In theory, we would expect rational people to be entirely outcome driven and single-minded in their purpose. In practice, while there is no doubt that people strive purposefully in their choices toward outcomes that are in their interests, they also demonstrably choose to do the right thing: to be fair, cooperative, and trustworthy in their dealings, even in fabricated, one-off situations where there is no obvious motive for such behavior.

The distinction between the purposeful mentality and the "do the right thing" mentality has parallels with the two main contrasting schools of thought that underpin commercial ethics: teleology and deontology. The word "teleology" is derived from the Greek *telos*, which means end or purpose. Ethics based on teleology is often described as the "ethics of what is good." A teleological ethical decision looks at rightness or wrongness, based on the results or outcomes of that decision. The word "deontology" is derived from another Greek word, *deon*, which means obligation or duty. Ethics based on deontology is often described as the "ethics of what is right." A deontological ethical decision looks at the moral obligations and duties of the decision maker, based on principles and rules of behavior.

Commercial folk, like bankers, traders, and professional service providers, tend to lean toward teleological thinking. In contrast, people like tax inspectors, ecologists, and philosophers prefer deontology.

Table 3.1 illustrates the distinction between teleology and deontology. Yet our perception of fairness, trustworthiness, and the "right thing" can be distorted quite easily depending on context. Our ethical compass can be pushed and pulled in all directions in somewhat predictable yet seemingly irrational ways.

Table 3.1 Teleology and deontology compared

TELEOLOGY	DEONTOLOGY
Telos: end, purpose	*Deon*: obligation, duty
Ethics of what is good	Ethics of what is right
Rightness or wrongness based on outcomes	Obligations based on duties, principles, rules
Legal positivism	Natural law
Enlightened self-interest, utilitarianism, consequentialism	Moral absolutism, Kantianism, categorical imperative

We argue that ethics should be embedded in the ways people do business at all times, while recognizing that many of the ethical choices people need to make are not clear cut. We should recognize the nuances in the ethical choices we make and try to make them both sound and consistent. We should consider our ethical choices from both a teleological (outcome-based) and a deontological (process-based) perspective.

Figure 3.2 shows a model for thinking through commercial ethical choices, illustrating what we call the zone of ethical nuances:

- *Don't Do It*: If your proposed action would lead to a result that is clearly both a bad commercial outcome and the wrong thing to do, then it doesn't require much thought to decide not to take that action.
- *Just Do It*: If your proposed action would lead to a result that is clearly both a good commercial outcome and the right thing to do, then it doesn't require much thought to decide to take that action.
- *Patsy*: If your proposed action would lead to a result that is a bad commercial outcome although it is the right thing to do, but you choose to go ahead with that action anyway, you are behaving like a patsy. Your commercial career is likely to be short and none too sweet.
- *Spiv*: If your proposed action would lead to a result that is a good commercial outcome although it is the wrong thing to do, but you choose to go ahead with that action anyway, you are behaving like a spiv. Your commercial career might be both short and sweet—perhaps you'll be over the hills and far away with your profits or bonuses before the chickens come home to roost as a result of your ethical choices.

In reality, of course, very few commercial ethical choices are entirely clear cut. Most choices fit within the zone of ethical

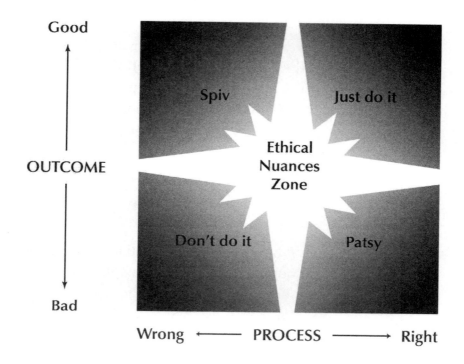

Figure 3.2 Zone of ethical nuances

nuances where we need to apply judgment. We have illustrated the zone sitting nicely in the middle of Figure 3.2, with potential judgments to be made at all the joins between good and bad. However, where the ethical nuances zone sits depends very much on context. We have already shown in simple experimental examples how ethical choices can be predictably changed with pictures or spoon-fed moral thoughts.

In organizations, it is very easy to create a context where certain behaviors or choices are acceptable or unacceptable. A corporate culture is simply "the way people decide to do things around here." If a solid ethical framework is embedded in that corporate culture, you are unlikely to get many Spiv choices. Nor, indeed, should you get Patsy choices either. In the absence of such a framework, ethical compasses within a large organization are likely to be pointing in many different directions in different

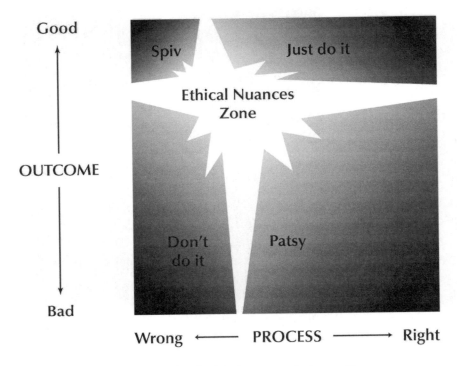

Figure 3.3 Perceived ethical nuances in boom times

contexts, with perhaps examples of both Spiv and Patsy ethical choices being made. And of course, some organizations have an unsavory corporate culture, leaning strongly toward Spiv choices as the default. When a corrupt organization finally tumbles, a pattern to the culture is usually revealed: "Don't ask too many questions"; "The bosses know best, just obey their instructions"; "Everyone was expected to turn a blind eye to those things"; "It seemed too good to be true"; "Profit was the only thing that mattered."

The same contextual issues can apply to prevailing economic conditions. During boom times, when profits tend to be high and risks tend to be downplayed, the perceived sizes of the quadrants tend to shift. Figure 3.3 illustrates this shift.

Because the benchmark for profits is higher in boom times, managers have a tendency to perceive themselves to be in the

Patsy quadrant more readily. Of course, in boom times it also should be easier both to do the right thing and to achieve good outcomes, but only if you retain a realistic perception of what a good outcome is. Also, in boom times the perception of what comprises Spiv-like activity is more rarely identified.

For most of the 1980s, for example, although insider trading was technically prohibited, it was more or less ignored. Of course, the big-name traders, deal-makers, and bankers had inside information; that's how they made things happen. Much of the City of London operated as an informal club of lucky people who knew what was going on better than anyone else. It was a tough club to join unless you had the right connections or exceptional skill, and therefore usefulness to someone within the club. Regulatory changes in 1986 and the market crash that followed a year later changed the mood considerably. Scapegoats needed to be found and on that occasion it was insider traders. The rules were tightened considerably and some of the high-rollers ended up in court. Many insider-trading activities were illegal as well as unethical. Many were borderline legal, but, as the mood changed, shifted from ethically acceptable to ethically unacceptable.

Another good example of this form of ethical shift took place in Japan after the decades of high economic growth gave way to the years of slump in the 1990s. This is vividly documented in *Ethics and Finance* by Avi Persaud and John Plender.[9] During the boom years in postwar Japan, certain practices became commonplace between senior civil servants and top business-men. One well-known practice was *amakudari*, meaning "descent from heaven." Senior civil servants would customarily retire from the service in their early 50s and "make their pile" for a few years in businesses that they had previously regulated and supervised.

Another interesting practice became famous in Japan in the 1990s, the *no pan shabu shabu* scandal. The Ministry of Finance was regarded as an austere and hard-working environment, and perks were provided by top businessmen who might want favors from officials. One such perk was banking officials being entertained by bankers with lavish meals at an expensive Chinese restaurant, Lo Lan, which specialized in *no pan shabu shabu*. *Shabu shabu* is a tasty Japanese beef hotpot. *No pan* means that the waitresses wore short skirts and an absence of pants. The savoriness or otherwise of this combination is a matter for personal taste ("*no pan* sushi and sashimi" might have been a more appropriate example for this book), but it became clear that the times and locations of banking regulatory inspections were being leaked to bankers by ministry officials during the course of these meals.

When the scandal broke, the Japanese economy had shifted from boom to financial crisis and the slump had started. Several banks, such as Hokkaido Takushoku and Hyogo, collapsed, several other banks were in deep trouble, and the real economy was suffering. Unemployment was high and the prospects for economic recovery were poor. When the chief inspector of banks, Koichi Miyagawa, was taken into custody, he stated that he did not believe the entertainment had gone "beyond acceptable social limits." However, those acceptable limits had shifted. These shifts are depicted in Figure 3.4, where the ethical nuances zone has shifted and enlarged considerably.

From a purely teleological point of view, the question of whether or not society has an orderly banking system is a binary one: either it is orderly or it isn't. Therefore, when the banking system ceased to be orderly, the benchmark for good outcomes shifted down a long way, making the Spiv quadrant much bigger. At the same time, the court of public opinion also shifted its judgment on what constituted acceptable and unacceptable behavior. Behaviors were far less likely to be questioned while the outcomes were acceptable. Once the outcomes became unacceptable, there was huge public outcry against the officials and businessmen involved.

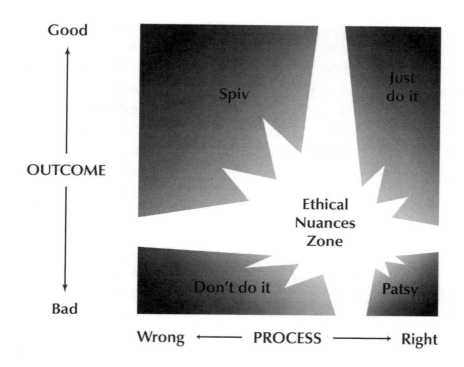

Figure 3.4 Perceived ethical nuances in a slump

Surely humanity should aim for a more consistent ethical framework in which ethical choices are made, be they at an individual, organizational, or societal level? We shouldn't consider certain ethical choices acceptable in boom times if we consider them to be fraudulent in slump times. While recognizing that emotions and feelings are an important part of ethical choices, society perhaps needs to aim for a more systematic approach to ethics, especially where those ethical choices have significant commercial and/or societal consequences.

BEHAVIORAL UNCERTAINTY

Chapters 2 and 3 have explored choice, the first of our four streams of thinking for making better decisions about wicked problems. Decision making is the process of selecting a course of action from a number of alternatives in conditions of uncertainty. Studying decision making makes a large intellectual contribution toward our journey, but focusing on decisions alone is not sufficient. We need to apply choices across space and time. Concepts of time and uncertainty lie at the heart of choice. Unfortunately, human beings make poor intertemporal decisions; that is, decisions in which differential timing becomes part of the decision. The involvement of periods of time complicates decision making; the longer the periods, the more complicated the decision making.

Chapter 4 traverses topics of choice through time, such as intertemporal behavior and long-term investment appraisal. In the process, it initiates our economics stream. Chapters 5 and 6 will continue to intertwine economics and choice.

4 | CHOOSING TO STEAL THE FAMILY SILVER

Many of the more important personal decisions we make are long term, such as pursuing more education, purchasing a home, or saving for retirement. Yet individuals, organizations, and governments alike tend to struggle to make sound, long-term choices, usually favoring and justifying short-term gains over longer-term planning. Perhaps that explains why each generation decides to steal the family silver from future generations, and why such choices can nevertheless be perceived as rational and even fair at the time they are made.

TIME TO MAKE DECISIONS ABOUT TIME

Decision making gets even more interesting once differential timing, or intertemporal choices, is part of the mix. Richard Thaler, George Loewenstein, and Drazen Prelec made a successful niche for themselves experimenting with many types of intertemporal decision.[1] In one experiment, individuals were asked to make two decisions, with a week elapsing between them.

Decision One: Your job allows you 30 days' holiday a year. To reward you for excellent performance, your boss offers you an additional 14 days of holiday. You are given two choices:

- Choice A: take all 14 extra days this year.
- Choice B: take 7 of your extra days this year and 7 next year.

Would you go for Choice A or Choice B?

Decision Two: Your job allows you 30 days' holiday a year. To reward you for excellent performance, your boss offers you an additional 14 days of holiday. You are given two choices:

- Choice Y: take 44 days of leave this year and 30 days of leave next year.
- Choice Z: take 37 days of leave this year and 37 days of leave next year.

Would you go for Choice Y or Choice Z?

Most people opt for choices A and Z, although A and Y are identical choices, as are B and Z. If you frame this decision in terms of extra days, people tend to want the additional holiday benefits now, not later, yet when you frame the exact same decision in terms of overall holiday benefits, people show a preference for spacing out their benefits evenly. Whether they envisaged the extra benefits being used for fishing holidays was, sadly, not asked in the experiment.

In another Loewenstein experiment from the 1980s, students were promised a $7 gift voucher for a local music store (sufficient for one sizeable item or a few small items at the time) and randomly told that they would be receiving the gift in either one, four, or eight weeks' time.[2] Each student was then asked if they were prepared to trade their voucher for a less valuable voucher to be received more quickly (a deduction for speed-up) or for a more valuable voucher to be received later (a premium for delay). Table 4.1 shows the various responses, indicating the average percentage premium or deduction the students were prepared to accept.

People show a far higher propensity to be rewarded for delay than to pay a penalty for speed, although clearly the same question could be framed in terms of either a delay premium or a speed penalty, depending on the reference points given when framing the question. In short, the way a question is framed

Table 4.1 Premium for delay or deduction for speed-up

TIME INTERVAL	PREMIUM FOR DELAY	DEDUCTION FOR SPEED-UP
1–4 weeks	16%	4%
4–8 weeks	12%	5%
1–8 weeks	25%	7%

often predetermines the answer. Preferring delay rewards over speed penalties is very similar to the loss aversion highlighted in prospect theory. Indeed, Loewenstein suggests that intertemporal decision making has a great deal in common with prospect theory; you can observe seemingly inconsistent behavior by changing the point of reference for the temporal aspect of the decision.

In a third experiment, students were offered choices between free dinners, either in a "Modest Greek" restaurant or a "Fancy French" restaurant (most favored Fancy French), and then asked whether they wanted their choice in one month or two months' time (most favored a one-month over a two-month wait). Those who had expressed a preference for Fancy French food in one month's time (the vast majority still) were then offered two free meals, one Modest Greek, one Fancy French; one of which would be given to them in one month's time, the other in two months' time. The seemingly consistent answer would have been for all to choose to have the Fancy French meal in one month's time and the Modest Greek meal in two months' time, but a significant majority opted to have the lesser meal first. Most people seem to prefer a pattern of increasing utility over time, such a preference being a stronger influence on the two-meal decision than the time preference expressed in the one-meal decision. In short, we like our gratification to increase over time. Fish lovers among you will be delighted to learn that some of the experiments involved an additional choice of a Grand Lobster Supper at a very swanky restaurant.

INVESTING FOR THE FUTURE

Given that it is difficult to make consistent intertemporal decisions about gift vouchers, holidays, and lobster suppers now or a few months hence, how on earth can we make important decisions about long-term investments? Economic and financial theory claims to have an answer: compare long-term investments with short-term decisions using the concept of net present value (NPV).

Let us define some terms. Most people know what an *interest rate* is, for example the percentage applied to your deposit every year in a simple deposit account. The underlying assumption is that cash today is worth more than the same amount of cash tomorrow. We need to be paid for saving or investing today, which is equivalent to deferring gratification until tomorrow. The term *discount rate* can mean exactly the same, but in the context of computing present values in discounted cash flow calculations. This is the meaning we shall use for the rest of this chapter and indeed the rest of this book.[3]

Net present value (NPV) is a common method used in business to make capital investment decisions. Basically, all future costs and cash flows are expressed in terms of the value of money today. There are a number of concepts related to NPV, for instance *discounted cash flows*. Many analysts value the shares of a company based on discounted cash flows. They take the company's future expected cash flows and discount them back to a net present value, using a discount rate typically based around the cost of capital or the interest rate one might get on deposit or a government bond. Thus the value of a company is the net present value of all its future cash less the cost of its shares.

Within businesses, decision makers are deciding all the time whether to invest in one or more projects. The basic idea is simple: will the investment produce more cash than it consumes? Discounted cash flow calculations illuminate decisions such as:

- Can the company afford an investment, (perhaps with debt, perhaps without)?
- When will an investment yield returns that exceed its cost of capital?
- What are the expected profits compared with returns available elsewhere?

Let us take a simple example of three options for a business-person with $100 and ten years of time: Keep-the-Cash, Micro-Project, and Mega-Project. Keep-the-Cash says don't spend the $100, Micro-Project requires $100 investment, and Mega-Project requires $400 investment. The businessperson believes that she will make a 25 percent return per annum on the Micro-Project and/or the Mega-Project expenditures.

Figure 4.1 illustrates that, in this simple example, the most money is made with Mega-Project, $500 more; the second most with Micro-Project, $50 more; and nothing with Keep-the-Cash, leaving the businessperson with $600, $150, and $100 respectively at the end of 10 years.

There are two immediate problems with the simple NPV shown above. The first is that the businessperson wouldn't just sit on the cash. At the very least she would put it on deposit with a bank. With an interest rate of 5 percent on the cash, taking the Keep-the-Cash option results in about $163 after ten years of compound interest. Micro-Project is now $13 less attractive than Keep-the-Cash. The businessperson is better off keeping the cash in the bank than investing in Micro-Project.

The second problem is that the businessperson doesn't have all of the $400 for Mega-Project and will have to borrow $300.

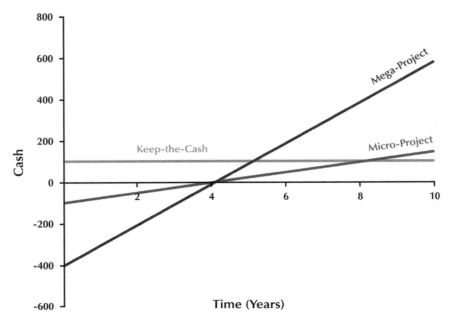

Figure 4.1 Simple net present value

The lender will require a return on the money. If the money must be repaid in equal installments over 10 years with a 10 percent loan interest rate, then Mega-Project yields just $35, Micro-Project returns $50, and just putting the cash on deposit, Keep-the-Money, returns $63, as illustrated in Figure 4.2.

Einstein supposedly said that compound interest was "the greatest mathematical discovery of all time." Of course, that implies that compound debt might just be the worst mathematical discovery of all time. The linkage between compound interest and economic growth is intriguing. In *The Future of Money*, Bernard Lietaer says:

> the rate of interest fixes the average level of growth that is needed to remain in the same place. This need for perpetual growth is a fact of life that we tend to take for granted in modern societies and that we usually do not associate with either interest or even our money system.[4]

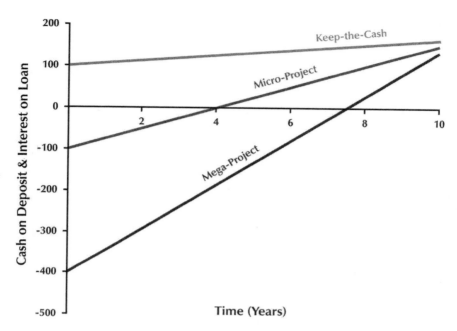

Figure 4.2 NPV with cash deposit and loan interest

In *The End of Money*, Thomas H. Greco, Jr. goes further:

> Those who recognize the impossibility of perpetual expo-
> nential growth and who understand how compound interest
> is built into the global system of money and banking expect
> that there will be periodic "bubbles" and "busts", each of
> increasing amplitude until the system shakes itself apart.[5]

Returning briefly to the underlying mathematics, NPV is very
sensitive to the interest rate the organization might pay for borrowing and receive for lending. Most projects require investment,
so people normally use the concept of negative cash flows and
discount rate (the deemed interest rate or hurdle rate the organization uses for computing net present values) to produce a simple equation.

For a multiyear project, say that where $CF(x)$ = cash flow in year
x, d = discount rate, and n = the number of years in the project:

$$NPV = CF(0) + CF(1)/(1+d) + CF(2)/(1+d)^2 + ... + CF(n)/(1+d)^n$$

Note that $CF(0)$ would typically be negative for most investment projects.

Consider something similar to Mega-Project but on a grand scale. This is Garga-Project, which spends about 1 percent of the world's $50 trillion GDP—that is, $500 billion—on something really useful globally. Garga-Project is so useful that it will produce $50 billion of value in nominal terms for ever. You can expect Garga-Project to produce a 10 percent return in the very next year; that is, $50 billion of value. But given a 10 percent discount rate that $50 billion is worth a bit less next year, about $45 billion in today's money.

You can subtract the $45 billion return from the $500 billion cost and move to the next year. The following year you get another $50 billion, but that's only worth $40.5 billion in today's money. The following year, the $50 billion is worth just over $36 billion; and at the end of the 10th year it's worth only $17 billion in today's money. In this example, despite a 10 percent return, Garga-Project would take some 60 years to break even.

To illustrate the sensitivity to the discount rate, Figure 4.3 sets out a number of discount rates for Garga-Project, from 2 percent to 14 percent. You can see that with discount rates above 10 percent, Garga-Project never moves into positive numbers; that is, it never pays off. Discount rates below 10 percent take varying degrees of time to pay off. Rather obviously, if Garga-Project produced higher returns, then the discount rates would matter less and the payoff dates would be sooner. You'll be relieved to know that we don't intend to take you through any more calculations. But please hold on to the idea that this technical matter of discount rate is fundamental to evaluating long-term investment decisions. It is also fundamental to questions of long-term economic growth and sustainability.

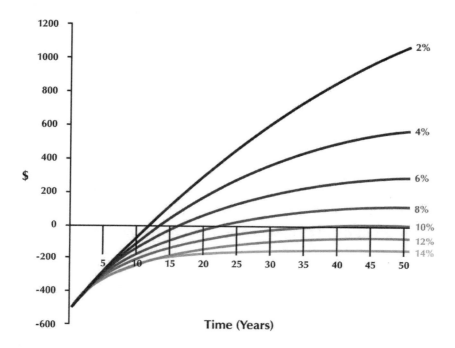

Figure 4.3 Discounting investment

AT ANY RATE?

In business, the correct discount rate is not necessarily obvious and can be the cause of heated discussion. Typically, for business projects a "cost of capital" is calculated to arrive at a discount rate. Cost of capital can be a fairly complex calculation that employs the *capital asset pricing model*, which in turn depends on factors such as the risk-free rate of return, the equity rate, the bond rate, and the debt/equity structure of the organization. We have ignored any attempt to take account of inflation and taxation—some taxation systems favor expenditure over capital investment, or vice versa; some favor debt over equity, or vice versa. Somewhat ironically, despite all these machinations, the discount rate used in low-inflation circumstances by most businesspeople most of the time seems to circle around 8 to 10 percent, inferring perhaps that discount rate calculations are often used to justify decisions that have already been made.

More crucially, we have ignored risk: whether the projects achieve their objectives at the cost stated when the decision is made, or achieve their objectives at all. Micro-, Mega-, and Garga-Projects might overrun and need more money. Even with more money, they might only partially succeed. They could fail and be a complete waste of money. There are more advanced techniques for investment appraisal used by the cognoscenti, such as real option theory, portfolio analysis, and many more, but we shall ignore those additional complexities too for the time being.

Discounting future consumption can lead to more than one conundrum, particularly over finite resources. Global fishing is a $55 billion industry, possibly on its way to extinction. Taken to the extreme, eating a $6 fish tonight can be calculated as worth more than consuming all the fish in the world a couple of millennia from now at a discount rate of 1 percent. At a discount rate of 10 percent, tonight's $6 is worth all the world's commercial fish stocks 260 years from now. Such calculations mean little, of course, if you believe that all the world's commercial fish stocks might be extinct in as little as 60 years.

THE PRICE OF DEFERRED FISH

Just in case you were starting to think that intertemporal decisions based on NPV and discount rate can be reduced to classical economic assumptions about rational decision making, it's time to remind you that intertemporal decisions are affected by framing and reference points, as shown in the experiments described earlier in this chapter. Here is one more example, adapted from the Loewenstein, Prelec, and Thaler experiments with promises of future tasty meals. The subjects were asked whether they would prefer a fish supper in a swanky restaurant in two weeks' time or the same fish supper, but in six weeks' time. Assuming they would prefer to have the meal in two weeks' time, how much money would they need to receive on the day of the supper in six weeks' time to compensate for the four-week delay?

Between 80 and 90 percent of the students (where were these experimental meals and payments when we were students?) chose to have their meal sooner and asked for several dollars in compensation for the four-week delay. The same students were then offered the following, subtly different choice: a fish supper in a swanky restaurant in one year's time or the same fish supper, in one year and four weeks from now, with $2 less compensation than the amount they asked for in the first experiment. Most (about 70 percent) of the students who had asked for more than $2 compensation in the first experiment were happy to accept $2 less in the second. This is an interesting finding, as the time delay between the two options in each of the choices is exactly the same, four weeks.

If people really were applying straightforward discount rates to such decisions, they would be consistent in their decision making. It seems that we have a natural tendency to increase our perceived value of the discount rate for more proximate delays and reduce that value for more remote timeframes.

NO INTERTEMPORAL SELF-CONTROL

Intertemporal choices can also be considered in terms of self-control. The additional value we place on wanting something now rather than deferring gratification is to some extent determined by our patience, or our self-control of our impatience. Commerce depends on self-control and patience. Social research indicates that children who are able to defer gratification are more likely to be successful and happier in later life. In 1981,

Thaler and Shefrin wrote an influential paper on intertemporal choice and self-control, examining the internal conflict individuals often face in their simultaneous capacity as "both a far-sighted planner and a myopic doer."[6] This conflict is akin to the principal–agent problem we discussed in Chapter 3, except that, in this instance, different sides of the same individual's personality replace the potentially conflicted parties of the conventional agency model.

Furthermore, the same two techniques that are used to try to resolve principal–agent problems—alignment of incentives and the imposition of rules—are often deployed to encourage intertemporal self-control. For example, many people who are trying to save more money or pay off debts set themselves targets and psychologically reward themselves by meeting those targets. Others impose rules on themselves by, for example, setting up automatic transfers for a set amount of money each month to a savings or debt-repayment account.

Some intertemporal choices seem so remote that people struggle to impose their own rules on themselves. A well-studied example is workers' contributions to pensions and savings plans. Most workers, when interviewed, confess that they do not save enough toward their retirement. Indeed, about half will state that they will save more next year (their farsighted planning selves talking) but do not do so (their myopic doing selves not acting). Many state-run schemes have a default contribution rate of zero percent and zero is precisely the level of contribution most workers make. An element of paternalism in pensions policy,[7] or libertarian paternalism along the lines discussed in Chapter 2 (automatic enrollment with the ability to opt out), could help boost take-up rates enormously, as shown by Madrian and O'Shea.[8] Thaler and Benartzi go further, advocating Save More Tomorrow schemes, with automatic increases to the default contribution rate over time, which participants can (but normally don't) adjust to suit their own circumstances.[9] Default settings tend to be sticky, even if it only requires a few clicks of the mouse, or the equivalent effort, to change them.

Neoclassical economics suggests that each individual should make intertemporal choices based on their marginal rate of time preference, which should equate to the relevant interest rate for them.[10] Demographic factors such as age, marital status, current income streams, expected future income streams, and the like might all be expected to affect an individual's borrowing rate and therefore their marginal rate of time preference. Intertemporal choices are clearly affected by crowd behavior—doing what everyone else is doing. Development economists in particular are interested in the impact of poverty on people's marginal rate of time preference.

In recent years, Sendhil Mullainathan and others have been researching fruit, vegetable, and flower vendors in Chennai, India.[11] Most vendors endure extremely high discount rates, paid to money lenders, just to be able to trade; this can often equate to about half their income. Such circumstances are often described as poverty traps. Yet those Chennai vendors typically buy a couple of cups of tea during the trading day, despite the fact that they could become debt free in about a month, thus doubling their take-home income, simply by abstaining from one of those cups of tea each day for that period. A minority of the Chennai vendors have the self-control to escape this poverty trap, but the majority persevere within it. Mullainathan argues that scarcity (of which poverty is one example) causes a unique pattern of psychological responses to intertemporal choices, essentially nonoptimal choices or bad allocation decisions.[12]

Most people make similarly poor decisions in respect to allocating their scarce time. You'll recognize the failing in yourself if you have ever looked at your diary and wondered: "Why on earth, given that I am so busy, did I ever agree to attend that event/give that lecture/do voluntary work that day/write a book to that deadline…" Those facing money poverty, like the Chennai vendors, tend to find themselves in an especially difficult decision-making environment, because the small temptations to which most humans can easily succumb, such as a cup of tea or a tasty snack during the trading day, have such a pronounced effect on their economic position. Extreme scarcity is maintained or even exacerbated all too easily in environments where a small deficit of self-control makes all the difference.

The 1981 Thaler and Shefrin paper on self-control draws out a similar point, quoting an intriguing study by Jerry A Hausman[13] suggesting that there was more to intertemporal choice than simply the borrowing rate for individuals. Hausman looked at household purchases of air-conditioning units, which were sold on a variety of capital outlay and expected operating cost bases. From the payment choices people made, it was possible to calculate the inferred discount rate of the purchases. People on low incomes tended to buy air conditioners with slightly lower capital outlay prices but high operating costs (and therefore high inferred discount rates), whereas those on higher incomes tended to buy the slightly more expensive capital items with significantly lower operating costs and therefore much lower inferred discount rates. The inferred discount rates varied between 5 percent for the wealthiest group of buyers to 89 percent for the poorest, while the average was around 20 percent.

It is especially difficult to be a far-sighted planner when you are living from hand to mouth, needing essentially to be a myopic doer simply to get by. It is therefore unclear whether poorer people are poor because they have less self-control, or are less able to exercise self-control because they are poor. What is clear is that proximate rewards are perceived to have a high discount rate, whereas more distant gratification is perceived to have a much lower discount rate. This intertemporal anomaly is fundamental to the rest of this chapter and its central question: How do we end up inadvertently choosing to steal the family silver, appropriating resources from our children's future for our own current use?

STEALING THE FAMILY SILVER FROM FUTURE GENERATIONS

People don't aim to be outright thieves, but we do have a habit of mucking around with the discount rate, usually by claiming that future expenditure is worth a lot less than today's. There are three common reasons for discounting future consumption:

- Consumption levels will be higher in the future, so the marginal utility of additional consumption will be lower.
- Future consumption levels are uncertain.
- Future consumption should be discounted simply because it takes place in the future and people generally prefer to benefit in the present than in the future (whether the benefit is money, gift vouchers, or fish suppers).

One of the biggest issues in economics is the discount rate to use under various circumstances. The term *social discount rate* is often employed when computing net present values for social investments or public works. This is technically the same factor as the discount rate (or hurdle rate) described above for businesses making investment decisions, but in practice the social discount rate used for public works tends to be significantly lower than the equivalent corporate rate. Businesses have to use something close to their cost of capital, but governments have more leeway. In 2002 the British Treasury stated:

> the current discount rate is being "unbundled" so that the new rate reflects only one factor (the social time preference rate), set at 3.5%. The current rate of 6% implicitly allows for such factors as risk, optimism bias, and the cost of variability. It is now proposed that these are dealt with separately and explicitly.[14]

For economic evaluations across society, discount rates are typically lower. When considering intergenerational transfers, people attempt to estimate the "pure rate of time preference"—the rate people would ethically use to evaluate transfers to future generations. To get there, analysts sample the population using ethical questions about saving lives versus costs to try to find these utility functions, often struggling through a thicket of contradictions to arrive at an estimate of around 1.5 percent. The average annual death rate for adults is about 1.5 percent, so this is not a surprising number. In some ways, there is no such thing as society, only individuals. Society, if it had a mind, might think that it will live for ever and try to balance income across everyone in all generations. Individuals quite rightly want to see payback in their lifetime. No wonder old people can be crotchety about long-term investments. It will be interesting to see if the trend toward longer lives, perhaps becoming substantially longer with some foreseeable medical breakthroughs, starts to decrease the pure rate of time preference.

Having established a pure rate of time preference, we still need to establish a pure time discount rate for investment decisions. The pure time discount rate should be higher than the pure rate of time preference, reflecting the fact that we can't do everything. If we set the pure time discount rate to zero, we find that future offspring are too numerous and infinity is a long time. Very tiny income streams have enormous net present values. Thus we find ourselves having to do everything now for infinite generations yet unborn. Once again, the British Treasury's social time preference rate seems reasonable at 3.5 percent.

One way to estimate the pure time discount rate is by examination of global long-term real interest rates, now about 2 percent for the industrialized nations. But a decade ago, global long-term real interest rates were about 4 percent. Do we care more about the future now than we did a decade ago? Did the Victorians, who made things to last for 150 years, apply a very much lower discount rate to their descendants than the current generation does? Or did the Victorians inadvertently over-engineer their infrastructure?

OVERENGINEERING DECISIONS OR DECIDING TO OVERENGINEER?

One of the hardest things to avoid is overengineering, of which Victorian engineers were masters. Overengineering is when something is designed to last longer or in worse circumstances than is needed. If you think about planned obsolescence from an engineering perspective, the ideal situation is when everything fails at once, or at least around the same time. If you think about a fishing boat, you would like the engine, the hull, the safety equipment, the periodic cycle of net replacements, and everything else to collapse at a specific time. Nothing is wasted. The boat fails when everything coincides with its own obsolescence. The ultimate nautical engineer would plan that everything collapsed at some specific point, say 880,000 hours on the engine. In the ideal situation, the fuel tank would be empty and the boat would coast in and beach itself by the scrapyard before it sprang a leak.

Making do while systems start to fail can lead to complicated systems interactions and decisions. After several decades of neglect and poor maintenance—to some degree due to lack of water pricing and nonrecognition of the value of the assets on their books, leading to false profits—leakages from UK water systems were especially high in the first decade or so of the twenty-first century. Historically, water pressure was anywhere from 3 to 4 bar; that is, enough to raise water another 30 to 40 meters from where it leaves a water company's pipes (3 bar is a good shower pressure). The pressure levels may not have been statutory, but they were relied on. By comparison, in Utah for instance, the statutory requirement is around 2 bar. In order to reduce water leakages, UK water companies reduced water pressure. Hopefully at some point their maintenance programs will allow them to restore traditional pressure, but in the meantime thousands of homeowners are installing water pressure pumps and consuming electricity locally to get the system pressure back to normal for showers and other machinery. Of course, if water companies do restore traditional pressures, we might expect to see quite a few leakages in homes that, during the intervening period, haven't installed systems robust enough to handle higher pressures.

The Victorians overengineered, intervening politicians took credit for cost savings that were really underdeployment of maintenance, and everybody tried to hand problems on to the next generation if at all feasible. So in a sense, our generation stole from the Victorians, but our parents stole from them and from our generation, while our generation tries to steal from its own children. Unfortunately, in the "hot potato meets musical chairs" nature of long-term infrastructure, our generation happens to be the one left with creaking Victorian infrastructure at the time it needs replacement. While the utility companies may try to blame their Victorian forebears, we suggest that the blame lies closer to the modern era. Successive generations failed to make adequate provisions for maintenance and replacement. The long-term investment cycle does not resonate well with the shorter-term political cycle.

Discount rates much above 3 percent often render major long-term investments unattractive. Governments take a short-term view of certain long-term investment issues that matter to them, such as "Will investment affect our re-election?" or "Does today's tax pain help us in the next election?" This implies that they will often use relatively high discount rates, perhaps 20 percent, when evaluating investment decisions because they want quick returns. Discount rates such as 3, 5, and 10 percent are widely used in economics, but there is little consensus on what value is appropriate in any given circumstance.

The truth is that governments, like individuals, have a tendency to discount the remote future too much, otherwise known as underprovisioning. We have already discussed this with the Victorian infrastructure example, but another gargantuan underprovisioning problem concerns pensions. The actor George Burns once quipped, "If you live to be 100, you've got it made. Very few people die past that age." He was right; he died in 1996, aged 100. Fortunately for him, he didn't die while poor.

Globally, pensions are an enormous future burden. In 1950 there were 12 people aged 15–64 for every person of retirement age. Today the global average is 9 to 1; by mid-century it will be 4 to 1. These statistics have hit hardest in Europe and Japan, but they will soon affect Eastern Europe and Asia. Not surprisingly, the combination of long timeframes and government has led to a huge crisis in most countries: 40–80-year pension plan decisions meet 4–5-year political cycles. In the early twenty-first century, increased accounting transparency and mistakes in actuarial estimates coincided with bear market revaluations to the point that many large companies are pension fund liabilities with an incidental car company or steelworks attached.

Estimating potential pension liabilities is another area where the discount rate that is used really matters. For example, based on a discount rate of 3.5 percent, the UK government admitted that the unfunded public-sector pension fund liability amounted to £460 billion, less than 40 percent of one year's GDP. However, in a world of lower than expected long-term returns, within the space of just three years the Government Actuary's Department revised the discount rate to 2.8 percent and then further lowered it to 1.8 percent for pension liabilities. On that basis, some actuaries estimate UK public pension fund liabilities to be in excess of £1 trillion; that is, close to 100 percent of one year's GDP and more than double annual public expenditure.

In a fascinatingly honest and nonpartisan critique of government debt, Mark Field MP critiqued the lack of transparency surrounding public works and pensions. In the UK Parliament on 20 February 2007, he stated:

> there is no easy way out. In essence, today's pensioners and those retiring in the near future will be able to rely on considerably more generous benefits than those just entering the workplace, who will pay for those liabilities. Given that there are twice as many voters over 55 as there are under 35, and that they are twice as likely to vote, it is unrealistic, to put it mildly, to expect anyone in the political arena—on either side of the political divide—to stand up and state some fairly bald facts on this matter. We are consuming what we believe we are entitled to without regard to the costs, and future generations will have to meet the liabilities for that short-sighted and selfish approach.

Given all this uncertainty, it probably helps to know that there are two types of economists:

- Those who cannot calculate the correct discount rate.
- Those who do not know that they cannot calculate the correct discount rate.

As individuals, firms, and economists show so little aptitude for intertemporal decision making and so much aptitude for "stealing" from future generations, it is tempting to conclude that governments ought to do something about such problems. But governments seem to show no more aptitude for long-term planning than the rest of us. In any case, surely there are fundamental questions to ask about the appropriateness (or otherwise) of governments' roles in areas such as commercial infrastructure and pensions. We explore such questions around the role of government in the next chapter.

In the final section of this book we revisit questions of long-term decision making and discount rates, when we discuss wicked problems such as climate change and sustainability.

STREAM B | Economics

5 | GOLDILOCKS GOVERNMENT AND THE MARKETS

This chapter delves into the relationship between governments and markets. Despite hundreds of years of deep thought about economics, government, and commerce, our society has yet to determine successfully what should be done in the private sector and what should be done in the public sector by or through governments.

TWO OR THREE SECTORS?

We tend to think of markets as either centers of innovative wealth creation, or nests of self-centered, profit-maximizing capitalists. We are equally dualistic about government as a benevolent enforcer of equal opportunities or a "Bureaucratic Big Brother Bogeyman."

The vocabulary falters even more on the third sector, frequently described in negative terms as not-for-profit or nongovernmental organizations. These days we tend to use more positive terms, such as charitable, civil society, social enterprise, voluntary sector, or activist organizations. Nevertheless, we can be just as binary about charities: they are run by either caring humanitarians organized for the common good, or interfering, self-righteous busybodies.

Looking at society through commercial eyes, it is easy to conclude that there are three main groups: markets, governments, and not-for-profits. Easy, but perhaps wrong. A glance at basic economic statistics might quickly dispel the third way and get us to focus on the public–private divide alone. The not-for-profit sector is, despite much growth and noise recently, by far the smallest at a couple of percentage points of GDP and about the same in employment, though it is very hard to estimate the contribution of volunteer time. John Hopkins' Center for Civil Society Studies provides enough information across 22 developed nations to guess that even with volunteer time, around 5 percent of labour activity is in the not-for-profit sector.

We return to the increasing importance of the not-for-profit sector in later chapters, but for now we focus on a private sector employing nearly 80 percent of the workforce and a public sector employing some 20 percent on average in the developed world.[1]

GROW YOUR OWN

The public sector in the UK spends well over 40 percent of GDP. About half of this expenditure consists of transfer payments such as welfare or pensions, so perhaps it is fairer to focus on either the slightly more than 20 percent of general government final consumption expenditure, or the 20 percent of the workforce in government employment, indicating that at least that percentage of the economy is under public-sector decision making. Still, it is difficult to examine government expenditure without realizing that much of it is circular, finding its way back into the private sector. It is like continually opening a series of Russian dolls, one within the next, where each doll has within it other private- and public-sector dolls.

This trend of increasing government expenditure is not confined to the UK. People like to imagine that the US is more free market, but the same effect is obvious there. If anything, the growth in US federal spending has been more rapid over the past century, rising by five times in the past 100 years.

An interesting trend to examine is the long-term growth of the public sector. Figure 5.1 is a graph of twentieth-century US

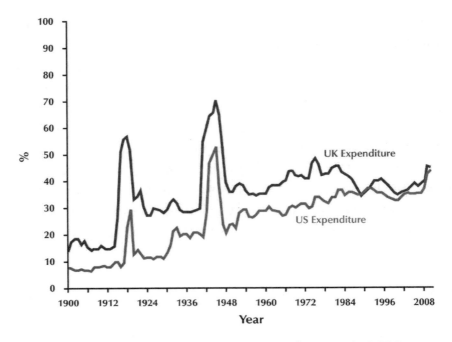

Figure 5.1 US and UK government expenditure as % of GDP

and UK government expenditure as a percentage of GDP. The wartime periods predictably result in a steep climb, followed by a decline, but there is no denying that one of the most important changes of the twentieth century was the manyfold growth of government expenditure.

This rise in the scale of government leads to the natural question: Is this good or bad? Developed economies exhibit a wide range of supposedly orthodox structures. Government can be anywhere in a range of 15 to 50 percent of the economy, without much ability to distinguish one form of economy from another on most measures of performance. The only factor that seems to be negatively affected by large government is GDP growth, though even that relationship is keenly debated at times. The risk of constraining GDP growth through too much government is an important factor to consider over the long term, but it is rarely a compelling short-term reason to induce government to cut its own scale. It is reasonable to ask: Does the public sector have an inbuilt bias for overexpansion?

A number of economists have put forward arguments that the public sector might have a malignant, inbuilt propensity to grow beyond an optimal level. Starting at least as far back as Charles Dodgson (Lewis Carroll) in the 1800s, scholars have pointed out that majority voting systems have inbuilt biases that can make them unfair for certain types of decisions. Adolf Wagner noted in 1883 that industrializing countries' public expenditure would increase in absolute terms and relative to the rest of the economy, his Law of Increasing State Activities.

In more skittish terms, C Northcote Parkinson developed Parkinson's Law, initially in a 1955 article in *The Economist*, latterly in the eponymous book.[2] Starting with the "commonplace observation that work expands so as to fill the time available for its completion," Parkinson developed a pseudo-scientific law of time elasticity. His "killer stats" were comparative admiralty statistics from 1914 and 1928. Despite a 68 percent decline in ships and a 32 percent decline in Royal Navy officers and men, all the other admiralty staff numbers increased. "The officials would have multiplied had there been no seamen at all," he commented wryly.

H R Bowen in 1943 and K J Arrow in 1963 wrote papers considering whether majority voting decisions on spending and taxes have an inbuilt tendency to creep upward.[3] It is clear that voters tend to underestimate the costs of public expenditure. Surveys show that they are confused over capital versus long-term running costs, such as Private Finance Initiative (PFI) programs. Voters struggle to reconcile the apparently small direct costs to themselves of any specific program and the large price tags they read about. Nor can they easily distinguish direct tax rates such as income tax from the myriad of other taxes they face directly or indirectly, such as excise taxes, value added taxes, sales taxes, corporation taxes, or inheritance taxes.

IF IT MOVES, TAX IT

The history of public expenditure is inexorably intertwined with the history of taxation. The latter is the history of peoples' relationships with their governments and with each other. In an interesting contrast across two millennia, Marcus Tullius Cicero averred that "taxes are the sinews of the state," while Robert Orben joked that "Washington is a place where politicians don't know which way is up and taxes don't know which way is down."

Many people welcome the benefits of taxation, regardless of the cost. As the public sector grows, more voters depend on the public sector sustaining them and may well vote to maintain or increase its size. In *Moralizing Criticism and Critical Morality*, Karl Marx noted:

> civil servants and priests, soldiers and ballet-dancers, schoolmasters and police constables, Greek museums and Gothic steeples, civil list and services list—the common seed within which all these fabulous beings slumber in embryo is taxation.

There have been numerous attempts to bring taxation into line with expenditure, and vice versa. While the debt markets allow governments of all types to borrow in frighteningly sophisticated ways, the electorate and the tax authorities are locked together in annual rituals. Despite the ability to borrow and invest over the economic cycle, taxpayers claim to like the simplicity of annual balanced budgets.

However, taxation levels and tax rates do not necessarily correlate with tax revenues. Indeed, most economists believe that there is a maximum tax rate beyond which tax revenues will decline rather than increase. This effect is often referred to as the Laffer Curve, after the supply-side economist Arthur Laffer who helped to popularize the effect in the 1980s. He himself believed that the phenomenon to which he donated his name has probably been around for almost as long as taxation itself. Keynes, in his General Theory,[4] certainly refers to a point at which increased taxation will lead to lower tax revenues. Where economists cannot agree is where on the curve the rate is so high that revenue starts to fall. It is increasingly hard to predict, given the many forms of tax everyone faces and the ability (at least for some people) to switch jurisdictions to avoid certain taxes.

There are really only three ways in which substantial imbalances in public borrowing can be corrected in the future: increased taxation, large-scale cuts in government expenditure, or inflation. Governments often find the inflation route the least painful from their point of view, especially if the inflation caused by the excesses of Governing Party A conveniently occurs when Governing Party B happens to be in power.

INFLATE AWAY

Both banks and governments can create money and thus trigger money inflation. Banks create money through a process known as *fractional reserve banking*. When a bank makes a loan, it does not match that loan directly with a deposit; it simply writes the loan as an accounting entry. Regulators require banks to retain a fraction of their deposits in reserve, but in essence, whenever a bank writes a loan, the bank is creating most of the money represented by that loan. It isn't just governments that can roll metaphorical printing presses and create money; banks do so all the time when making loans. When economists talk about a country's broad money supply, they are talking about a combination of commercial bank-created money and government fiat money. That comprises the bulk of the modern "money system."

When the financial going gets tough, the periodic bubbles and bursts that are, it seems, inevitable with such a financial system, this (perhaps unholy) alliance between banks and governments allows the money creators to inflate away unwanted debt.

A novel phrase that arose from the developed world's response to the early twenty-first-century "bubble burst" is *quantitative easing*, also known as QE. This is a form of open-market operation in which the central bank electronically creates, from nothing, the money with which it purchases real assets such as government bonds, gold, or currencies. People often refer to this as "printing money," but these days the money will almost certainly not be printed, it is simply added to the electronic books of the central bank. That newly created money then enters the banking system when those open-market purchases are made, thus adding to banks' reserves and enabling them to lend a great deal of money, potentially far more than the value of the QE injection—the multiple effect described above.

It is clear that government interventions were needed to stave off the worst possible effects of the global financial crisis in the early twenty-first century, but the longer-term implications of those interventions are less clear. How much does a dose of QE actually add to the money system? It depends on how much lending and therefore additional fractional reserve money results from the central bank injection. No one knows the consequences before the injection of QE and even after that event, economists will ceaselessly debate the extent to which government intervention staved off economic depression and/or got out of hand. By "out of hand" in this context we mean inflation and more asset bubbles. One thing we very rarely hear about is a government deploying a dose of quantitative constipation to deflate a galloping economy. In troubled times, government debt tends to be high and inflation conveniently reduces the burden of unwanted debt.

Milton Friedman, always keen to discourage big government, famously said: "inflation is the one form of taxation that can be imposed without legislation." John Maynard Keynes similarly stated: "by a continuing process of inflation, governments can confiscate, secretly and unobserved, an important part of the wealth of their citizens." It is hard to find a subject on which the grand economists Keynes and Friedman agree, but their objection to government-induced inflation as a backdoor way of taxing the masses is one such subject.

PUBLIC CHOICE

A number of economic arguments have been labeled the Public Choice School, arguing for a more rigorous setting of thresholds before things are allowed to move into the public sector and an aggressive campaign of reducing the scale of the public sector to an optimum level, presumed to be somewhat below its current size. Paul Starr summarizes:

> In short, starting with an individualistic model of human behavior, the public choice school makes a series of empirical claims:
> - That democratic polities have inherent tendencies toward government growth and excessive budgets.
> - That expenditure growth is due to self-interested coalitions of voters, politicians, and bureaucrats.
> - That public enterprises necessarily perform less efficiently than private enterprises.[5]

On the other hand, arguing against a simplistic view that private-sector operations are intrinsically superior to the public sector, it is easily possible that voters are not aware of the scale of the benefits they receive. Galbraith pointed out that private goods and services are more aggressively promoted than public goods and services. Many benefits, such as the beauty of national parks, are intangible. Others, such as long-term welfare provision, are spread over long periods.

In a review of a book by Benjamin Friedman, Joseph Stiglitz remarks:

> American economists tend to have a strong aversion to advocating government intervention. Their basic presumption is often that markets generally work by themselves and that there are just a few limited instances in which government action is needed to correct market failure; government economic policy, the thinking goes, should include only minimal intervention to ensure economic efficiency.
>
> The intellectual foundations for this presumption are weak. In a market economy with imperfect and asymmetric information and incomplete markets—which is to say, every market economy—the reason that Adam Smith's invisible hand is invisible is that it does not exist. Economies are not efficient on their own. This recognition inevitably leads to the conclusion that there is a potentially significant role for government.[6]

Despite the political rhetoric of privatization, private finance, and public–private partnerships, over the past four decades a number of European countries seem to have stabilized at around 40 percent of GDP being spent by the government; and the US, while until recently a bit less at around 30 percent, has also accepted a rather significant part of the economy coming under public control. The differing ways of accounting for state purchasing partially explain the difference between Europe and the US. Healthcare provision, for example, is counted as government spending in Europe, while in the US it is essentially private-sector provision part paid for by government transfer payments. Nevertheless, there remain significant differences in the scale of the public sector around the world.

CONTRACTING WITH THE PEOPLE

One of the hottest topics for millennia has been the idea of representative democracy versus true democracy. While nodding respectfully at Plato, Aristotle, Spinoza, Hobbes, Locke, Rousseau, Jefferson, Hamilton, Madison, *et al.*, it is interesting that the issue in former times was the structure of government and the right, or lack thereof, of people to extract "rent" from society due to a position of privilege, whether that position be monarchy, nobility, monopoly, or clergy, while the modern approach is to take government as a given but to wonder about its scale.

Joseph Schumpeter wrote that the kernel of democracy was an "institutional arrangement for arriving at political decisions in which individuals acquire the power to decide by means of a competitive struggle for the people's vote."

Individuals and organizations need to be able to "contract" with society, perhaps implicitly, perhaps explicitly, but in any case with enough stability to make the risks and rewards inherent in those contracts clear and reasonably certain. In the eighteenth century, the key advantages of a republic were seen to be its ability to handle greater numbers of citizens and greater distances. Further, a representative democracy in the form of a republic tends to be more stable over time than a true democracy. The Federalist Papers, a series of 85 essays by Alexander Hamilton, James Madison, and John Jay, published in the 1780s, advocated the adoption of the US Constitution. They are a seminal source of modern constitutional thinking. Numbers 10 and 51 are generally regarded as the most influential; Number 10 advocates a large, strong republic, while Number 51 explains the need for the separation of powers.[7]

Benjamin Franklin famously said: "those who would give up essential Liberty, to purchase a little temporary Safety, deserve neither Liberty nor Safety." He meant, of course, that even seemingly minor or transient curbs on freedom should not be tolerated. Yet American representative democracy required a compact with markets that did give up some essential liberties in order to purchase a little temporary safety. This contract was recognized as new, but not alarming. On the other hand, it is clear from Federalist Paper Number 56 that the authors did not anticipate the regulation of commerce growing remarkably:

> A proper regulation of commerce requires much information, as has been elsewhere remarked; but as far as this information relates to the laws and local situation of each individual State, a very few representatives would be very sufficient vehicles of it to the federal councils. Taxation will consist, in a great measure, of duties which will be involved in the regulation of commerce.

We suggest that the Lockean principle of the American Revolution, individuals delegating their power and allowing social compacts, seems to provide more stable markets than the Rousseauian principle of the French Revolution, the majority expressing individual rights. The checks and balances inherent in the American federal model with separation of powers appear to reduce uncertainty and increase confidence when individuals and organizations make long-term contracts, either with the government or among themselves within markets. It might indeed be that the key criterion for successful government and market interaction is stability of commercial contract. Checks and balances prevent governments from changing direction rapidly, which might result in a somewhat weaker social contract but are accompanied by stronger social and commercial stability.

Markets seem to emerge anywhere humans stand to gain from exchange—markets can and do emerge outside democracies. For instance, the Chinese government has done more in recent decades to reduce poverty than probably any single entity. It is not democracy that makes this possible, but the reasonable certainty over a reasonable length of time that commercial entities are able to contract with the Chinese government. Such certainty is usually "part of the deal" with democracy, but some democracies deliver that certainty better than others. Similarly, a government does not necessarily have to be a democracy to deliver commercial certainty.

GLOBAL CONTRACTING

It is interesting to note that in an age of global trade, which is also an age of global privatization of assets such as the right to pollute air, we see the conflict of an open system within a closed system. The closed system is the earth, a biosphere that is effectively closed except for the injection of energy from the sun and the radiation of energy into space. The open system is the market. The market system has two salient characteristics that create dissonance with the biosphere system: it is anthrocentric and it relies on extensive, enforced property rights. Conflict can arise when some people ignore the impact their activities might have on future generations or on people far away. In any case, enforcement of property rights such as emissions protocols is highly problematic. For example, which government is going to send in the gunboats to a small island nation that decides to receive every wayward tanker and export electricity, while polluting away in flagrant breach of international agreements?

The global financial system presents many opportunities for similar conflicts between governments about markets. The deployment (or should we say misapplication) of UK anti-terrorism law to freeze the assets of a defaulting Icelandic bank during the global financial crisis of the early twenty-first century is a relatively small but illustrative example. The same financial crisis spawned rumblings between the US and China about currency manipulation and trade imbalances. Legislative rumblings had the potential to trigger severe trade wars and yet deeper financial crisis.

Such conflicts are also evident in the world of fish, where the closed system is the capacity of the earth to sustain edible fish species and the open system is the market for fish. There are increasing concerns globally that several major sources of fish are being harvested unsustainably and that stocks are possibly close to collapse. At a national level, there is often antagonism between the government (putative owner of the fishy assets) and the managers (fishermen and fisheries), with very little trust between these parties. Individual governments, together with the scientists who advise them, try to think about the long-term future of fish stocks, but the only tool they seem to deploy is annual (short-term) fishing quotas. Quota ownership is uncertain and leads to complications in managing and financing the industry. More sophisticated and perhaps more suitable longer-term instruments, such as individually tradable fishing quotas, would require unprecedented levels of international cooperation to work effectively.

The human race is taking baby steps toward addressing some of these big issues of the global ecosystem. Market advocates fervently believe that enforceable property rights and trade will achieve an optimal distribution of activities. Government advocates believe that the ultimate solutions are political, nation to nation. To date, markets have only weakly embraced ideas such as emissions trading and many governments have done daft things on property rights, such as levying windfall taxes on energy, thus harming investment in sustainable energy at the same time; or playing fast and loose with emissions quotas, thus damaging the value for early purchasers of such quotas.

THE GOVERNMENT OPTIMETER: HALF FULL OR HALF EMPTY?

Naturally, everyone wants just the right amount of government: not too much, not too little, but just right. This reasonable request brings to mind the story of Goldilocks and the Three Bears, in which Goldilocks rejects Daddy Bear's porridge for being too hot and rejects Mummy Bear's porridge for being too cold, only to eat Baby Bear's porridge, which was just right. Putting aside the distributive injustice within this story (Baby Bear is the least blameworthy bear yet is the one who suffers the most), the story also gets us thinking about measuring government. Wouldn't it be nice to have a handy-dandy meter to assess the scale of government and help to keep it just right—a Government Optimeter.

If the Government Optimeter goes red, too much of the economy is being swallowed by government; or at the other extreme, the economy has too little government. If the Government Optimeter goes green, the economy is in an optimal range. What a seductive idea—just set out the key measure and it's highly likely that, even if politicians don't immediately enthuse about it, through the discipline of voting the democratic process gets them to come round.

However, there are a number of significant measurement problems that make it difficult to specify our Government Optimeter. Examples that might lead to overstating the scale of government include the size of the informal sector or black economy, the extent of tax evasion or corruption, how public involvement in commercial operations is accounted for, the receipts people get from government, and the amount of benefits such as public education or health. On the other hand, the Government Optimeter could understate the scale of government, by not taking account of price controls, regulations, licenses and permits, barriers to competition, barriers to ownership, tariffs, or indirect administrative overheads such as tax collection and rule enforcement imposed on businesses.

The Government Optimeter might not be sustainable if borrowings are not taken into account; as Sir John Hicks pointed out, "the purpose of income calculations in practical affairs is to give people an indication of the amount which they can consume without impoverishing themselves." It might also be easily influenced by changes in demographics, for example construction activity might fall in the future as people need fewer living quarters, yet the administration of pensions by the state might naturally increase.

Moreover, how is one to analyze the sheer variety of mixed-economy models? For instance, there are government franchises for services, nationalized industries, Government-Owned-Contractor-Operated (GO-CO) companies, government-backed companies, insurers-of-last-resort, trusts, agencies, quangos, government-funded charity work, grants, vouchers, tax rebates, subsidies, tolls, service charges, and many other permutations of private and public. Truly a mixed, and mixed-up, economy. The Government Optimeter could be easily skewed if it turned out that future income is being consumed through increasing debt or by handling resources in a nonsustainable way. Once the media latched on to the Government Optimeter as a vital measure, you can naturally anticipate some intriguing accounting mechanisms that would make public–private partnership (PPP) deals and off-balance-sheet financing look positively transparent.

THE COMPETITION OPTIMETER AND THE COMMUNITY OPTIMETER: MARKETS AND COMMUNITIES

Furthermore, competition plays a very important role. We could achieve a tremendous move of resources from the public to the private sector, yet find that we have not provided competition. In Tudor times, there was a proliferation of monopolies and patents on things such as salt or soap. While Tudor monopolies were largely in the private sector, the value of the monopoly derived from the lack of competition.

There are a number of theoretical arguments supporting the case for privatization, such as the Public Choice School's criticism that the incentive structure of the public sector is inefficient, or the "property rights" school's criticism that public ownership does not stimulate efficiency. While there are many difficulties of comparing like for like, it turns out that, while there are typically lower costs of production in the private sector and asset values are higher under private-sector ownership, in industries where there is competition or the threat of real competition, there is relative efficiency, regardless of ownership.

Thus we not only need a Government Optimeter but also a Competition Optimeter for areas outside government. There is little point in privatizing a section of government without introducing competition. Perhaps we could introduce a Competition Optimeter for areas inside government. Why can't there be two Passport Offices, three Health and Safety Inspectorates, or four Internal Revenue Services?

At the start of this chapter we talked about the public sector, the private sector, and the not-for-profit sector, promising to consider the role of communities later in the chapter. So while we're at it, what about the idea of a Community Optimeter or a Cooperation Optimeter? The whole concept behind open markets is that selfish behavior leads to common good—that is, cooperation—even if this is unintended. Of course, it's easy to quip that communities are not the realm of economics or commerce. We happen to disagree with that view. We believe that real commerce is not only about exchange, it is about the *community* of exchange. Furthermore, the growth of government has occurred alongside the growth of collective organizations, such as trade unions and other social movements. Advances in social legislation, in areas such as human rights, education, and health, often originate through community activity, have a direct impact on the scale of government, and are in areas of endeavor that don't naturally lend themselves to competition. A Community Optimeter would make the picture more complete, as long as you can determine some measures for it.

A Danish friend once remarked to us that Danes are the most associative people in the world: they belong to the most clubs and societies and are most active in local organizations. It is an attractive assertion, but we have often wondered how we might measure this associativity. In *For the Common Good*, Daly and Cobb suggest:

> community is precisely the feature of reality that has been most consistently abstracted from in modern economics. The need is not for one more theorem squeezed out of the premises of methodological individualism by a more powerful mathematical press, but for a new premise that reinstates the critical aspect of reality that has been abstracted from—namely, community.[8]

Thus we should try to understand and measure the totality of exchange, commerce as both markets and communities, rather than merely private-sector economics. Of course, just as definitions and measures for government are difficult, it is difficult to define and measure a community. We can start with the idea that communities define themselves—"we are accountants," "we are entrepreneurs," "we work with charities," "our firm reports to X regulator," or "our families have ties with Y." However, this illustrates the complexity: people belong to multiple communities, some voluntary, some imposed, some a source of pride, some of which they wouldn't consider communities at all. Anthropologist Arian Ward describes these as "Constellations

Figure 5.2 Characteristics of a community

of Communities" and sets out several common elements to describe a community.[9]

We like to define communities based on six characteristics, developed in part from Ward and in part from our own experience, illustrated in Figure 5.2.

Below are those six characteristics of communities using the Fishmongers' Company, also known as the Worshipful Company of Fishmongers (Fishmongers), as an example:

🐟 *Common purpose*: Fishmongers is a guild for the sellers of fish in the City of London. It is one of the oldest guilds, receiving its first Royal Charter in 1272 and existing in some form for a great many years before that. A guild is basically a co-fraternity of craftsmen who associate to educate trainees, maintain quality standards, and promote their trade. Historically guilds were often cartels; Fishmongers had a monopoly on the sale of fish in the City of London for several centuries. Its modern purpose focuses on quality control and charity.

- *Co-located spaces*: Fishmongers Hall has been located on its current site since 1434, although several replacement halls have been built over the centuries. Fishmongers is also a fixture at Billingsgate Market in London, as explained in "consistent methods" below.

- *Cultural alignment*: Fishmongers follows the cultural traditions of London's livery companies (most of London's guilds have, historically, been granted livery by the City of London). While in modern times Fishmongers tends to align around ceremonial and charitable activities, working fishmongers are still well represented among the livery members.

- *Coherent interests*: In common with many livery companies, Fishmongers is especially active as an educational charity, with particularly close connections with Gresham's School in Norfolk, but also providing scholarships and exhibitions to other schools. In addition, it provides almshouses and pensions for poorer members.

- *Consistent methods*: although no longer a monopoly, Fishmongers retains the power to inspect all fish coming into the City of London. In particular its inspection staff, known as fishmeters, are a constant presence at Billingsgate Market, having fulfilled the quality assurance role for over 400 years, originally by royal decree in the charter of 1604, more recently delegated powers from government under the Food Safety Act 1990.

- *Co-created future*: Fishmongers' role continues to evolve over time. It was instrumental in setting up the Atlantic Salmon Research Trust and it represents the shellfish industry nationally. It also supports the work of, among others, the Marine Biological Association of the United Kingdom and the Scottish Association for Marine Science.

The financial services sector provides a very different example, virtual financial communities. From this you can see that it is possible to be a member of multiple communities—banking, insurance, repo-trading, or interbank loans—while still belonging to a more nebulous community of wholesale banking:

- *Common purpose*: The fundamental reason or passion for joining is clear—making money—and there is also a great sense of time, for example banks that can trace their origins back centuries, such as Monte dei Paschi di Siena (1472) or British merchant banks.

- *Co-located spaces*: There is shared physical and virtual space with known periods of interaction. Although there is a move online, historically financial communities have congregated at a limited number of international locations, for example London, New York, Hong Kong, Zurich, Tokyo. Why else would every trading room need to show the time at key locations around the world? Even in virtual space, online exchanges find that they need to schedule times for particular markets in order to ensure liquidity.

- *Cultural alignment*: There is a common cultural context, principally risk and reward, for determining "how people decide to do things around here." "Risk transfer" and "who gets the rewards?" are common ways of viewing problems. There are strong, informal cultures, as described in books such as *Liar's Poker*, with its tales of "big swinging dicks," or strong, formal cultures such as those imposed by trade associations or professional bodies for accountants, actuaries, or stockbrokers.

- *Coherent interests*: Lobbying takes place as a group for their own interests. There is intense lobbying of regulators, governments, and transnational organizations in order to ensure the proper functioning of markets. Furthermore, financial communities create common utilities to further their shared interests, such as exchanges, clearing houses, or technology networks.

- *Consistent methods*: There are known procedures and benchmarks for operations and conduct. In finance, many of the products are well-known commodities arranged in new combinations. Even shared jargon indicates that consistent practices proliferate.
- *Co-created future*: Financial communities have shared visions of the future: smarter, cheaper, faster, integrated, such as an all-electronic world of straight-through processing, real-time settlement, and online anomaly detection combined with intense visualization. Financial communities cooperate in building toward these visions, though some efforts are open-ended research, and many fail.

Too often people look at the level of central or federal government and forget that not only are there many levels of government, there are also many levels of community that solve many problems that might otherwise go to government. Indeed, it is too often assumed that the only way of managing common resources is via government. The academic arguments began when ecologist Garrett Hardin reified the Tragedy of the Commons using a number of topics, such as pollution and over-population, to illustrate his point that people need to submit to "mutual coercion" on their activities in former areas of freedom such as waste disposal or breeding.[10] His influential paper has polarized subsequent debate. At one extreme is the assertion that public assets must be publicly governed. Coercion via government is a natural enforcement mechanism, and ultimately all use of public resources must flow from government. At the other extreme, the claim is that only by allocating property rights over formerly public assets will people care enough, in their own selfish interest, to defend and maintain those assets. This feels like those old battle lines again: socialism or capitalism?

What is interesting is that when you look at communities and how they handle common resources, you realize that they can be effective if they control the local market. Influential academic and winner of the Nobel Prize for Economics in 2009, Elinor Ostrom, assembled empirical research on a number of long-term, common-pool resource-management systems such as agriculture, fishing, forestry, and water, showing that not only was there an alternative to the old battle lines, but that the alternative had been around for some time.[11] The systems she studied ranged in age from a minimum of 100 years to well over 1,000 years, including communal tenure in Switzerland, common lands in Japan, the *huerta* irrigation institutions of Spain, and the *zanjera* irrigation systems of the Philippines. She pointed out that there are many, enduring, alternative approaches that are neither "socialist leviathans" nor privatization.

Ostrom derived eight design principles for systems that successfully manage common-pool resources:

- Clearly defined boundaries.
- Equivalence between costs and benefits (appropriation and provision rules) in local conditions.
- Collective-choice arrangements.
- Monitoring.
- Graduated sanctions.
- Conflict-resolution mechanisms.
- Recognition of rights to organize.
- The use of nested enterprises.

Communities can do much through their own control of markets. It should be no surprise that "ever closer union" in Europe began with a common market and a European Community.

Nevertheless, today communities may be in peril. In *Bowling Alone*, Robert Putnam questions whether society is weaker with fewer interactions and an increasing social-capital deficit:

Television, two-career families, suburban sprawl, generational changes in values—these and other changes in American society have meant that fewer and fewer of us find that the League of Women Voters, or the United Way, or the Shriners, or the monthly bridge club, or even a Sunday picnic with friends fits the way we have come to live. Our growing social-capital deficit threatens educational performance, safe neighborhoods, equitable tax collection, democratic responsiveness, everyday honesty, and even our health and happiness.[12]

GOLDILOCKS GOVERNMENT? THE BEAR-EST RECIPE TO GET THE SCALE JUST RIGHT

Without some clear principles, it is difficult to force activities into either the public sector or the private sector. We would hope that by keeping the scale of government under discussion, we at least keep people aware of the issues. Others might find it disturbing that one of the greatest tools for resource allocation, the market, fails to make its case vigorously, and that economic analytics fail to provide people with an optimal setting. Yet markets do work well with communities; Daly and Cobb again:

> The market does only one thing: it solves the allocation problem by providing the necessary information and incentive. It does that one thing very well, when supplemented by enough community or collective action to maintain competition, restrain self-interest and deal with public goods and externalities.

So what might we conclude about the public sector versus private sector divide? There are a few simple items:

- We need to find more ways to give communities genuine power and genuine responsibilities, including bearing the consequences of their actions. Increasing centralization of power at a national level reduces the variety in economies. If you don't see local solutions to local problems, or local failures, you don't have local responsibility.

- Political positions need to be remapped. A number of people have tried to gain acceptance for mapping political positions on more than one axis, to get away from a one-dimensional view of politics as a spectrum ranging from anarchists through Marxist Socialists, Social Democrats, Fabians, Liberals, Conservatives, and Fascists. Why aren't there parties that recognize that huge numbers of responsible, overlapping, and competing communities are feasible within a market society, or that while there is no such thing as a global community, globally dispersed communities do exist today?

- Metrics are crucial. Society should encourage the development of more sophisticated measures of government scale, competition, and community, and publicize them.

In summary, there is no right or wrong answer to the question of what should be done in the public sector and what in the private sector. There is firm evidence that the public sector (and taxation along with it) tends to grow by stealth over extended periods. It becomes increasingly difficult to justify the scale of government in the economy, yet global problems such as climate change and unsustainable levels of commercial fishing require large-scale interventions that markets alone struggle to make.

We believe that the study of real commerce requires an understanding of government, market, and community forces. We encourage the development of more sophisticated measures of government, competition, and community influence through which societies can try to optimize their respective levels.

6 | NETWORK ECONOMICS: LOCAL, GLOBAL, OR SOCIAL

This chapter continues the discussion with a focus on local and global economies, starting with the thorny question of whether economies work better when centralized or decentralized.

Some governments are predisposed to centralization, such as the UK and France. If you look at a map you see that all roads and railways lead to Paris or London, the main decision makers reside in Paris or London, even the night sky points you to both capitals. The governance of both countries might be described as centralized or unitary. Every government review of two or more functions seems to conclude that centralization could result in savings. Central government bureaucracies might employ 10,000 people just to ensure that two people don't end up duplicating some effort.

So are we advocating decentralized government, operating more local or federal models such as the US or Germany? Not necessarily. Decentralization too incurs waste and duplication, though of a different nature. In many countries the various branches of government quarrel with each other. There are immense turf squabbles among federal authorities, state authorities, counties, and cities. Savvy actors play off various parties against each other. Furthermore, isolated communities can lose diversity and virility. Isolation from market forces tends to render closed networks suboptimal.

The type of governance reflects the underlying structure of the country or association. Figure 6.1 categorizes governance based on central or local operations and intrinsic or delegated legitimacy.

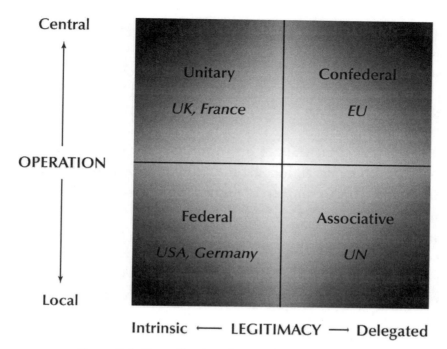

Figure 6.1 Centralized or decentralized governance

STARFISH AND SPIDERS

Brafman and Beckstrom's book *The Starfish and the Spider* puts forward a helpful metaphor in this regard. The spider is centralized, the starfish decentralized.[1] If you cut bits off a starfish they may regenerate or even replicate, but cutting off its head will kill the spider. In relation to organizations, Brafman and Beckstrom ponder "what happens when there's no one in charge... when there's no hierarchy." Traditionally companies were centralized, emulating military command-and-control systems, but now highly decentralized organizations have developed such as Alcoholics Anonymous, Apache Software Foundation, Craigslist, Gnutella, Linux, Skype, and Wikipedia. With decentralization have come new structures of commerce and ways of making money, such as indirectly via advertising, donations, many very small transactions, or selling information about transactions. Such organizations can be quite innovative at finding new customer needs. InnoCentive, for example, is an exchange that connects scientists and engineers ("solvers") to corporations ("seekers") offering cash prizes for finding solutions to their technology problems.[2]

As well as decentralized organizations, social networks such as LinkedIn or Facebook abound, fulfilling social purposes but also acting as real commercial exchanges. The new exchanges are social in two senses: they promote more direct social interaction and they are often socially responsible. They are creating new communities. For example, Kiva is a social exchange that helps people lend to small entrepreneurs in the developing world in order to assist them in escaping poverty. Intriguingly, in the developed world too there are several analogous exchanges for people who want to lend directly to other people, such as the UK's Zopa (a peer-to-peer social money-lending service) or the US's Prosper (an online auction site for borrowers and lenders).[3]

GLOBALIZE IT, LOCALIZE IT, OR CRITICIZE IT?

Given that these emerging network structures have the ability to change social, environmental, or economic structures, we should think about the impact they might have on the globalization or localization of real commerce.

There are six basic factors of globalization: goods, services, capital, people, culture, and commons.

◆ *Goods*: Trade in goods underpins the rosiest views of globalization among economists. From Adam Smith's Invisible Hand, to Robert Torrens and David Ricardo on the Theory of Comparative Advantage, to empirical studies, free trade in goods seems to benefit all except those who bear the transition costs (see below). There are some richer points in all this—specific structures where free trade might be harmful and legitimate questions over the full cost of externalities such as transport and pollution—but for these purposes we take free trade in goods as largely good in itself. As Jagdish Bhagwati states in *In Defense of Globalization*: "the modern evidence against an inward-looking or import substitution trade strategy is really quite overwhelming."[4]

- *Services*: Trade in services is widely seen by economists to be good as well, but this was the big battleground in the World Trade Organization's faltering Doha trade rounds and will continue to be problematic for global trade agreements. Intellectual property is another increasingly contentious field of battle that is impairing open trade. Bhagwati remarks, "particularly onerous problems arise for the poor countries, in my view, not over opening their markets through trade concessions, but when the pressures are applied on them to consent to extraneous and harmful demands aimed at appeasing the domestic lobbies in the rich countries on trade-unrelated issues such as intellectual property protection and labor..."

- *Capital*: Economists have significantly changed their thinking on free capital flows. The widely cited case of Malaysia benefiting from imposing capital controls during the East Asian crisis and other theoretical and empirical evidence has led to statements such as this from *The Economist*: "If any cause commands the unswerving support of *The Economist*, it is that of liberal trade... It seems natural to suppose that what goes for trade in goods must go for trade in capital, in which case capital controls would offend us as violently as, say, an import quota on bananas. The issues have much in common, but they are not the same. Untidy as it may be, economic liberals should acknowledge that capital controls—of a certain restricted sort, and in certain cases—have a role."[5]

🐟 *People*: Free movement of people can correct imbalances in national and local labor markets. Although economists seem to be fairly indifferent about free flows of people, people in general seem to object to noticeable flows of newcomers. Whether the newcomers bring wealth and riches or do the jobs others find distasteful, they tend to be unwelcome in large numbers. John Plender points out an obvious dilemma in *Going Off the Rails*: "a more far-sighted realpolitik would acknowledge a moral ambiguity in the developed countries' advocacy of a globalization process that does not extend to labour markets. If the west will not accept many of the developing world's immigrants, it has to export more capital to the developing world to help prevent it from becoming a breeding ground for disaffection and, in extremis, terrorism. That is in its own interest."[6]

🐟 *Culture*: This divides into two elements, in country and out of country. In country most people are happy with a blend of ethnic restaurants and a few exotic folk at dinner parties and receptions. However, many seem to rebel when these numbers exceed a genteel level. Out of country, people love the idea of wild frontiers until their yachts founder or their mountain climbers fall, whereupon they expect global standards of rescue. They want to get far from the beaten track, but not to contract dysentery or lose their iPhone's reception. They excel at getting deep into the culture of a country, but expect to be bungee-jump rescued when they have an anaphylactic shock. There are deep, uncomfortable, cultural issues in the McDonaldization of the world, the loss of languages and customs. One person's quaint rural lifestyle is another's poverty. There must be ways to recognize that culture is more profound than building styles, food preferences, and clothing.

🐟 *Commons*: The global commons is the biggest area for future conflict. Although the basics might seem sorted—national boundaries, sea boundaries, basic property rights—in fact this isn't the case. We expect the big battlefields of the future to be fought on the commons—climate change (actually setting global emissions that matter), pollution, water scarcity, and fisheries are clear natural resource conflict zones—but we equally expect the intellectual commons of trademarks, patents, copyrights, and designs to hot up.

Sociologist Manuel Castells, in his seminal work *The Rise of the Network Society*, describes such a society as a major, transformational change:

> the informational economy is global. A global economy is an historically new reality, distinct from a world economy. A world economy, that is, an economy in which capital accumulation proceeds throughout the world, has existed in the west at least since the 16th century... A global economy is something different: it is an economy with the capacity to work as a unit in real time, or chosen time, on a planetary scale.[7]

However, such transformational and global change does not occur without *transition costs*. That's a great phrase, a tidy, abstract euphemism, a bit like "collateral damage." Sadly, real people wind up taking "friendly fire"—real people lose real jobs, real livelihoods, real health, and real opportunities. Transition costs have victims. Too often the question should be: Why hasn't society changed this inequitable situation earlier and borne the costs so these people weren't in this situation to start with?

Critics have valid points against globalization on a number of dimensions:

- *Poverty*: Where trade has increased, poverty has diminished unevenly. The International Monetary Fund notes, "as globalization has progressed, living conditions (particularly when measured by broader indicators of well being) have improved significantly in virtually all countries. However, the strongest gains have been made by the advanced countries and only some of the developing countries."[8] So there is clearly some increased inequality and more work is required to understand why some countries gain and others stagnate.

- *Women and children*: It is easy to blame globalization for women or children being in near or actual slavery when their goods turn up in our shops. However, perhaps poor local government is more to blame than globalization. Numerous studies have shown that overall women and children gain from globalization, especially when multinational buyers insist on reasonable standards of employment conditions and pay.

- *Antidemocracy*: Matters could be improved here, particularly with regard to international representation in global forums or trade bodies, as well as much better control over the corrosive effects of corruption. However, on balance globalization seems to have increased the democratic voice, as people have more ways of expressing themselves, attracting support, and exercising their commercial freedoms.

Globalization brings growth in GDP; but of course, GDP growth isn't everything. GDP is certainly not the best measure of happiness, and many economists welcome analytical work on happiness and distribution of wealth. Nevertheless, in the developing world, without GDP growth above population growth there is a low likelihood of happiness. As John Kenneth Galbraith teased, "wealth is not without its advantages, and the case to the contrary, although it has often been made, has never proved widely persuasive."[9]

Joseph Stiglitz, winner of the Nobel Prize for Economics in 2001, says in *Globalization and Its Discontents*:

fundamentally, it is the closer integration of the countries and peoples of the world which has been brought about by the enormous reduction of costs of transportation and communication, and the breaking down of artificial barriers to the flow of goods, services, capital, knowledge, and (to a lesser extent) people across borders.[10]

So globalization has led to more integration, but inequality remains. He goes on to make some pointed criticisms of key institutions, particularly the IMF. These are quite telling, as he worked at the World Bank as a chief economist and senior vice president. He notes: "fiscal austerity, privatization and market liberalization were the three pillars of Washington Consensus advice throughout the 1980s and 1990s." Stiglitz identifies situations where fiscal austerity is dangerous, where competition matters much more than privatization, and where too-early capital market liberalization needs to be avoided. To him, there are two types of error—poor recognition of local circumstances and errors in sequencing liberalization—although the general benefit of globalization is not in doubt. Stiglitz and Bhagwati both prioritize better governance structures over technical economic solutions.

SUSTAINING THE NETWORK

Another appealing call for structure comes from those arguing for *sustainability*. For people to live sustainably, our planet's resources must be used at a rate at which they can be replenished. There are many calls for sustainability: sustainable cities, energy, agriculture, architecture, or business. Cutting through much debate, there is broad agreement that a simple model of sustainability consists of three factors (sometimes expressed as pillars, sometimes as overlapping circles): social, environmental, and economic.[11] All three factors must be present in order to support sustainability.

As with any taxonomic structure, one can argue at length about other factors or groupings that might constitute a structure for sustainability. Many people suggest additional factors, such as culture or education or technology; others claim that the three factors are fuzzy or at least need more precision.

Nevertheless, the basic structure suggests that where social and environmental factors meet, society develops a bearable system for the planet, for example preserving wilderness. Where economic and social factors meet, society ensures equity, for example eliminating poverty while accepting income variations. Where environmental and economic factors meet, society creates processes that are viable over time, for example not over-consuming resources. Clearly, the ideal scenario is one where social, environmental, and economic factors are balanced and society can claim to be sustainable. Figure 6.2 illustrates these intersections.

It is not such a leap to suggest that this chapter should further examine network economics using these three factors: social, environmental, and economic. We start with the social factor.

SOCIAL ELEMENTS OF NETWORK ECONOMICS

Dr. Matthew Haigh emphasizes the importance of combining economics and sociology. He points out that economic assumptions of perfect competition, perfect information, and no external shocks are artificial-world, not real-world, assumptions. In contrast, economic sociology should attempt to examine networks, for example how social relations structure investor, producer, consumer, or agent behavior. The effect of trying to develop economic sociology is to undermine neoclassical assumptions of profit maximization and provide richer views of

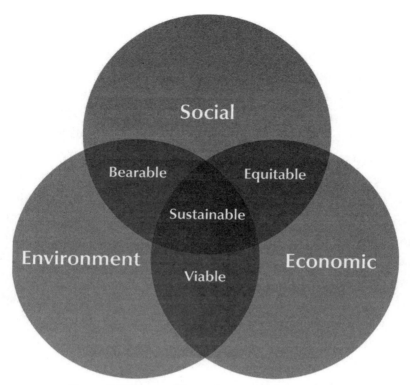

Figure 6.2 Three pillars of sustainable networks

Source: http://en.wikipedia.org/wiki/File:Sustainable_development.svg

economic relations such as fiduciary trust, value, responsibility, or incentives.

Many influential thinkers have attempted to enrich economics with sociology, or sociology with economics. Pierre Bourdieu extended ideas of capital, such as social capital, symbolic capital, and cultural capital. To him, power derives from connections and responsibilities. In his 1973 paper "The Strength of Weak Ties," Mark Granovetter united micro and macro sociological theory by pointing out the richness and complexity of social networks.[12] He developed a sociogram-based diagrammatic approach to examining social relationships. Granovetter diagrams are often used to model social interactions in economics or computer systems. His key insight for economic purposes is that economic actors value the relationships within networks as well as the economic value. Granovetter saw early that changing social relationships in commercial relationships leads to fads and "tipping points," later popularized by Malcolm Gladwell.[13]

Lately the social context has been more strained. There are more of Granovetter's weak ties at the expense of strong ones. Studies of heavy internet users show that they tend to have larger overall networks of contacts, but difficult relations with family members. We struggle to know which method of connection is best for our various contacts: email, text, instant messaging, broadcast, phone call, video conference, even a visit. We know how to mash up web applications, but not how to make a cup of tea and listen. These strains can profoundly affect the nature of commercial networks as well.

Many new networks of contacts are social networks first, then opportunities to influence economics. Perhaps a corollary is that all meaningful social networks do affect economics. Henry Markowitz grounded much of modern finance using portfolio optimization. The implication of Bourdieu and Granovetter is that, when associated with many forms of social interaction, "maximization" is pathological. Economic sociology points out how artificial any maximization seems in social contexts. Yet many global social structures are cold, distant, and artificial, lacking in humanity. We have grown distant from our fellow humans, more accustomed to terms such as "collateral damage" and "strategic necessity" than "natural law" or "human rights."

In *The Great Transformation*, Karl Polanyi first mooted the idea of "embeddedness," the economy being embedded in social institutions that control the market so that it does not endanger other aspects of human life.[14] Thus Polanyi sees embeddedness as an essential control of markets, while Granovetter sees embeddedness as an essential viewpoint. Markets grow from social relations, but social values and market values are often inconsistent with each other. We gladly pay for a restaurant meal when dining out with our parents, but would not even dream of paying for a meal our parents cooked for us in our family home. Socially sensible interpretations of economics explain why we may deal with a particular fishmonger despite them not having the lowest prices, why there is such emotional stress over small shops, or why we value personal medical advice at certain times and impersonal medical advice at others.

ENVIRONMENTAL ELEMENTS OF NETWORK ECONOMICS

The biggest change to the environment surrounding new network economics is the World Wide Web. New networks are grounded in the assumption that the cost of connecting people over distances and time has fallen significantly, for ever. That is a big assumption and makes it interesting to revisit historical claims about the internet. Michael Wolff, writing about his net adventures in his 1999 book *Burn Rate*, describes the internet in 1994:

> Internet users, working in ASCII text and UNIX commands, were really very modest in their claims about the medium. The grandest metaphors had to do with community, with town meetings and bulletin boards. No one was saying that the Internet had anything to do with TV or entertainment. (Even if you could, why would you want to turn this into a medium that mimicked television? We already had television.)[15]

The internet has been more than a social or technical change. By changing connections, information, and the costs of both, it has transformed the environment too. The internet is a surprise generator or a global innovation engine. Equally, any major change to the assumption of low connection costs spells upheaval.

Networks such as the World Wide Web and citation networks are believed to be scale free: they obey a power law. A power law distribution means that very few people or websites or blogs get most of the traffic, though everybody gets a bit—a few Googles or Yahoos or Amazons, and lots and lots of holiday snap sites. In a normal distribution the mean and the median are similar, so most sites are average, with a few very large or small. Following a power law, some people have 10 times the average number of connections, a few 100 times, even fewer 1,000 times. People are beginning to analyze the internet, and thus its economic connections, with a greater appreciation of what it means to have non-normal distributions, so-called fat tails and long tails.

Equally, connectivity has led to a bit of fun. Small-world networks epitomize the idea behind *six degrees of separation*, an idea set out in a short story, "Chains," by the Hungarian author Frigyes Karinthy. He surmised that each person is separated from every other person on the planet by only six connections. The internet allowed Karinthy's idea to be tested, and in the 1990s websites were developed such as SixDegrees. One connectivity measure is the Erdös number. The prolific Hungarian mathematician Paul Erdös, who wrote joint papers like there was no tomorrow, is taken to be the core of many mathematical collaborations. Mathematicians now have an Erdös number—how far they are removed from collaborating directly with Paul Erdös.

Taking the idea a step further, actor Kevin Bacon stated in a 1994 interview that he believed he was at the most two degrees separated from everybody in Hollywood—so media people (especially actors) now have a Bacon number. This has spawned the idea of "extended Erdös numbers" to encompass all forms of published collaboration, including the arts. Indeed, there are many related connection games: one such is to find, through Wikipedia links, the fewest number of pages between any two random subjects. The person with the fewest links to topic wins.

At this point we envisage many readers disappearing to their computers for a quick game or to check their links. We thought we should publish our own Bacon and extended Erdös connections to demonstrate the idea. We are both "Bacon Three" through different connections. We thought our Erdös connections were more remote, but while finalizing this book we discovered that we can both boast "extended Erdös Three," through our friend and one-time collaborator Dimitris Fatouros.

Of course, the value of such connections is questionable. If we wanted to discuss this book directly with Kevin Bacon, for example, we would almost certainly simply write to him stating that we were authors writing up the concept of Bacon numbers and his SixDegrees.org charity. And we would not expect to find much favor through our Bacon Three connections. Indeed, our friend John Random, who sometimes appears in films and whom we approached to try to track down some of these connections, makes some telling points. John can claim a Bacon Two by having worked with Charlize Theron and an extended Erdös Three by having worked with Matt Damon, so he knows what he's talking about:

> I actually read a biography of Paul Erdös, *The Man Who Loved Only Numbers*, and he struck me as a likeable but tragic figure. I felt so sorry for him. It also strikes me that talk of being "x" degrees away from anyone fosters an illusion of closeness to other people. If only. Like most people with a job, I spend far too much of my life with people I don't know and don't love, struggling to find the few times a year I can actually get to be with the people I do know and do love.

Still, "six degrees" experiments and games retain their fascination for a great many people. Of course, people can and do use network tools to connect with the people they know and love; social networking and genealogy websites are among the most popular uses of the internet, mechanisms for connecting with friends, relatives, and loved ones. Yet pornography and online gambling are also two common uses of the internet, activities unlikely to be ranked highly on the basis of the social value of the connections, despite being potentially valuable activities and connections for the businesses behind the websites.

Mathematicians, technologists, and thinkers have come up with many ways of trying to value network connections. Researchers apply these network techniques to a variety of subjects. For example, Professor Geoffrey West at the Santa Fe Institute asks: "Why are large cities faster?" By implication, how does one take the social temperature of a city? The Boltzmann Constant relates particle energy to the temperature of a gas. Is there a Boltzmann Constant linking the energy consumption of a city to its social temperature, or the metabolic rates of cities and villages?

Net popularizers invoke Metcalfe's Law or Reed's Law. Robert Metcalfe helped develop Ethernet technology, thus George Gilder coined Metcalfe's Law as: "the value of a telecommunications network is proportional to the square of the number of connected users of the system." One telephone is worthless; two telephones are a bit limited; five telephones are getting somewhere; many telephones are worthwhile. So a network with 20 telephones is four times more valuable than a network with 10. There are some arguments about users versus devices, that all connections are not equally valuable, logarithms versus exponents, and the rate of growth, but the main point of Metcalfe's Law is the observation that the growth in value of a network is not linear. Naturally, people apply Metcalfe's Law to social networks.

Equally, David P Reed coined Reed's Law, stating that the value of the utility of large networks, particularly social networks, can scale exponentially with their size. His contribution is to note that subgroups, each of which has value, create a value for the larger group, a "group-forming" law. Is there a richer equation that points out when some networks begin to exhibit diseconomies of scale? Does Metcalfe's Law ever go into reverse and, if so, when? Does Reed's law have subtractive subgroups, for example terrorist cells?

ECONOMIC ELEMENTS OF NETWORK ECONOMICS

Many people extol the idea that changes in both the cost and availability of information, combined with new social networks, will transform markets, their scale and their logistics. Of this we have little doubt. Today's day traders can move across borders and buy and sell currencies, stocks, and commodities on a global basis. In a decade, society has gone from the idea of car boot or garage sale or flea market being local affairs for the school or church or community center, to the great, global jumble-sale-in-the-sky of eBay.

Entrepreneurial Law Professor Yochai Benkler, in *The Wealth of Networks*, makes three powerful observations about "the networked information economy":

- "Non-proprietary strategies have always been more important in information production than they were in the production of steel or automobiles," leading to the increasing importance of nonmarket motivations, actors, and organizational structures.
- "Ee have in fact seen the rise of non-market production to much greater importance," leading to multiple sources of information: market and nonmarket, state based and non-state.
- "The rise of effective, large-scale cooperative efforts—peer production of information, knowledge and culture."[16]

A PRICE OF FISH SUSTAINABILITY NETWORK

Robert Jensen studied the introduction of cellphones among fishermen in Kerala, India in 1997. By 2001, nearly 60 percent of the Keralan fishing fleet had cellphones, which meant that the fishermen were able to learn about market prices while out at sea and pick the best market to land their fish. In "The Digital Provide," Jensen concluded that "fishermen's profits increased on average by eight percent while the consumer price declined by four percent."[17] Technology and commerce increased the wealth of the disadvantaged and their ability to make their livelihood. Wasted fish decreased, from between 5 and 8 percent of the catch to almost nil. This is down-to-earth proof of the importance of information.

In a broader, statistical analysis, "The Impact of Telecoms on Economic Growth in Developing Countries," Leonard Waverman and others went further to estimate that, across the developing countries he and his team studied, "a developing country that had an average of 10 more mobile phones per 100 population between 1996 and 2003 would have enjoyed per capita GDP growth that was 0.59% higher than an otherwise identical country."[18]

By way of contrast, an April 2008 Reuters news report from Hong Kong described how three anglers landed an 85kg, 1.68m Bahaba fish after a 90-minute fight. This fish is colloquially called a giant yellow croaker. The fishermen (actually one was a woman) thought they had also hit a big jackpot when they sold the fish to a local fish buyer for HK$20,000, about £1,300. But the fish buyer sold the massive fish, which is highly prized for its swim bladder, to a local restaurant for HK$580,000, about £38,000. And the restaurant sold the fish to a mainland Chinese buyer for HK$1,000,000, about £65,000. The three anglers clearly undervalued their catch.[19] Here is evidence of how lack of information can hurt, and also of how trade and commerce manage to balance risks and rewards through exchange.

Perhaps those anglers are the people in Hong Kong most in need of a cellphone in order to sustain their businesses; or perhaps not. The giant yellow croaker is critically endangered, nearly extinct, and few survive to maturity given overfishing. Such commercial transactions might help sustain businesses for a short while, but networks don't assure sustainable business, however ingenious those networks might be.

BANKING ON TIME

We have talked about global social, environmental, and economic trends, but let's look at something very local, Rushey Green Time Bank near Catford in London. Rushey Green is based on the Time Bank model developed in the US by Dr. Edgar Cahn in the 1980s. Cahn's journey is well documented in David Boyle's book *Funny Money*, which comes with the enticing tag line: "Only our limited idea of money is keeping us poor."[20]

A "time bank" is an enduringly popular local approach, where people can swap hours of each other's time. Cahn's line of thinking had been pursued before, most notably in the labor theory of value arguments from Aristotle to Ricardo to Marx, but Cahn tried to put time and labor exchange into practice. For every hour you spend helping someone at Rushey Green, you are entitled to an hour's help in return. Since 1999 this has proved to be a radical, empowering, and transformational form of volunteering that gives self-confidence and stewardship to people who have previously been marginalized or at least passive recipients of care. Numerous mutual exchanges take the form of simple housework, clearance, shopping, DIY, befriending, cooking, babysitting, paperwork, massage, IT help, walking someone's dog, picking up mail, lifts to hospital or doctor's appointments or exercise classes.

The Time Bank movement tends to distinguish time banks from Local Exchange Trading Systems (LETS), but we think it is more accurate to describe time banks as a particular type of LETS. LETS can be defined as locally initiated, democratically organized, not-for-profit community enterprises that provide a community information service and record transactions of members exchanging goods and services by using the currency of locally created LETS Credits. They blur the distinction between givers and receivers and encourage more vulnerable people such as the elderly and those with mental health needs to get involved. They also help to build grassroots community-based self-help and mutual support, promoting coproduction, the idea that services are successful only when the people being served are involved.

LETS are, themselves, one form of local currency, of which there have been many examples in the last 100 years or so—Ithaca dollars, Brixton Bricks, Manchester Bobbins. One of the best-documented examples is the WIR, a local currency for small and medium-sized enterprises established in 1930s Switzerland in the aftermath of the monetary squeeze resulting from the Great Depression. The WIR is still thriving today.

There is something inherently attractive about these ideas. Directly valuing people's time has an intuitive fairness about it, although different schemes will have different views on whether every hour is treated as being of equal value—does an hour of babysitting exchange fairly for an hour of legal or medical help, for example? Time banks tend to value every hour as equal, whereas other forms of LETS have various ways of computing what the currency, including various uses of time, is worth. Locally initiated and democratically organized sounds like a wonderful "power to the people" motif and rings an appealing note with those of us who grew up reading and embracing E F Schumacher's *Small Is Beautiful* ideas; indeed, the Schumacher Society and its partner organization the New Economics

Institute are excellent sources of information on local and community money.[21]

While LETS are a good example of community exchange, they supplement rather than supplant traditional money. Very few LETS make a transition from community organization to influencing significant chunks of local business. A waggish adage comparing conventional money with LETS money is that the former is hard to earn but easy to spend, whereas the latter is easy to earn but hard to spend. Furthermore, word from the front line of LETS is that organizing a currency, even a simple, local time bank one, can be very hard work. Many volunteer-based schemes disappear as rapidly as or even faster than they appeared. The problem is that "community finance" can be many things, ranging from lending to people with similar ethnic, gender, or religious biases, to investing locally.

Levels of penetration are also very low at the moment, just a few hundred LETS in the UK and several hundred in the US. Time banks have a tax dispensation, effectively allowing the currency to operate outside the tax system; we don't think HMRC and the IRS are quaking in their boots about lost revenue through such sources just yet. Still, LETS are trying to link up: there is a UN program, UNILETS, and a shareware system, Ripple.

Cooperation does not only occur on an individual basis; businesses are forming communities too. Businesses in isolated areas often miss out on spatial economies of scale. Such economies exist, but they do not need to be national. Clusters of furniture makers across northeastern Italy or manufacturers in central Germany demonstrate that strong clusters do not have to be that large, and that a global customer base and competition can ensure connection rather than isolation.

Clustering does not only apply to businesses that require physical distribution: many people also want to lend and invest within their communities. Geographic risk is real, so if you want to invest wisely, it can make a lot of sense to invest in firms you see daily. As you pass by you can see the customers' cars or bicycles, you can meet the employees socially, you can tell whether the firm is well off or not. Studies of venture capitalist investment note that there is a bias for successful investments to be closer to headquarters. Geographic proximity reduces uncertainty by improving information quality and interpretation. The "local" venture capitalist knows more things of more relevance, and makes better investment decisions as a result. As a simple but real example, when accompanying one venture capitalist on a tour of a potential foreign investment, he remarked how "quiet" the local economy seemed, not realizing that it was a local religious holiday. He declined to invest in what turned out to be a fantastic company.

In the US a century ago there were hundreds of stock exchanges, but they consolidated on a handful of national platforms. In the UK, a host of regional stock exchanges had died by the 1980s as trading centered on London. This national consolidation was not just due to competitive success, or "liquidity begets liquidity," it was frequently driven by regulators or legislators who believed that centralization, consolidation, or size was important to regional or national success. We suspect that the financial crises of the early twenty-first century may cause that centralization trend in finance to go into reverse.

The reciprocal trade movement is potentially a massively multiplayer, modern form of barter. Its current global scale is hard to determine, however. In *The Future of Money*, Bernard Lietaer quotes IRTA (the International Reciprocal Trade Association) estimating $650 billion in 1997,[22] but today IRTA doesn't boast trade volumes. It does claim that several hundred thousand companies use reciprocal trade, that several hundred companies act as reciprocal trade exchanges, and that some tens of billions of dollars' worth of potentially lost and wasted capacity is utilized as a result of reciprocal trade. Many of these reciprocal trade organizations issue their own currencies or trading tokens and operate clearinghouses for trade among members. A few aspire to back their nascent currencies with available barter trade and the balance sheets of the larger global companies. The aspirations to harness global resources more efficiently and effectively must be good for business and good causes alike.

EXTRANATIONAL CONSIDERATIONS

Traditional analysis evaluates issues using national boundaries. Yet online movements tend to transcend national politics. Boundary-crossing ventures are likely to create new communities and new elites, as Professor Ian Angell predicted in his 2000 book *The New Barbarian Manifesto*.[23] Expect more confusion over boundaries and natural communities as people find more and more ways of linking up; Reed's Law again. What is the boundary of an organism or a city or a network? We have enough trouble defining cities already; imagine the difficulty of establishing the boundary of an online network. Registered users? Frequent users? These questions may start to affect real-world measures such as GDP or value added for tax purposes.

Furthermore, expect challenges to the idea that government controls trade. New communities might be much more vocal about how governments inhibit their effectiveness through trade restrictions, and might have the democratic clout to do something about it. In fact, these new networks transcend physical geography. Expect in the future to see novel definitions of social geography, leading to novel definitions of taxation.

Modern definitions of money state that money is a medium of exchange with two properties: it can be used as a unit of account and as a store of value. Every time we deal with the world, we need a rate of exchange for the unit of account. For some time government has held the monopoly of force on our assets and labor and dictated the value of the unit of account. An hour of labor stored in a time bank doesn't sound a bad idea in the face of sometimes wild fluctuations in the value of state currencies.

Pierre-Joseph Proudhon, a nineteenth-century radical anarchist, proposed a People's Bank, similar to many cooperatives or mutuals. In the aftermath of the early twenty-first-century financial crises, it is intriguing to remember the deluded demutualization that preceded them. In the modern three-way taxonomy of public, private, nongovernmental organization, society seems to have lost a key fourth category, mutuals. Mutuals were dull, whether they were building societies or stock exchanges or insurers or credit unions or cooperatives; someone stood to gain when they were incorporated and sold. But risk then became disassociated from the holder: it lost its social contact. One person sold a mortgage, another funded it, yet another raised the savings for the funder, still one more sold the funded mortgages as packages to a disassociated third party. We advocate supportive conditions for mutualization so that social connections can keep things more in kilter.

Local currencies take such notions to their logical conclusion. In contrast, Muhammad Yunus believes that eliminating poverty means moving to a single global currency. If you have new networks but money still talks, then local currencies might start to confound economics and democracy. If democracy gives each person a voice, in local currency terms those voices may deserve different volumes, just as shareholders vote with different voices depending on the number of shares they own. Perhaps communities and time banks should give each person a vote based on their net community contribution represented as currency. For different communities one person might equal one influence unit, but that influence unit might be time, wealth, talent, or military contribution. While this sounds radical, current voting structures are weak feedback mechanisms, used infrequently.

NEW ECONOMY?

So what can we anticipate emerging in network economics? First, look to see ideas and structures flowing back across the internet. Too often people seem to view the internet as peer-to-peer communication in the developed world, but broadcast to the developing world. Many of the so-called third-world or developing economy micro-finance models seem equally appropriate in the developed world; it has poverty too. Moreover, if necessity is the mother of invention, look to harsh conditions in the developing world for inspiration. Expect more ubiquitous application of developing-world ideas, such as mobile-telephony-based exchange applications developed in Africa moving to the streets of American and European cities, or cellphone crop insurance in rural Kenya becoming cellphone life insurance in urban America.

Secondly, networks and exchanges need to promote more direct social and local interaction. Too many networks and exchanges seem to believe that globalization should reduce direct social interaction: let's be all virtual. In fact, the more social interaction exchanges can provide, the more likely they are to keep their members or customers. Perhaps networks should be more modular, cells, cascading groups of ten, cohorts, fractal units. Technology can help here, using geo-referencing and networking tools to create micro-clubs, but society needs the human aspect of real people meeting other real people, not just cyberbots transacting with avatars. So expect to see as much investment directed toward social networking and tools (such as interest group meetings, conferences, or magazines) as toward trading technology.

Thirdly, there will be many changes in the ways we analyze businesses. There are far too many exchange opportunities left wherever risk or opportunity can be exchanged—direct peer-to-peer insurance, peer-to-peer pensions, property exchanges—for any existing exchange to try to develop them all in-house. Consider Amazon providing a set of books for a study program that is audited by a testing network and underwritten by a network of mutual employment insurance. If you read the books and pass the tests, you're guaranteed to get a job, or else draw unemployment benefit from your peers.

Network analysis will be deployed more and more. Instead of focusing on optimal firm size in a debate around marginal cost equaling marginal revenue, we could debate optimal network size. That might be measured on many dimensions: social, environmental, and economic. Like marginal revenue and cost, each addition to the network should increase the value of the network more than it costs, or the network is beyond optimal, but then there are networks of networks and portfolios of relationships, not a straightforward corporate delivery model.

Customers may want scale in technology and reach, but they also want it hidden behind a local face. If social networks are changing, then real commerce is changing too.

In summary, there is no universal right or wrong answer to the centralize or decentralize question, although new networks make it more likely that decentralized organizational structures are feasible, and barriers to network growth have fallen dramatically. Similarly, there is no simple answer to the question of whether globalization is beneficial: global problems perhaps need global solutions, but large global institutions rarely fill people with confidence that they might deliver technical solutions. However, perhaps global institutions can help to deliver the governance structures society needs, enabling local delivery of the actual solutions.

We have examined three factors for sustainable networks: social, environmental, and economic. Real commerce is a combination of all three factors. The challenge for those seizing the opportunities of network economics will be to think global, act local, and be social.

POLITICAL ECONOMY

We have now explored two of our four streams: choice and economics. Many other topics could have been examined, for example theories of corporate finance or macroeconomic choices such as interest rate policies or monopolies regulation. We could have written an entire book on "equality of outcomes verses equality of means."

We have grappled with some of the big questions that bridge politics and economics. What is an appropriate scope of government? Should economies be centralized or decentralized? When does commerce work better at a local level and when does global commerce operate more effectively?

However, choice and economics are not sufficient for making sense of the way the world really works. While we have mentioned the importance of measurement and forecasting in passing, we haven't yet discussed them. Measurement and forecasting can be good things when you get them right and bad things when you don't.

Chapter 7 focuses on various topics related to measurement and forecasting. It initiates our systems stream, blending choice, economics, and systems thinking. Chapters 8 and 9 continue to intertwine systems, economics, and choice.

7 | THE PERVERSE AND THE REVERSE: MEASURES AND FORECASTS

Why do measures matter? Imagine a world without commercial measures. You are ready to buy a fish, but without a measure you don't know how much fish you need, and you have no idea whether the amount you're told you're being sold is correct. And is the currency you're using valid, of value, convertible, at what rate? If it's a wholesale fish trade, perhaps you have no idea who the counterparty really is, who vouches for that party, what the payment terms are, or where disputes will be adjudicated. A market without measures is a market without reason, yet ill-thought-out measures can lead to perverse outcomes and increased uncertainty. So measures do matter.

Around 450 BC, Protagoras of Abdera, a Greek Sophist, noted: "of all things, the measure is Man; of the things that are, how they are; and of things that are not, how they are not." This statement is of fundamental importance to commerce. Over the years, we too have found questions of measurement important, in particular, "How will you measure the success of *X*?" Measures that people care about are the only measures that matter for markets. In real commerce, the ultimate determinant of value for markets is the value given by people. Human interests drive markets for cloves, nutmegs, pepper, tulips, tea, coffee, sugar, fish, and precipice bonds. If you want people to use what you think is the correct market value for something, you have to make it valuable to them. By helping people value sustainable fishing through a consumer label, for instance, the Marine Stewardship Council strives to give sustainably fished fish more value.

Markets cannot function without measures. It is no coincidence that Section 8, Clause 5 of the US Constitution specifically gives Congress the power "To coin Money, regulate the Value thereof, and of foreign Coin, and fix the Standard of Weights and Measures."[1] Indeed, markets pay a lot for measurement, whether it be to auditors, actuaries, rating agencies, laboratories, standards agencies, or inspectors. Equally, markets benefit from measures. Measurement reduces market volatility and information asymmetries. If we can trust the moisture content measure in the cargoes of wheat we are trying to buy, everyone has saved a lot of time, bother, and unnecessary calculations about future volatility in outcomes. If we can trust the weight and quality measures on the bills of lading for the consignments of fish we are buying, then that element of assurance has reduced somewhat the information asymmetry in those transactions.

In fact, the evolution of a market from an innovative product or service, to a widespread product or service, to a commodity is frequently accompanied by an evolution in measurement. Breaking from a commodity back to an innovative product or service is often accompanied by a revolution in measurement.

As an example, take telecommunications. In the very early days there were a variety of billing methods. Globally, the industry evolved to the point that most twentieth-century telephone bills were based on measurements of time, distance, and national borders. With the long payback on the fixed assets, these charges became increasingly divorced from the underlying costs of delivering telecommunications and a number of people predicted the "death of distance." Over time, technical innovation led to a demand for a flat charge for internet usage, so data bills were based, initially at very high charges, on connectivity. This led to unprecedented innovation, to the point at which Voice Over Internet Protocol (VOIP) is cannibalizing traditional telephony; connectivity measures are losing their relevance in telephony pricing. A cycle from innovation to commodity and back again, accompanied by or instigated by changes in measurement. On the other hand, a market that relentlessly enforces an outmoded measurement may avoid evolution for a time. Measures can skew markets and markets can skew measures.

Protagoras understood that measures are not as objective as we like to think. All measurement is political and takes place by one of three methods:

- Assessing against a standard.
- Comparing against like objects.
- Evaluating against a prediction or model.

These three means of measuring—respectively standard based, comparative, and predictive—can be fused, for example average the comparisons and we might have a standard, or we might consider a prediction to be just another comparison. The first is an absolute measure, the second is a conditional measure, and the third focuses on expected outcomes. Measurement immediately begs the questions: By whom? and For what end?

WHAT HAVE MEASURES EVER DONE FOR US?

Managers often abide by the rule of thumb "What gets measured gets done," but they should also realize that they may fail to find great measures that can handle the intangible or the serendipitous. Descriptive measurement—"the fishery contains X tonnes of suitable fish"—would seem to be different from success measurement—"the fishery is well suited to its purpose: providing enough protein for the community, livelihoods, exports, tourism..." The unbounded nature of direction (people may change where they are heading or what they are becoming) complicates measuring success. Before you have achieved your goals, you have often established new ones. And goals may not be directly measurable. "Profit maximization," for example—how do you know this is the most profit you could have made?

We contend that most measurement is in aid of one or more of four general purposes:

- *Setting direction*—the intention is to achieve X.
- *Gaining commitment*—agreement with the audience that they should expect X to be achieved.
- *Keeping control*—knowing what the key measure is and how "on target" you are.
- *Resolving uncertainty*—believing in X as a key measure, regardless of some of the volatility around you, and being confident.

Here's an interesting statement from Warren Buffett that embodies all four purposes:

> Our long-term economic goal (subject to some qualifications mentioned later) is to maximize Berkshire's average annual rate of gain in intrinsic business value on a per-share basis. We do not measure the economic significance or performance of Berkshire by its size; we measure by per-share progress. We are certain that the rate of per-share progress will diminish in the future—a greatly enlarged capital base will see to that. But we will be disappointed if our rate does not exceed that of the average large American corporation.[2]

Note that Buffett has incorporated all four purposes:

- He has set direction, as this "average annual rate of gain in intrinsic business value" is a long-term economic goal.
- He has gained commitment from shareholders by focusing on a per-share basis.

- He has kept control by showing he realizes that increasing scale will make the measure more difficult to achieve.
- He has resolved uncertainty by acknowledging that Berkshire Hathaway's "per-share progress will diminish," but also by comparing its performance to the average large American corporation. If Berkshire Hathaway fails to beat the average, then things are below expectations; otherwise, they're on target.

That seems straightforward enough in Warren Buffett's hands. So why do we end up with so many bad measures and skewed markets? We tend to mess up measures in two big ways: we obsess about targets and we overrely on single numbers.

OBSESSING ABOUT TARGETS

A measure associated with an incentive becomes a target. Professor Charles Goodhart was Chief Adviser to the Bank of England when he formulated an observation on regulation, Goodhart's Law, the original formulation being: "as soon as the government attempts to regulate any particular set of financial assets, these become unreliable as indicators of economic trends." Goodhart's initial observations emerged from monetary policy and regulation. The law has subsequently been reformulated as "any observed statistical regularity will tend to collapse once pressure is placed upon it for control purposes," or, even more broadly, "when a measure becomes a target, it ceases to be a good measure."[3]

An example of Goodhart's Law in action has been the focus on benchmarks for investment managers. Initially, the statistical measurement of investment managers made a lot of sense. Investment management benchmarks emerged, from Morningstar ratings to comparisons with the S&P 500. However, investors frequently have conflicting objectives. For instance, a typical investor might wish simultaneously to beat the annual performance of a benchmark index, to minimize the variability of annual returns, and to avoid significant losses. While luck might permit all three objectives to occur in any particular year, over time the three will naturally conflict. If you want to beat a benchmark you have to accept either higher variability of returns, significant losses, or both.

Beating a benchmark has moved from being a statistical measurement to being a target, because potential investors tend to obsess about watching the single measure of "performance against the benchmark." Investment managers need to beat the target in order to attract investors. They know that investors, especially pension fund managers, want excess return over the benchmark, "without risk." While this excess return over an index (often known as "alpha") is desirable, it is also technically impossible. Nevertheless, honesty can be a poor sales policy. In order to attract investors, investment managers find themselves stuck, either having to breach some technical portfolio issues or credit quality; the latter is easier.

For instance, investment managers may add to their portfolio a one-year corporate security that pays 100 basis points more than an equivalent one-year Treasury bond. The security and the bond have the same duration, but the credit quality is different. As long as the corporate security pays out, the investment manager is able to claim that he or she beat the benchmark by delivering more than alpha. Corporate securities rarely fail, but on the rare occasions that such failure does happen, the investment manager folds up his or her tent and walks away. A small change in credit quality allows the benchmark to be beaten. Goodhart's Law is alive and well. Because those benchmarks become a target, they cease to be good measures.

Goodhart's Law bears gentle comparison with Heisenberg's Uncertainty Principle. Heisenberg noted that the more precisely the position of a particle is determined, the less precisely its momentum is known. Measuring a physical system disturbs it. In biology, measuring a cell may well kill it. While many are loath to apply lessons from physical systems directly to social systems, it is true that measuring social systems disturbs them and alters their behavior. If measurement did not alter behavior, you would hardly see such an emphasis among politicians, managers, and others on measurement. In some ways, the more precisely people try to measure things, the worse these measurement problems become.

Yet appropriate measurement in many particular situations is a good thing; indeed, we often consider someone to be an expert in their field precisely because that person is very good at understanding and articulating appropriate measures in specific circumstances. It can be a delight to watch a professional at work pursuing the following line of questioning in a professional services firm, say a legal or accountancy or architectural practice:

- How do you define utilization?
- How do you incorporate overtime in utilization?
- Does utilization include all working days, or just days that people turn up for work?
- Are bonuses based on utilization or on value added?
- Therefore, how closely do aggregated bonuses correlate with profitability?

NOT QUITE THE MEASURE OF THINGS INTENDED

Now consider a related, but subtly different law, the Law of Unintended Consequences. There are many versions of this law, but ours is: "Action to control a system will have unforeseen results." This is a law people hate to love, but love it they do. Most of us like to support the underdog and experience a small thrill when we see authorities humbled trying to control things they possibly shouldn't have a say over. Supposedly, when authorities in the state of Vermont tried to control roadside advertising in 1968 by banning billboards, instead of obtaining clear views of the countryside, they found that local businesses had acquired such intense artistic interests that an auto dealer commissioned and installed a sculpture of a 12-foot high, 16-ton gorilla clutching a Volkswagen Beetle, and a carpet store erected a 19-foot high genie holding aloft a rolled carpet as he emerged from a smoking teapot. On the other hand, Adam Smith's Invisible Hand is a rarer case of the Law of Unintended Consequences having a beneficial effect: huge numbers of selfish people create mutual benefits.

There is a lovely acronym for one straightforward approach to setting objectives, SMART. A SMART objective has five characteristics: it is specific, measurable, achievable, realistic, and timely. As an example, think of a call center:

- *Specific*: A number, percentage, or frequency should be used—"answer the phone within 10 seconds" is much clearer than "answer the phone promptly."
- *Measurable*: the measures must be taken consistently and communicated—"you don't seem to be answering the phone as quickly as yesterday" is not an adequate measurement.
- *Achievable*: the objective must be realistic for a reasonable amount of effort—you can't ask people always to answer the phone within one second given that they have to breathe and drink.
- *Relevant*: the objective must be within people's control—you can't ask call-center agents to increase market share.
- *Timely*: you must clearly set out timescales—do you mean calls within the next month?

Nevertheless, this tidy SMART edifice falls down if you set the wrong measures or obsess about the targets. As Alastair Bryburgh, Chief Contrarian at Akenhurst Consultants, puts it, "Hmm. So something measurably average is better than something clearly outstanding but hard to quantify." Here is an example we encountered in a financial services organization that was struggling with its helpline. In order to improve efficiency, the call-center agents were given time targets, such as "so many minutes to be spent per customer query." As it happens, this target was SMART, but not exactly what we would call "smart." As bonuses were tied to the targets, the agents rapidly found that they could hit the minutes-per-customer target fairly accurately. It didn't matter that many of the big, profitable transactions, such as "I'm thinking of taking out a mortgage," or the ones that matter to customers, such as "I need to change a regular payment," took more than the allotted time, because the agents found mysterious ways for such calls to end abruptly as the time limit approached. Many unfortunate customers would retry a few times before concluding that the one transaction that could occur within the narrow time window available was terminating their account.

Soon the financial services organization noticed two things: the popularity of its helpline seemed to be rising rapidly and customers were leaving in droves. Action had to be taken. So a special, second helpline was set up to catch customers who made noises threatening to leave. As soon as they talked about leaving, they were transferred to the special helpline. This second helpline was given two special powers. The first was a small amount of money to grease the path for the customer back into the high-quality service. And the second power? An unlimited amount of time to deal with queries. Of course, because of the higher call volumes, the regular agents were now stretched handling all the phone calls from customers within the allotted target, so their target time per customer was reduced. Strangely, although the special helpline was reasonably successful at retaining customers, the rate of customers threatening to leave increased yet further when these changes were implemented.

Naturally, the increased dissatisfaction and continuing loss of business had to be investigated further, so an ultra-special third helpline was set up to find out why customers were dissatisfied. This third helpline had one role: to listen. Completely unlimited time to talk to customers. In a final ironic twist, the chief executive of this company was in the media talking about the need to "get close to the customer" and special "listening to customers" research he was commissioning.

Yes, it is fun hearing tales showing that "action to control a system will have unforeseen results." Plucky call-center agents triumph over the wicked control system, albeit by throwing a spanner in the works, while disconnected managers get their comeuppance. Less fun, though, is the huge amount of wasted time for customers and call-center people; and/or the potential loss of jobs because the financial services firm is clearly less competitive. While it was relatively easy to unpick the root causes and resolve the problems within a few weeks, many targets create malignant problems that are prone to escalate out of control and much harder to resolve.

So how can you avoid these unintended consequences? Well, first recognize that there is a big difference between measures and targets. Measures are, in theory, isolated facts. Targets are things where some remuneration or incentive is implied. You could argue that there is such a thing as an objective, nonhuman measure, but you certainly can't imagine a target that doesn't involve people and some form of incentive intended to motivate them. The problem is that such incentives, however well intended, can easily become perverse.

There used to be a lot of Soviet-era jokes about targets taken to the absurd. Once upon a time there was a steel factory that made railroad equipment, especially locomotives. The target was changed to output as much steel as possible, therefore the managers made the locomotives with as much steel as they could, so heavy that the locomotives broke the rails. Central planning converted the locomotive factory to focus on making rails for the railroads. The new target was set as the maximum number of pieces of finished steel, so the managers decided to make exceedingly thin rails, as thin as pins. Thus central planning decided to convert the factory to make pins, but the railways were too weak to deliver the ore or ship the pins.

Such examples do not emanate solely from a bygone Soviet era. The UK government has been frequently pilloried for its overly enthusiastic use of targets in the health service. A commitment to cut hospital waiting lists, for example, leads to a target of, say, "reducing the number of people on a waiting list for treatment by 100,000." The target is met, to fanfares and hurrahs—until observers spot that an increasing number of people are waiting to be put onto waiting lists.

You can expand on this theme of distorted measures across Europe as agricultural subsidies distort decisions in transportation, energy, and the environment. Similarly, in the US, the Merchant Marine Act of 1920 (the Jones Act) requires all goods carried between US coastal ports to be on US-flag ships, which reduces intracoastal shipping markedly and directly affects the price of fish.

Mundane measures start out with good intentions: "We need to measure such and such to ensure that the organization's objective is truly met." But often the really valuable measure that might deliver the objective is beyond people's ken, difficult to define or difficult to measure. So we find a cheap proxy for the valuable measure: some paper target that will more or less do. While the people we are trying to measure will almost certainly change their behavior to meet their targets, they almost certainly will not look beyond the measure to the original objective. After all, it is much easier, and cheaper, to deliver the measure that has been set.

This brings to mind Gresham's Law, which is often mistakenly paraphrased as "bad money drives out good," although the economist Robert Mundell deftly debunks the attribution to the Tudor merchant Sir Thomas Gresham (the idea at least dates back to Aristophanes). Mundell expresses the thought more accurately as "cheap money drives out dear money if they exchange for the same price."[4] In the measurement field, the phenomenon can be described as Gresham's Measurement Corollary: cheap (or poor) measures drive out dear (or rich) ones if they are deemed to have equivalent value. Think back to the call center example. Poor measures such as "minutes per call" are deemed valuable in the hands of call-center agents (that is, they are rewarded for meeting call volume productivity targets), whereas the true value lies in richer measures such as satisfied customers, increased revenue, or improved profits. The adverse consequences might be unintended, but surely they are predictable if one thinks about the mismatch between the intended value and the value being measured.

So why do firms and governments measure what they do? In part, they measure what they can. Sometimes this is fine, sometimes it is a big mistake. A lot of current thinking tries to get managers to think as scientists: How can you measure impact and what measures relate cause to effect? The measurement of impact may relate to long-term goals and the structure may be fairly stable, but the measures of cause and effect should change over time. As you learn what causes success, those causes of success should become normal. As you learn what causes failure, those causes of failure should be made rare. In turn, new measures should evolve.

OVERRELIANCE ON SINGLE NUMBERS

Take one fundamental and universal area of commercial measurement, financial accounts. Accounting measures are presented as specific numbers, not ranges, despite their inherent uncertainties. When Global Megacorp states its turnover as $71,393,224,326.73, you know this number is a fiction. This is typically an estimate of the mean of turnover, but you don't actually have the distribution of values to know more. Accountants grapple with significant uncertainties when computing turnover. Auditors have materiality issues with the consequences of that uncertainty. Realizing the obvious absurdity and statistical improbability of purporting to know a huge corporation's turnover to the penny, accountants laugh and happily round things off, but still neglect to give us any idea of the range of the distribution. One number alone is sought to describe complex distributions, typically the mean.

The three frequency charts in Figure 7.1 show the same mean turnover, $71,393,224,326.73 under today's deterministic "one number" paradigm. However, that mean turnover has a very different meaning in each case. Scenario A is the least of anyone's problems. The differences in values across the range $71,393,224,325.75 to $71,393,224,328.50 are infinitesimal, each of the potential individual differences making up that range amounting to pennies. Scenario B has an alarmingly wide range ($50bn to $90bn), normally distributed around the same mean turnover figure. In fact, there is a 90 percent chance that the turnover will fall between $61bn and $84bn, which doesn't exactly increase confidence in the mean value. In Scenario C, the distribution is heavily skewed, with the most likely outcomes being significantly lower turnover than the mean outcome (median turnover is $50bn). There are possible outcomes at significantly higher turnover than the mean. All that we can say with 90 percent likelihood is that turnover falls within the range $0bn to $172bn. Much like Scenario B, Scenario C is a dream for the accountant who is being asked "just give me the figure," but a nightmare for the auditor trying to work out whether that figure is justifiable.

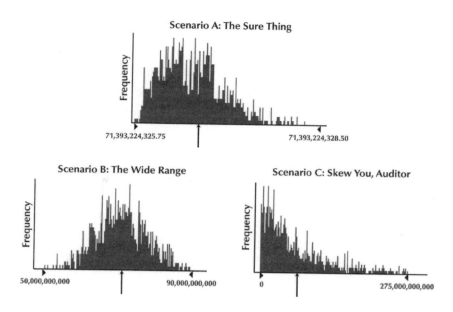

Global MegaCorp turnover: exactly £71,393,224,326.73?

Figure 7.1 Too mean to mean much

As in all accounting statements, too many measurable items that end up in a profit figure are ranges, from the estimate of gains in freehold land value to the likely profit on individual contracts to the value of insurances. To ensure total clarity, we litter accounts with explanatory footnotes to the point that only highly sophisticated financial analysts can understand them. When the accounts are presented, these financial analysts tear them apart in order to try to rebuild estimates based on ranges.

Audit is all about measurement, yet in practice financial audit is virtually bereft of all the usual scientific terminology one finds around measurement: confidence intervals, range estimates, sampling techniques, probability distributions. In short, we believe that financial audits need to be more scientific. If auditors do practice risk-based auditing, then why can't we see the odds they face? This simple question raises a number of concerns about the approach to financial statements in auditing by today's accountants. Balancing the odds might well give a truer and fairer picture of accounting than traditional ways of balancing the books. We call this probabilistic or *confidence accounting*.

Much like the Soviet era, there is a surfeit of old jokes in which an accountant delivers the punch line: "What do you want the number to be?" The uncomfortable truth is that accountants have quite a bit of influence over the final number. Indeed, accountants and auditors throw away tremendous amounts of information, as they principally use fixed numbers in almost all their calculations. The financial community knows that the annual report is subject to tremendous uncertainty, but will find little evidence therein. The key community for the annual report, investors, spend more of their time on reconstruction of the underlying ranges or guessing other investors' sentiments than worrying about the annual report's singular guess at what reality might be. Surely no theory of measurement has wasted so much effort ignoring the real world.

Intriguingly, the overreliance on single numbers ensures that auditors get off very, very lightly, practically skipping away. How do you hold an auditor to account? If you can prove that the profit figure is incorrect by $1, is that enough to claim that the accounts are invalid? Certainly not. $100? Well, when? In fact, auditors have cleverly avoided giving us anything substantive to go on, such as "The auditors are 95 percent certain that profits were between $X and $Y." We believe that the auditing profession would benefit from such disciplines and that audit failures (of which there are far too many for comfort) would then become that much rarer. We advocate forcing auditors to lay these ranges out clearly and to provide indemnities to support their ranged opinions.

The term we use to describe this approach, confidence accounting, has an intriguing double meaning. It uses confidence intervals rather than absolute numbers, plus we believe that the approach should cause people to have more confidence in accounts. For example, once profits are expressed as ranges after allowing for doubt, users of those accounts should have more confidence in the profits thus recognized. Furthermore, we believe that the approach introduces useful feedback and control loops into the regulatory system. Regulators could, in changing circumstances, change the confidence limits to be applied to certain accounting factors. For example, following a banking crisis, confidence intervals used by banking regulators to determine reserve levels could be tightened or loosened in order to restore market confidence and/or vary liquidity.

We use the acronym BET% to describe this approach: Bottom, Expected, Top, and the percentage likelihood. We have talked about overreliance on single numbers in the context of financial accounting measures, but the principle of using ranges instead of discrete numbers applies to all manner of measures. In fact, we advocate pinning down all commercial measurers to their estimates using BET%.

BET%ING ON THE FUTURE

BET% comes into its own in the forecasting field, a discipline related to measurement but one in which the person "just giving you a number" can at least subsequently make the excuse that that number was merely a prediction. John Kenneth Galbraith famously quipped: "the only function of economic forecasting is to make astrology look respectable." Or, our favorite, "prediction is difficult, especially about the future," variously attributed to Niels Bohr, Yogi Berra, Mark Twain, and Sam Goldwyn. Who could have predicted so much attribution confusion for that simple quote?

Instead of a single number that is almost certainly going to be wrong, our firm, Z/Yen, has used probabilistic modeling and fan charts since the mid-1990s for our revenue forecasting. We assess each opportunity individually on a BET% basis and then, once a month, produce a statistical model of the portfolio of opportunities to generate probabilistic revenue-prediction charts and fan charts. We advocate the use of such methods for many forward-looking measurements, in particular future company results.

A good example (on a slightly grander scale) is the Bank of England's use of fan charts to predict inflation, published since 1996.[5] Expected outcomes spread out in bands from the most likely path of inflation. Fan charts are not new, dating back several decades, but even actuaries are finally getting excited about probabilistic mortality models that provide fan charts instead of discrete numbers, because the fan charts permit the range of error to be evaluated after the event.

A range of possible outcomes is no longer a sign of imprecision, it's a sign of maturity. John von Neumann, who claimed "there's no sense in being precise when you don't even know what you're talking about," would surely have supported fan charts. Ranges of forecasted outcomes with their probabilities allow us to achieve a better assessment of the accuracy of the forecaster over time. According to Richard Feynman, "the first principle is that you must not fool yourself—and you are the easiest person to fool." Presenting forecasts as probability ranges is a first step toward being honest with yourself and allowing evaluation of your forecasting accuracy in the future.

DIFFICULT TO PREDICT

So we really want to make predictions, but it is really difficult to tell how good we are at it. Sometimes we can generalize confidently from experience, at other times not. But in any case, we need to deploy some form of statistics if we want to predict.

There are two major schools of statistics: frequentist and Bayesian. The *frequentist* school is the version most people are exposed to at school or college. Find a lot of examples of something, see how they are distributed, and predict on that basis. The *Bayesian* school approaches the problem the other way around: it says, in effect, have a good guess at what you think the distribution will be in advance and then modify it based on experience. The Bayesian school can work with very little data, making use of *priors*, the distributions we assume apply to the experiences we have had so far, even from very little experience. For example, the normal or Gaussian distribution, the *bell curve*, is something that we use intuitively to estimate a lot of things, for example height, age, and weight. If asked a question such as "What is the weight of most 40-year-old British men?" you would implicitly use a bell curve; while if you were instead asked "What will the box-office takings be for the next Bond film?" you might well use a different distribution function.

Experiments aimed at identifying the priors people use for a variety of common-sense questions suggest a "close correspondence between people's implicit probabilistic models and the statistics of the world."[6] Striking a blow for common sense, one experiment even found that ordinary people guess telephone-queue waiting times using a power law distribution. Telecommunications engineers worldwide are slowly realizing that this might be more accurate than their traditional Poisson distribution. Such research suggests that evolutionarily developed guessing mechanisms may be quite sophisticated, and adequate for many purposes. This idea is closely related to the question of heuristics and biases we discussed in Chapter 2— humans have developed these intuitive methods because they tend to work for most purposes.

However, we need to understand the limitations as well as the benefits of intuitive methods. Superstition is the mistaken belief that accidental correlation is causal. In a less sophisticated world, the time and energy wasted on those false priors is probably worthwhile, to avoid greater risk—of death, perhaps—if a genuine piece of causal evidence is erroneously ignored. Such a frequentist of the prehistoric world would be too busy gathering additional data for his frequentist experiment to avoid the present danger—say, a man-eating saber-toothed tiger—from which the prehistoric Bayesian would already be fleeing.

Nevertheless, the philosophical challenge remains to choose between a successful inductive theory and a wrong one. The experimental approach of science isn't always possible in commerce. Once you admit that the trial is dangerous in some way—jobs will be lost or customers will leave—then you are very unlikely to get people to agree to a scientific test. You could be more creative in many cases, for example conducting scientific trials of several ways to run schools or hospitals before you launch yet another new management approach, but it's never an easy sell. People want to select a solution, not to test possible answers. This leads many organizations to follow what others do.

A good example here is the assumption by many in government and NGOs that the correct form of procurement is an open, competitive tender, with all the bureaucracy and perverse results that seem to accompany public-sector tenders, as we discussed in Chapter 2. They rarely evaluate the alternatives used by many other organizations, and would find an experimental test terrifying, because their principal driver is conformity, not economy, efficiency, effectiveness, innovation, or even reducing corruption.

PERFECTLY UNPREDICTABLE

Further good news for the future of forecasting is often missed by those who judge computational advances from their desktop.

The deep structure of computer systems is moving confidently toward dynamic, anomaly, and pattern-response systems. By *dynamic*, we mean systems that are adaptive and able to learn from new data in real time. By *anomaly*, we mean systems that can identify unusual behaviors or outlying data points. By *pattern response*, we mean systems that can help reinforce successful behaviors and/or initiate real-time actions.

New technology architectures support new applications for communities, trading, sales, or customer relationship management, for example handling all of the incoming emails for an auction site; directing consumers to the goods they're most likely to buy; or appealing to a customer's likely charity or political affiliation. Growing computational capability and increasing quantities of data give organizations the power to spot incipient trends early. Firms are taking advantage of their internet traffic of all forms—emails, website hits, orders, and searches—to build increasingly fast, adaptive response systems. No successful global web-business owner can respond to commercial requests without automated systems; the volumes are too high. In short, we envisage more automated decisions, real-time analytics, visual presentation, and machine-created strategies from transaction and text processing.[7]

Price isn't everything, particularly when you know so much about your customers and their likely responses. And recommendations that jar can lead to hilarious consequences at the consumer end. Writing in the *Wall Street Journal* in 2002, Jeffrey Zaslow's article, "If TiVo Thinks You Are Gay, Here's How to Set It Straight," highlighted machines presuming too much, from their owners' sexual orientation and resulting choice of films to watch, to Amazon's computers' public recommendation of pornography for its founder, Jeff Bezos.[8] The emerging power of interacting directly with people's desires enriches, rather than undermines, our view of real commerce, but it is also very likely to impair elements of our privacy.

One suggestion we sometimes hear is that predictive software will end up replacing markets. We disagree. We believe that markets now matter more, but in different ways. In the past, prices were the single most important piece of information. Prices and the resulting information that could be inferred about supply and demand were critical factors. Now, there are enormous prediction markets. H G Wells is said to have mused about the future that "statistical thinking will one day be as necessary for efficient citizenship as the ability to read and write." It has taken a long while for this insightful forecast to approach reality—indeed, such a long time that the quote is sometimes attributed to the statistician Samuel S Wilks—but intriguingly, today's systems allow us to take the thinking of the citizenry and represent it statistically more easily than ever.[9]

There are many examples of highly active betting exchanges, such as the University of Iowa's Electronic Markets for US elections set up in the 1990s,[10] as well as markets such as the Hollywood Stock Exchange or the Foresight Exchange. These betting exchanges have moved from being laboratory playthings, to being used inside many large companies for sales forecasts, to being fun public tools in their own right, used on a large scale for gambling and trading. The largest exchange by volume of transactions in the UK is not the London Stock Exchange, nor is the London Stock Exchange (founded in 1761) valued as highly as this new, largest exchange, which was founded in 1999—it is Betfair, processing bets among both companies and individuals. Prediction markets supplement real markets by anticipating movements. They are incipient trend detectors.

Extrapolation or interpolation can be myopic, ignoring large-scale qualitative issues. Yet we increasingly have the ability to incorporate the qualitative with the quantitative. So-called *imperfect-knowledge economics* strives to recognize the importance of qualitative regularities: patterns that are observable, durable, and partially predictable.[11] A good example is the long-term forecasting of exchange rates based on purchasing power parity. We expect purchasing power parity to affect the long-term equilibrium, yet the short-term equilibrium often fails to materialize. Forecasters can use imperfect models, relying on large-scale regularities in human nature and the environment to keep their model within bounds.

Quantitative models are great from day to day, but we need to keep in mind the overall picture. Know when to throw them out and start afresh. Too often model failure induces a religious response: "What you need to do is to model harder!" When quantitative models become less valid, we need to think about using a fundamentally new model rather than necessarily fixing today's. Increasingly, thoughtful forecasters are employing ensemble forecasts and scenarios to break out of day-to-day model loops. Instead of trying to find a best model, they are trying to build sets of robust models. Using scenarios, we can break out of today's models to build consistent pictures of alternative worlds based on different assumptions with new parameters. For example, in the London Accord work on climate change, the jump was to ignore day-to-day prices and models and just assume that the cost of CO_2 would exceed $\text{\euro}X$/tonne. This new scenario suggested novel questions. Scenarios are about recognizing that prediction is futile, while helping to identify the decision of most reward and least risk that provides the most future options.

Scientific and economic models have become the basis of speculative news—"the model is the message" perhaps superseding or supplementing Marshall McLuhan's slogan "the medium is the message." More and more media speculations are about model outputs, not real outputs. This thesis equally applies to interest rate models, inflation models, GDP models, credit models, or any other model that is reported in the press. The model's outputs and future outputs can become the news, and a feedforward loop has developed predicting with some accuracy what the "true" news will be. A simple example is that some researchers use searches on the words "depression" or "recession" in the media to create leading indicators of business sentiment. Of course, they publish articles on the frequency of word occurrences that themselves increase the frequency of mentions of "depression" or "recession" in the media and influence our opinions of what other people are thinking. Many indices and models—inflation, interest rate, financial center performance, GDP growth, and others—affect people's perceptions. Widespread reporting of these models brings about self-fulfilling prophecies. One of forecasting's principal benefits should be volatility reduction, yet the very models we use now seem to increase instability. To paraphrase Goodhart's Law, "When a forecasting model becomes a media model, it ceases to be a good forecasting model."

In short, measures are mainly a good thing in real commerce, but there is a tendency to obsess about targets to such an extent that the measures around which the targets are set cease to be good measures. We rely too much on single figures, even in circumstances where uncertainty should encourage us toward ranges of numbers rather than single numbers. Faced with uncertainty, we tend to fall back on heuristics and biases. Such "single number" reliance is even more worrying for forecasting than it is for measuring. Advances in technology enable us to invent analytical tools that can help us measure and forecast, yet those technological developments seem to be progressing more rapidly than humans' ability to analyze and use information well for measuring and forecasting.

In the next chapter we delve more deeply into market behaviors, which once again reflect the unpredictability of people making decisions about what might otherwise be predictable markets, in particular the notion of feedforward.

STREAM C | Systems

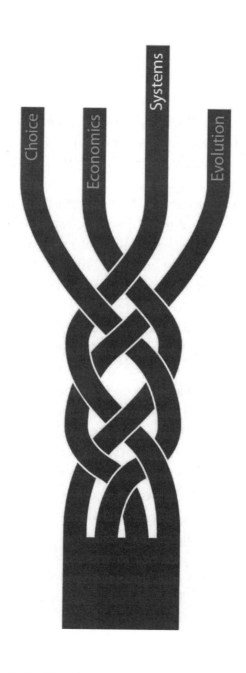

8 | PERCEPTIONS RATHER THAN RULES: PERFECTLY UNPREDICTABLE MARKET (MIS)BEHAVIORS

In this chapter we look more directly at systems theories. We also consider markets and how the combination of systems, economics, and people's behavior can make markets misbehave. We start by examining one element of systems theory, feedforward.

The following fishy story illustrates the idea of feedforward. Once upon a time there was a man who ran a fish and chip shop. People came from miles around to get tasty fish that was freely covered in thick egg batter, including his secret ingredient (beer), and thick-cut chips with plentiful sauces. In fact, the man was so successful that he could afford to send his son to complete an MBA at a top business school. After graduation, the son came back to work with his father. "Dad," he said, "based on the current economic statistics, we're heading for a recession. You've got to stop using all that thick batter, and you dish out ketchup as if it was free." The father was torn. He'd always been generous to his customers, but his very bright boy didn't get all that education for nothing. So, reluctantly, he cut back on the egg batter and the sauces. His son even convinced him to leave that pricey beer out of the batter. It was just in time, because it turned out his son was right—dad's business took a real dive.

This simple story illustrates an intricate truth about how systems around physical elements differ from systems around people. A physical system doesn't imagine what it could become. Yet what people think or believe will happen frequently comes to pass. You could say that people's self-fulfilling prophecies create chaos in the markets. And people's perceptions can cause markets to operate at the edge of chaos.

SYSTEMS THEORY BEGINS AT HOME?

The various theories and ideas we are about to explore have their roots in systems analysis, or cybernetics as it was called at the time it was founded by Norbert Wiener in 1948. Many people find that it only takes a brief introduction to enable them to start looking at the world slightly differently.

Systems analysis is the interdisciplinary study of the communication and control of many independent units acting toward a goal. It has had many noteworthy contributors, such as Ludwig von Bertalanffy, Claude Shannon, Alan Turing, John von Neuman, Stafford Beer, and Peter Checkland. With so many intellects, there have been a few wars and one needs to avoid falling into the trenches left behind. However, Gwilym Jenkins summarizes well a relatively accepted, traditional view of systems analysis from an engineering perspective:

- A complex grouping of human beings and machines.
- Able to be broken down into subsystems.
- Interaction between subsystem inputs and outputs.
- Part of a hierarchy of systems.
- Having an overall objective.
- Designed in a way that is capable of meeting its overall objective.[1]

The idea is that all systems exhibit seven components: inputs, processes, outputs, feedback, feedforward, monitoring, and governance. Acronyms such as mopffig, giffmop, and pigmoff don't work very well, but the mnemonic "In Parts Of France Fish Meals Gratify" (ipoffmg) is the best we can do and at least it

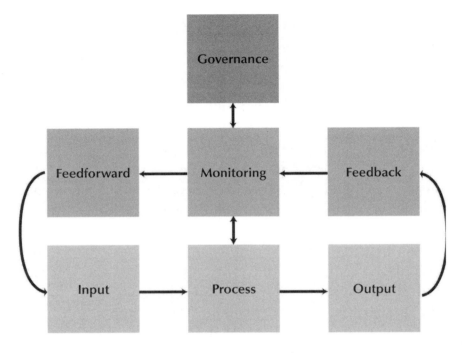

Figure 8.1 Systems theory in seven boxes

should whet your appetite for the ideas and those delightful fish suppers. Figure 8.1 may also help.

However, what do these seven components mean? Well, try considering an automobile as a system:

- *Inputs, processes, and outputs* are all the "doing" components: the engine, wheels, chassis, brakes, steering, and fuel systems of a car; note all the subsystems.
- *Feedforward* is a setting that anticipates something, perhaps using cruise control, signaling a maneuver, or sensing that the car in front is about to make a maneuver without signaling.
- *Feedback* is the one element of systems theory or cybernetics that most people have heard about. It relates to how the system reacts to news about how well or poorly it's doing, such as the vehicle's response when you brake, or accelerate, to

deal with the dual hazard of an unsignaled maneuver from the car in front and the cyclist alongside who is trying to overtake you.

- *Monitoring* is how you measure what's going on, such as the speedometer and the fuel gauge.
- *Governance* is how you adjust the system to meet your goal, such as deciding where to drive or choosing a hybrid car.

This may still be a bit abstract, so let's go into more detail with another example. Take a house with a heating system. It's a cool day and you want to regulate the temperature. You see the same seven components:

- *Input*: fuel.
- *Process*: burning the fuel to heat water.
- *Output*: pumping the hot water around the radiators.
- *Feedforward*: you set the thermostat based on your desired temperature.
- *Feedback*: a new, warmer temperature.
- *Monitoring*: comparing the new, warmer temperature with your desired temperature.
- *Governance*: your goal, a bit warmer, or a bit cooler?

Do note in Figure 8.2 the huge variety of subsystems that might be present: the pumping system for the radiators, the fuel-delivery system, the electrical system that powers the meters, the insides of the meters themselves. However, we want to draw your attention to the peculiar role of feedback and feedforward, so we built a small heating simulator. Unfortunately, though, we weren't able to get a very sensitive fuel input, so the temperature could, at random, either go up a degree or down a degree, not a lot in between. We used a computer-based random number generator to simulate that input. After debating the meaning of random and concluding that the computer-generated random

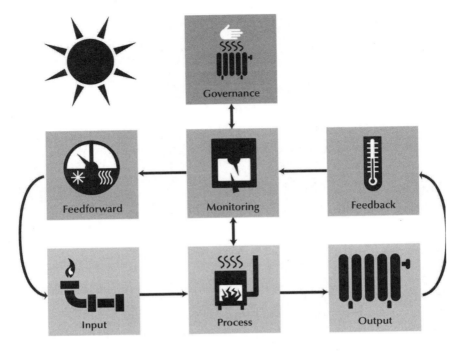

Figure 8.2 Systems theory begins at home

numbers should be random enough for our purposes, we then thought we'd better cool down by trying to keep the temperature at 20 °C.

Consider two other diagrams. Figure 8.3 shows a random walk of temperature around 20 °C—simply a process that follows the outside temperature. Figure 8.4 compares that random walk with three other components:

- A basic heating system that adjusts itself up when the inside temperature is below the target and down when the inside temperature is above the target. This simple feedback system is illustrated by the "T with feedback" line. It doesn't do too badly, but it's not perfect.

- A person trying to do without the temperature-control system. However, this person has some knowledge of whether the outside temperature is going up or down, so they inject

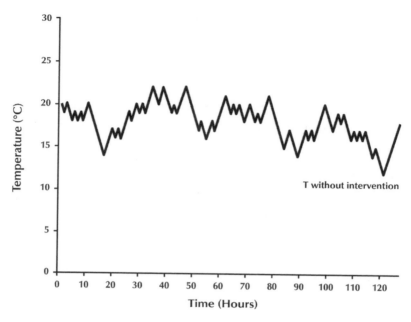

Figure 8.3 A heating system takes a random walk

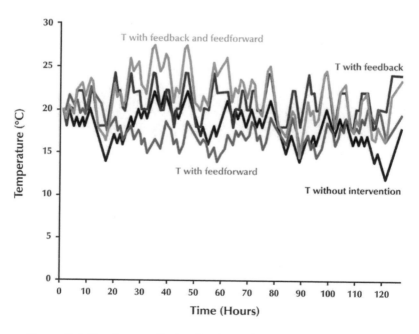

Figure 8.4 Random walk, feedback, and feedforward compared

161

some feedforward, the "T with feedforward" line. If the temperature is going to be cooler, say nightfall is approaching, they turn the heating up. If the temperature is going to be warmer, say the weather prediction is for a sunny day, they turn the heating down. Notice that the temperature is a little closer to target than random, but the feedback system was doing slightly better (although not significantly).

- Use the heating's mechanized feedback system and the knowledgeable person's feedforward together and surely things will be great. Well, here we have feedback and feedforward together, the "T with feedback and feedforward" line. Actually, this method does no better, as the feedback and feedforward often contradict each other.

The point here is that the heating system and the person, even with good foreknowledge, can't really improve on basic feedback; in fact, they can make it worse. Once they work out that they cannot really use that knowledge to cooperate, they might well start trying to game the system (see "Do not attempt systems theory at home") to try to get the result they want.

STOCHASTIC SYSTEMS THEORY

We have outlined systems theory and seen some diagrams that look very much like financial markets emerging from fairly straightforward interactions between system components. So where does the random or "stochastic" element fit in?

Stochastic, which comes from the Greek *stochastikos* meaning "skillful in aiming," is just a fancy word for conjecture; sometimes it is simply used to mean random. It is largely synonymous with chance. A good visual metaphor for stochastics is an archer aiming arrows at a target, shooting and then looking at the pattern of distribution around the target. Systems theory encourages us to decompose complex systems into subsystems, recognizing interlinked feedforward and feedback loops. Stochastic systems theory takes basic systems theory and asks us to realize that there are many imperfections at all points: what is the target; how do you know the value of the target; where is the target moving; what will this bow do; how well will this arrow fly; from your last hundred shots were you high, low, or all over the place? At each of the seven system components you do not have a single number, you have a potential range of numbers.

In the previous chapter, we discussed the benefits of looking at ranges rather than absolute numbers when considering accounting measures and real commercial predictions. A stochastic view of the world develops your appreciation of the roles of chance and imperfect information, both in planning forward and in evaluating backward. Stochastic systems theory asks you to recognize the role of chance and probability in systems, deploying the idea of ranging on systems generally.

DO NOT ATTEMPT SYSTEMS THEORY AT HOME

A vital element of these systems is the people who use them; in particular, how they interact with one another and the systems. The simple examples shown so far have just one person feeding forward. Most real-world systems, including financial systems, involve many people. In a spirit of scientific inquiry, some friends of ours, the Tiberelli family, volunteered to interact with their domestic heating system and let us observe the results. This was bound to be an interesting experiment, as Timothy Tiberelli is notoriously fond of extremely cold environments, whereas his wife and children tend to prefer something a little warmer. Or, as Timothy puts it, "Most people I meet are thermostatically challenged, whereas I am one of the very few temperate people I know."

This domestic situation should be familiar to many readers, whether the household is populated with housemates, lovers, a traditional family, or fictionalized characters. Rather than open warfare, the Tiberellis (in this experiment, primarily Timothy and his wife, Elspeth) engage in covert warfare. When he feels the temperature is getting down to just about right, he realizes that Elspeth is highly likely to put the thermostat up, so he turns it down a bit more, just to be sure. But she knows that Timothy is likely to behave this way, so she's highly likely to have increased the thermostat while he wasn't looking, maybe by about 10 degrees or so, just to be sure. Of course, in a one-person quest to save the planet, Timothy considers it to be his civic duty to turn the thermostat down again when Elspeth isn't looking. He might also open the windows for a while to ensure that the birds don't freeze.

Some readers will recognize the game theory implications of this domestic tussle. Game theory, covered in Chapter 4, is the study of behaviors in situations where one player's choices affect the choices other players might make. Traditional game theory seeks to look at such problems mathematically and find equilibria to solve them. A two-person thermo tussle as described above should lend itself neatly to an equilibrium solution.

Indeed, when we modeled the "Tiberelli marital strife" version of events, the results were strikingly similar to those of the reasonably efficient feedback line in Figure 8.4. Despite people adding some flavor to the situation, in this equilibrium-finding situation they end up reaching some strange form of stability.

However, add some more complexity to the mix and it becomes much harder to reach an equilibrium solution. In the Tiberelli household, two children have their own opinions on what a sensible temperature might be. They might also be engaged as proxies in the "thermo war," bribed by one parent or another (or both) to adjust the thermostat. Keen readers might have recognized plenty of potential for agency theory and information asymmetries (also discussed in some detail in Chapter 3) to come into play and add to the confusion. One of the strange things about complex systems is that, with enough actors and complexity, they can adapt to circumstances such that the overall system remains stable in a gross sense. For instance, share prices may be based on sentiment, but be attracted to the general region of "intrinsic" value.

We did once suggest to Timothy that it might be simpler for him and Elspeth to talk to each other and then discuss matters with the children to agree on a common temperature. He answered: "I'm led to believe that talking like this might upset our family harmony and possibly even place our marriage at risk." That, quite naturally, leads us to chaos.

THE EDGES OF CHAOS

Markets are always on the edge of chaos. Informally, we note the rapid changes in prices, sometimes commodity prices, sometimes equity prices on stock markets, sometimes exchange rates. We also note the rollercoaster ride of investment passions, technology shares, or Asian markets, all the rage at one time and then suddenly becoming pariah investments in what seems like the twinkling of an eye, only to bounce back into fashion again later.

Markets are anthropocentric: they are purely based on what people think. So how do these thoughts affect the numbers? More formally, we can look at an area of study called chaos theory and wonder about its applicability to markets.

Chaos theory is not in fact a theory, but a way of approaching problems, or a set of techniques and viewpoints that seem to recur in problems. It attempts to explain boundary conditions between order and disorder, between the easily modeled problem and the impossible-to-model problem. In Edgar E Peters' words, "many systems have now been found where randomness and determinism, or chance and necessity, integrate and coexist."[2] Chaos theory is not particularly interested in true chaos or true order, but it is interested in areas where things appear chaotic, even though they actually have a strong underlying order. Although earlier work by Georg Cantor, Waclaw Sierpinski, or Henri Poincaré has been a huge influence, "chaos" as a movement began in the early 1960s with the writings of Edward Lorenz and of Benoît Mandelbrot.

While chaos theory is not a formal movement, a number of strong themes recur. An initial theme is self-similarity or symmetry across scale. Self-similarity is often illustrated by fractals, geometric constructions that show dimensions between the integer dimensions. The term "fractal" was coined in 1975 by Mandelbrot from the Latin word *fractus* or "broken."[3] Simple equations can produce apparently complex, even beautiful diagrams that you can delve into at deeper and deeper resolutions unto infinity, yet they still seem similar at each scale. Self-similarity in fractals is thought to correspond to analogous similarity across scale in nature. Coastlines or clouds, for example, look similar whether viewed close up or far away. Mandelbrot believes that markets are strongly self-similar. Graphs of daily trading look similar to weekly, which in turn look similar to monthly or annually. He demonstrates that markets appear to exhibit a memory of their entire history contained within their fractal dimension.[4]

A second theme is the recognition that simple models can produce apparent complexity to an observer, such as the relatively simple algorithm that generates the Mandelbrot set, the set of points in the complex plane, the boundary of which forms a fractal. Furthermore, this apparent complexity seems, in many cases, to resemble the apparent complexity found in nature, such as trees, clouds, or coastlines. Graphs of deterministic nonlinear models that appear to generate complex behavior are popular in chaos theory because they illustrate well the existence of a region of models bounded by the organized simplicity of linear models, or continuous nonlinear models, and chaos. These models tend to have the characteristics of being aperiodic and having forms that change structurally given small changes to the model variables. At the same time, they exhibit an underlying order, with resonances and attractors that people perceive, or symmetry that people love. However, concrete analytical work sits alongside the heart-warming notion of making seemingly chaotic systems comprehensible and/or manageable.

A third large theme is said to originate with Poincaré: sensitive dependence on initial conditions. In one direction, we frequently examine financial-mathematical models and compare them with reality in hopes of finding a lasting comparison from which the existence of a theory may be inferred. Quoting Edgar E Peters again, this "can be confused with 'data mining' or torturing the data until it confesses... Actual results depend on many numerical experiments with varying test parameters. If this sounds unscientific, it is." Another direction is to take a theory, develop a model, and compare it with reality.

For example, in 1990 de Grauwe and Vansenten built a model of the foreign exchange market from generally accepted, though not uncontested, theory.[5] They demonstrated the chaotic properties of the model and contrasted it with actual exchange rate data, which showed numerous statistical similarities with the model outputs. The results illustrated that models can be constructed that may be perceived to mimic actual market behavior but are not predictive. However, minute changes to the model inputs resulted in new outputs that bore little statistical similarity to actual exchange rate data. The model was sensitive to initial conditions to such a degree that no data could ever be accurate enough to begin forecasting. The small degree of variance in normal input data accuracy was more than sufficient to change the model output markedly. Trivial facts or events could completely alter it. "Exact" knowledge of the environment would be necessary to use the model predictively and knowledge to that level of accuracy is unlikely. Moreover, the model was untestable, as there was no means of obtaining real-world data of sufficient quality to test it. So de Grauwe and Vansenten succeeded in proving that their foreign exchange model was useless in real life.

David Deutsch provides a summary:

Chaos theory is about limitations on predictability in classical physics, stemming from the fact that almost all classical systems are inherently unstable. The "instability" in question has nothing to do with any tendency to behave violently or disintegrate. It is about an extreme sensitivity to initial conditions.[6]

Three pointers from chaos theory can help us understand markets:

- Self-similarity at different scales.
- Simple models producing apparently complex behavior.
- Extreme sensitivity of models to initial conditions.

Chaos theory's distinctions among chaos, order, and the boundary between chaos and order are particularly useful as metaphors for markets. If there are nonlinearities in a system, then behavior may be as unpredictable as it is interesting. But you also need to be aware that the attractiveness of chaos theory may foster illusions. Einstein, echoing William of Ockham, warns us:

Although it is true that it is the goal of science to discover rules which permit the association and foretelling of facts, this is not its only aim. It also seeks to reduce the connections discovered to the smallest possible number of mutually independent conceptual elements. It is in this striving after the rational unification of the manifold that it encounters its greatest successes, even though it is precisely this attempt which causes it to run the greatest risk of falling a prey to illusions.[7]

CHAOS IS A BIT COMPLEX

As if chaos theory isn't complex enough, let's move on to complex systems, or complexity. Many ancient mythologies and religions dwell on the tension between order and disorder. The word "chaos" comes from the name of the progenitor of all Greek gods, Kaos. The link between chaos theory and complexity is the apparent emergence of order from chaos.

Another way of expressing this is that some systems are self-organizing or negentropic. Order emerges from them. For some period of time a negentropic system defies entropy, the second law of thermodynamics that states that all processes tend toward greater disorder. In some fashion, a self-organizing system gains energy from the wider environment and establishes or increases order. Biological systems such as slime and swarms and weather systems such as tornadoes and hurricanes are examples of this, at least until their death. Perhaps Adam Smith's espousal of the "invisible hand" is a seminal example of recognizing self-organizing systems emerging from apparent chaos in human organization.

Complexity is the multidisciplinary study of systems from which order seems to emerge. Bees within a beehive; cells within a human being's nervous system; a business unit within a company within a market within an economy—these all comprise complex networks of interrelated entities that interact and affect each other and seem to exhibit a deeper order, a group behavior.

Complexity asserts a commonality among these systems from which we may be able to derive common features and principles about how to treat these phenomena. Complexity studies tend to favor the modeling of complex systems using nonlinear mathematics embedded in software. Complexity is frequently bound up with the study of information, imperfect information, and the transmission of information among actors within the system. When Ikujiro Nonaka talks about new organizational orders emerging from business chaos, he notes that "the essence of self-organization is in the creation of information."[8]

A critic might note that we are talking about "perceived complexity." Humans perceive complexity and humans have a tendency to find patterns in anything. People are pattern-recognition machines, even when they're looking at white noise. We believe that Sir James Sutherland's Crabtree Orations, a set of satirical academic commentaries attributed to the fictitious eighteenth-century poet Joseph Crabtree, inspired the great intelligence expert R V Jones to coin Crabtree's Bludgeon:

> no set of mutually inconsistent observations can exist for which some human intellect cannot conceive a coherent explanation, however contrived.[9]

In short, humans have no natural tendency to sharpen their minds on Occam's Razor. On the other hand, to paraphrase the old joke about paranoia, "just because the brain sees pictures that aren't there, doesn't mean they don't exist."

A critical mind might also note that some of the observations from the complexity community could tend toward the vacuous or obvious—"life is complex" or "complexity is all around us," for instance. On the other hand, chaos theory and complexity have provided thrilling analogies to business, society, and nature. While to date few practical tools have emerged, surely it is right to explore the boundaries between order and chaos in nature and

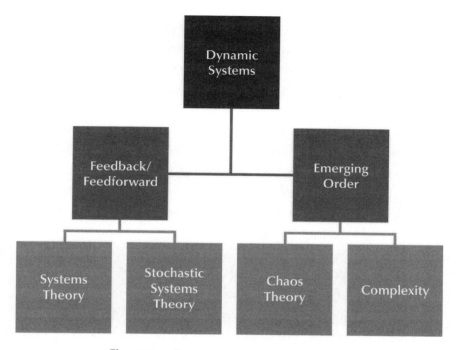

Figure 8.5 Dynamic systems summarized

see what learning emerges. Figure 8.5 summarizes dynamic systems theories in a simple taxonomy.

PREDICT THIS?

Chaos theory and complexity frequently use similar computer models. This interest has often taken the form of modeling evolution, for instance as "vivisystems," which in turn provokes thoughts of other living system metaphors for markets. Of course, the search for models is also the search for the ability to predict and the desire for predictive capability is deep-rooted. William Sherden devotes an entire book to examining the "second oldest profession," prognosticators. He estimates the market for prediction, "fortune sellers," as over $200 billion and then proceeds to demonstrate in most instances how poorly prognosticators perform against their own standards in areas as diverse as weather forecasting, economics, financial analysis, demographics, technology forecasting, futurology, and corporate planning.[10] As Paulos notes:

> if a system as trivial as this single nonlinear equation [of population] can demonstrate such chaotic unpredictability, perhaps we shouldn't be quite as assertive and dogmatic about the predicted efforts of various social, economic, and ecological policies on the gigantic nonlinear systems that are the U.S.A. and Planet Earth.[11]

Yet people keep trying to predict the unpredictable. That brings to mind an old Groucho Marx joke:

> "Doctor, Doctor, my brother thinks he's a chicken. Can you help?"
> "Why don't you stop him?"
> "We need the eggs!"

The desire to predict the unpredictable is deeply human. People need the "eggs," even if the result of their attempts to predict is simply egg on their faces.

Karl Popper doesn't need any eggs at all, however, commenting: "there can be no prediction of the course of human history by scientific or any other rational methods... We must reject the possibility of social science that would correspond to theoretical physics." He had a keen grasp of systems thinking's potential applicability long before complexity as a field of study emerged:

> There is no doubt that the analysis of any concrete social situation is made extremely difficult by its complexity... a complexity due to the fact that social life is a natural phenomenon that presupposes the mental life of individuals...

which in its turn presupposes biology, which again presupposes chemistry and physics. The fact that sociology comes last in this hierarchy of sciences plainly shows us the tremendous complexity of the factors involved in social life.[12]

Popper is correct, there are big problems involved in treating economics and finance as physical systems, but complexity's adherents persist in noting that lessons from other dynamic systems are as applicable to human organization as they are to nature, and that these approaches can afford insights into the limits of prediction.

Many people conclude that strategy or policy can emerge from environmental and organizational chaos, but paradoxically that some forms of chaos can be controlled toward certain ends. Many physical or ecological systems have implicit feedback. For instance, as predators' prey multiply, predators multiply, forcing a decrease in the prey population, leading the predator population to decrease, leading the prey population to increase, and so on.

PREDICTABLY CHAOTIC

As with the heating system metaphor described earlier, in addition to feedback, economic and financial systems exhibit feedforward. Our perceptions affect the probability of future events. Technology analyst Bob Giffords groups together feedback, monitoring, feedforward, and governance components as "feedthrough," highlighting the effect of people's perceptions on the probability of future events. If we change our perception of a risk, such as terrorism, that perception feeds through to alter future behavior, such as passenger levels on public transport.

We remember working on some strategic planning for London rail transport in the mid-1980s. Extrapolated employment in the financial services industry indicated that the number of people coming into the City of London would soon disastrously overwhelm the rail system at peak hours, particularly during the morning rush hour. The increasing growth of London as a global financial center in the 1980s, just before and after the Big Bang of 1986, meant that people were more integrated with global markets and needed to distribute their working hours to coincide with other markets. So, while in the event employment in financial services did rise, people stopped coming in during a very narrow peak period and started work both earlier and later, thus averting extreme overcrowding, although London's transportation system remains generally overcrowded at times.

People often wonder how financial market risk varies from natural risk such as earthquakes or hurricanes. Imagine that you know there is a hurricane coming to town. Imagine, too, that you run an insurance company that will have to pay out on damages. You do some calculations and in order to reduce likely injuries, you announce the hurricane's imminent arrival to everyone, with an enjoinder to leave town. You tell people that they ought to go, particularly as the police and emergency services are also on their way out. Unfortunately, that leads to some individuals staying behind to loot and you end up paying out much more for damage to property by people than the payouts faced from damage by the hurricane. The feedforward information had unintended consequences. There is a big difference between a natural risk and a human behavior risk.

The key distinction is that financial markets incorporate people's perceptions. Mark Twain puts these words in Huckleberry Finn's mouth, "Hain't we got all the fools in town on our side? And hain't that a big enough majority in any town?" Many people's perceptions matter to markets—and that leads to a majority view, including all the fools in town, deciding the fates of most financial markets.

Psychologist Herbert Simon said: "What information consumes is rather obvious: it consumes the attention of its recipients." Looking at financial failures, what failed often was not the firm, but people's perceptions of other people's perceptions. Bank runs are caused by people believing that other people will withdraw their money before they do. Clearly, the media have a big role in accelerating feedthrough.

The majority of share buying and selling is gambling against investor perceptions, not some "intrinsic" value (say, the dividend return) of the share. When you buy a share, you bet against past investors prepared to sell to you today. When you sell a share, you bet against future investors prepared to buy today. But it's not really that simple. A conventional bet crystallizes: "My football team lost and yours won, so I pay you." Shares are different. A traditional share may never crystallize. You might sell a share today whose intrinsic value (if there is such a thing) is as good as yesterday, but you believe that future investors will not value it so highly. Indirectly, you realize that might be the case because the "even more future" investors to whom they will need to sell may not value it so highly, and so on—feedforward on feedforward.

BEAUTY IN THE THIRD DEGREE

Keynes, in his General Theory, describes the actions of rational agents in a financial market in terms of a fictional beauty contest. Entrants have to choose six photographs of women whom they believe are the most beautiful from a large batch of photographs. Those who choose the six most popular faces win a prize.

A simplistic approach to this game would be to choose the faces that, in the opinion of the entrant, are the most beautiful. A more sophisticated contest entrant, wishing to maximize their chances of winning a prize, would think about what the majority perception of beauty is, and then select photographs based on their perception of public perceptions. This can be carried at least one step further to take into account the fact that other entrants would also be making their decision based on knowledge of public perceptions.

> It is not a case of choosing those [photographs] which, to the best of one's judgment, are really the prettiest, nor even those which average opinion genuinely thinks the prettiest. We have reached the third degree where we devote our intelligences to anticipating what average opinion expects the average opinion to be. And there are some, I believe, who practice the fourth, fifth and higher degrees.[13]

In this foresighted piece, Keynes was anticipating game theory and in particular the idea of the Nash equilibrium. An additional problem here is that you are betting on the future gambling propensities of future investors, not today's investors or today's facts. This leads to an interesting distinction between the prices of financial instruments and other physical systems: the importance of your perception of other people's perceptions today of yet other people's perceptions tomorrow, and so on ad infinitum; even if the prices, at times, seem utterly irrational. As Keynes is believed to have said: "the market can stay irrational longer than you can stay solvent." And as Jack A Marshall noted, "nobody perceives anything with total accuracy." Thus stochastic systems theory and feedforward on feedforward may well describe financial markets; a bit like the Tiberelli family with the individuals' perceptions about each other's heating cheating.

FAT TAILS

There is something statistically strange yet predictable about human games and market behaviors. Results are not normally distributed, they deviate wildly above and below a normal distribution. Many results, such as mean averages, might be close to a normal pattern, but some tend to be wildly different from these norms.

Indeed, the distribution of results in circumstances where feedthrough is involved, be that heating systems or financial markets, is not normal. Systems with feedthrough—and human systems are marked by this—typically have nonnormal event distributions.

Kurtosis describes the "peakedness" of a distribution and is informally described as the volatility of volatility. If a distribution has a higher central peak and "fat tails," typical of financial markets, then it is described as leptokurtic. Such distributions are increasingly important. The feedforward loop or feedthrough of people's perceptions might well explain the nonnormal distributions we encounter in finance. Financial markets are growing more accustomed to so-called three-plus standard deviation events. A more than three standard deviation event should only occur once in every 300 events if the distribution is normal. But if the tail of the distribution is unexpectedly fat or long, then events perceived to be extremely rare are less rare than we imagine.

Tsunamis in South East Asia, hurricanes in North America, volcanoes in Europe, and earthquakes in Central Asia—disasters seem to be increasingly common. Whether natural disasters are actually more common than they were previously is almost always a matter of complex analysis and debate. What is without doubt is that natural disasters are increasingly widely reported and financially important. Take hurricanes in North America. The public perception is of more frequent and more violent hurricanes. Hurricane frequency and intensity may, or may not, have increased slightly over past decades. What is certain is that financial damage has increased, though this can be almost wholly attributed to greater population, greater wealth, and greater insurance coverage in the areas at risk; decades of people moving to the Florida coast and buying expensive houses, for example. In other words, so far it is *people* who have caused the risk to increase, not nature, not hurricanes, not yet global warming. Financial analysts may moan about losses, but markets aren't failing because of these disasters. In fact, so long as natural disaster risk can be priced over a reasonable cycle, insurers ultimately make profits. Naturally, while hurricanes may follow typical natural distributions, the financial impact of hurricanes follows a leptokurtic distribution.

Let us be absolutely clear about this. There are many natural systems with nonnormal distributions. However, human systems, those that utilize people's judgment, are "normally" nonnormal and, importantly, are all too frequently mistakenly treated as normal. This, we suggest, is probably the root cause of the apparent increase in one in 300-year events, those well beyond the third standard deviation. The root cause is people. People-based systems tend not to be normally distributed yet we often treat them as such. Nonnormal distributions cause large problems for financial analysts. Analyzing them is hard work. First, you have to recognize that you are dealing with nonnormal distributions, then you have to deploy more sophisticated mathematics.

People are often guilty of confusing two types of events: natural events that will follow a normal distribution, and human systems that will frequently have leptokurtic distributions. These human systems are exacerbated by feedforward on feedforward. For instance, you can look at a number of financial failures and see that what failed wasn't the firm, but people's perceptions of other people's perceptions about the firm. Arthur

Andersen's involvement in Enron and other auditing disasters led people to realize that other people wouldn't respect the firm in future as an auditor. Future audit clients and future auditors willing to work for Arthur Andersen evaporated, forcing it to close. People tend to attribute these disasters to a lack of trust. Trust is often counting on people to behave as they did yesterday. That is true, but there is a more general point here too. Financial markets are about perceptions and the perceptions are the reality.

BUBBLE, BUBBLE, TOIL AND TROUBLE

In *The Wisdom of Crowds*, James Surowiecki shows that large numbers of people can be very good at arriving at correct answers to complex problems, but that to do so four conditions must typically be met:

- *Diversity of opinion*: Each person should have some private information, even if it's just an eccentric interpretation of the known facts.
- *Independence*: People's opinions are not determined by the opinions of those around them.
- *Decentralization*: People are able to specialize and draw on local knowledge.
- *Aggregation*: Some mechanism exists for turning private judgments into a collective decision, such as a price.[14]

Financial markets clearly meet three conditions: diversity of opinion, decentralization, and aggregation. However, those markets do not wholly fulfill Surowiecki's second condition, independence. When you give a bad weather forecast predicting rain tomorrow, it doesn't make rain tomorrow more likely. But when you give a bad forecast predicting that a share will fall tomorrow, you do make it more likely. People add a very strong feedforward loop to financial systems. Talking a market up or down frequently moves that market up or down. Financial bubbles are partially caused by the lack of independence of people's opinions; in many cases we follow what others tell us to follow.

Contrarian investors bet against the herd. They count on bubbles and believe, to paraphrase Keynes, that "in the long run, we are all wrong." You can imagine the funny stories in England during the Dutch tulip bubble, the tulipmania of the 1600s: "Hey, those crazy Dutch, you'll never believe what they think a tulip is worth. It'll never catch on here." And apparently, for the most part, it didn't. Nevertheless, the UK went on to produce a few good, home-grown manias over the centuries, such as the South Sea bubble. Then in the 1990s, "Hey, those crazy Californians, you'll never believe what they think an information technology company is worth. It'll never catch on here." This time it did; indeed, arguably Europeans were the bigger suckers, as the bubble was well advanced before most European investors piled in. The internet bubble proved to be the biggest financial bubble in history, until the asset price and subprime loans bubble just a few years later. Global information leads to global perceptions and therefore to global bubbles.

So what are the lessons from all this? Well, three things stand out:

- All information is only a guess, a stochastic stab at what the underlying reality might be. The world of commerce is one of nested sets of stochastic systems, based on people's perceptions, not on rules of "intrinsic" value.
- When you start looking for feedforward you find it almost everywhere. When fashion people tell you that "black is this year's new black," realize that they are trying to create momentum toward buying their large stocks of dark materials. When people tell you about property prices, remember

that feedforward can ensure a bubble is very hard to spot while it forms, but you'll almost always hear the "pop" because you're highly likely to be in the middle of it. Business is not immune to fashion.

- A bit like fashion and dress lengths coming round every few years, remember also that all markets have their favorite, recurring, no-lose investments. Whether it's tire recycling in the waste markets, ultra-efficient engines in the environmental markets, or funds of funds in the financial markets, the same stories come around with alarming frequency. One day they'll be at the top of the wheel, but perhaps not this time round.

And what does the future hold for the behaviors of markets? More and more people are joining the global economy. As perception is everything, we must attempt to understand their perceptions. These are people who are more likely to add diversity and opinions that we don't know or understand. Moisés Naim reminds us:

> Statistically, a "normal" human being in today's world is poor, lives in oppressive physical, social, and political conditions, and is ruled by unresponsive and corrupt government. But normalcy is not only defined by statistics. Normal implies something that is "usual, typical, or expected." Therefore, normal is not only what is statistically most frequent but also what others assume it to be. In this sense, the expectations of a tiny minority trump the realities of the vast majority. There is an enormous gap between what average citizens in advanced Western democracies—and the richer elites everywhere—assume is or should be normal, and the daily realities faced by the overwhelming majority of people. Information about the dire conditions common in poor countries is plentiful and

widely discussed. Curiously, however, expectations about what it means to be normal in today's world continue to reflect the abnormal reality of a few rich countries rather than the global norm.[15]

Unusually, this mutual ignorance might just be a good thing. Feedforward on feedforward is less likely to start when you don't know how to figure out what other people are thinking. The greater the diversity of opinion, the more likely it is that the herd of people will reach the right answer. The paradox today is how to ensure that global information does not overwhelm the diversity of local opinion, leading everyone, perhaps inadvertently, to misbehave. We know that large numbers of people can make good decisions if conditions are right. Improving the environment within which global markets behave is one of the biggest challenges facing real commerce.

9 | FINANCE IN MOTION OR EVAPORATION? VOLATILITY AND LIQUIDITY

In this chapter we look at some slippery ideas that affect the dynamics of markets, in particular volatility and liquidity. These are slightly difficult concepts but they are ever-present in real commerce, as the examples in this chapter illustrate.

UNCERTAINTIES GALORE

An abiding theme for the last couple of chapters has been uncertainty. Prediction, measurement, and feedforward are all subjects relevant to understanding real commerce because they help us to comprehend the systemic uncertainties with which we need to grapple. Trading on markets, managing organizations, and controlling personal finances all involve coping with uncertainty. Real commerce is essentially about making decisions in an environment of uncertainty.

We have spent most of our working lives advising organizations on how to make better decisions and have, over time, boiled down the universal question "How do you make decisions in conditions of uncertainty?" into a simple rule of three, which we call "Three Rs." In conditions of uncertainty, there are essentially only three things you can aim to achieve from a decision:

- Risk control.
- Reward enhancement.
- Reduction of volatility.

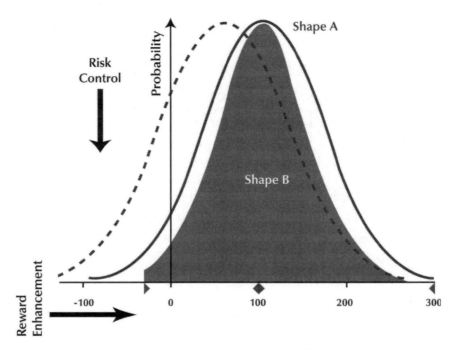

Figure 9.1 Three Rs for Rod

We can illustrate these three ideas with a humble sole-trader fisherman, whom we'll call Rod. Each day brings many commercial uncertainties for Rod. He might catch plenty of fish, he might catch very few. He might be able to sell his catch at a village near to home, he might need to travel some distance to offload his produce. He might get a good price for his fish today, he might have to settle for far less revenue than he'd hoped for.

Figure 9.1 illustrates the probability distribution of Rod's business. The dashed line is the current position. On average he clears $50 of profit a day, a decent return in his modest nation, Plaiceland, but not as much as he could earn. On an utterly exceptional day, when he finds a plentiful supply of fish while others struggle, allowing him to command the highest prices and sell all his fish at his nearest villages, Rod has been known to make $250 profit, which makes him very happy indeed. But on a really bad day, when everything goes wrong, he catches little and runs up a great deal of additional expense just trying to sell the paltry catch he did make. Rod has been known to lose as much as $175 in a day, which makes him extremely irritable. And the thing that really makes him lose sleep? He cannot tell from one day to the next how well or badly he is going to do. What can he do to make better decisions in the face of this uncertainty? Once Rod realized that decision making all boils down to the Three Rs, his local friends helped him to manage his uncertainty using each of the three areas in turn.

First, *risk control*. In Rod's business the main costs are all connected with the distances he travels in his fishing boat. Indeed, the only way he can lose as much as $175 in a day is by failing to bail out of a bad day early enough. If he were to reduce the distance he is prepared to travel to try catching and selling his fish, his costs would be much lower. For example, Rod has always refused to sell his excess catch to Mr. Fritto's chowder factory, as he thinks the sums that Mr. Fritto is willing to pay are derisory. But on a bad sales day, as his friends often tell him, you can at least recover a few dollars by selling to Mr. Fritto. If Rod would simply accept lower yields on poor catching days, and lower prices on bad selling days, he could limit his maximum potential loss for the day to about $80 while still maintaining an average return of $50. This category of decision, often described as risk management, is about accepting, avoiding, mitigating, or transferring the impact of adverse occurrences.

Secondly, there is *reward enhancement*. Some of the costs Rod incurs can be reduced. He has always insisted on using super-diesel for his fishing boat, although his friends tell him that the regular is just as good and costs 20 percent less; a potential saving of several dollars on an average day. Rod also has some old-fashioned ideas about sales prices. He always gives a whopping discount to his first sale of the day (for luck) and throws in a lot of small fry as free gifts even on tiny sales. His friends tease him: no one else does that stuff any more and he could regularly make more money, perhaps an extra $40 to $50 on average each day, if he gave up those ideas. This is illustrated in Figure 9.1 as the solid line, Shape A. Reducing costs and increasing revenues in these ways, although they would not reduce the amount of uncertainty Rod faces, would increase his returns on average. In commerce generally, this type of decision making is the domain of most professional managers. It is typically supported by cost–benefit calculations, although, as we discussed earlier in this book, the nonfinancial nature of some rewards and the human elements of decision making (such as heuristics and biases) will often lead to management decisions that are a mixture of quantitative and qualitative assessment.

Thirdly, and more subtly, there is *volatility reduction*. What can Rod do to reduce the uncertainties in his business? He cannot control the amount of fish in the sea, nor can he control what other fishermen are doing in their own attempts to make the most of things. However, some of his friends have recently combined forces, coordinating their fishing and selling activities. What each of those friends has found is that coordination reduces the variability of their daily profits considerably. They no longer get bonanza days when they can make two, three, or even four times their average daily profits, but they also no longer get many days when they lose money and now rarely lose more than a few dollars, even on a bad day. By coordinating their fishing activities, the supply of each type of fish seems to be more stable, which in turn has helped to stabilize prices. There is even talk of a wholesale fish merchant from the local large town placing a regular order for fish with this consortium, with guaranteed prices for species that the fishermen can supply in regular quantities.

In Chapter 6 we mentioned Robert Jensen's study on cellphone use by networks of fishermen in Kerala, illustrating the value of such networks for sustainability.[1] The primary use of the cellphones in that study was for fishermen to ascertain market prices in various local villages, helping them to minimize travel, maximize revenues, and reduce waste. The cellphone is a relatively simple and affordable technology that can help those fishermen (and many other similar networks of businesses) with aspects of risk control, reward enhancement, and volatility reduction. The effect of improving all three of these areas is illustrated in Figure 9.1 as the solid shape, Shape B.

VOLATILE PROFITS

Volatility reduction has a very significant value in real commerce. Rod loses sleep over the extreme uncertainty, or volatility, in his business because he knows intuitively that it is costly to him. It should be possible to value the difference between Shape A and Shape B in Figure 9.1. We know that the tighter shape, with low volatility, has more value to Rod (or to any manager trying to manage uncertainty) than the looser shape, but how do we value this difference?

The answer lies in techniques used to price financial derivatives, such as financial options. An *option* can be defined as a contract between two parties in which one party has the right but not the obligation to do something, usually to buy or sell some underlying asset. *Call options* are contracts giving the option holder the right to buy something, while *put options* entitle the holder to sell something. Payment for options takes the form of an up-front sum called a premium. Why would anybody pay for something as intangible (or derivative) as a right but not an obligation to do something? Because of volatility. In the absence of volatility, such derivatives would be worthless.

In his 1996 book *Against the Gods*, Peter Bernstein described the proliferation of derivatives as "a commentary on our times. Over the past twenty years or so, volatility and uncertainty have emerged in areas long characterised by stability." He cites the end of exchange controls and oil price controls in the 1970s as examples: "Derivatives are symptomatic of the state of the economy and of the financial markets, not the cause of the volatility."[2]

For example, we might buy a call option for a share you own in a large fishing fleet company. Today the company's shares trade at $100. We might pay you for an option to purchase the share at $100. You might agree with us that the option is for three months hence. If the company's shares are trading above $100 at the end of three months, we might decide to pay $100 to you and own the share. If the shares go down, perhaps to $90, we won't be interested in your share and will just walk away. As it is an option, we don't have to do anything at all.

The problem is agreeing how much we should pay you for that option. Let's look at two cases. If the share price is stable—say historically it has stayed mostly between $90 and $110—you might guess that the correct price for the option is a low number. If you take $5 now and if we decide at the end of three months to pay $100 more because against all expectations the share price hits $110, you've got your money and we made $10 on our $5 option investment. If the share price is wild—say historically it has fluctuated all over the place from $30 to $300—$5 for the option doesn't seem sufficient. If at the end of three months the share is at $30 then we won't want it, but if at the end of three months the share is at $300 then you'd rather keep the share yourself than sell it to us for $100 and watch us make $200. If both $30 and $300 are equally likely, you might agree that the option value is, say, $60. You can see through these examples that the option on a wildly fluctuating new-technology share is likely to be worth more than an option on a large, stable blue-chip share.

Derivatives trading is nothing new. Greeks, Phoenicians, and Romans traded options against outgoing cargoes from their local seaports. Options were bought and sold in Amsterdam in the sixteenth century. The Chicago markets brought futures and options to the American heartland. Starting in the late 1800s, option pricing models became increasingly desirable. Charles Castelli, Louis Bachelier, Vinzenz Bronsin, Paul Samuelson, Richard Kruizenga, and A James Boness all touched on this area, but Fisher Black and Myron Scholes are considered to be the fathers of modern option theory. Prior to the 1970s, financial theory was unable to supply a reasonable formula to calculate the price for an option and people found that they had frequently put themselves into a poor position inadvertently.

In 1973, Black and Scholes published a paper that revolutionized the financial markets in the latter part of the twentieth century. It was called simply "The Pricing of Options and Corporate Liabilities."[3] The Black–Scholes equation is one of the most famous financial equations. Analysts found that they could put in a few numbers and out would come a result that not only helped them agree terms, but was also mysteriously close to the actual prices for options on traded markets. Financial analysts were able to calculate, with great accuracy, the value of a stock option. Most of the models and techniques employed by today's analysts are rooted in the model developed by Black and Scholes. There are a number of simplifying assumptions within the original model, such as no dividends, no commission charges, normal distributions, efficient markets, constant interest rates, and European fixed-exercise dates. Thus, there have been many enhancements, interpretations, revisions, and refinements, but it is not an exaggeration to say that the Black–Scholes model allowed all of the derivatives markets to flourish from the 1970s onward, from basic equity and foreign exchange derivatives to the rise of credit derivatives at the start of the twenty-first century, because the formula provided reliable reference prices.

Black and Scholes, as did many others, realized that the volatility of the stock price made all the difference to the price of the

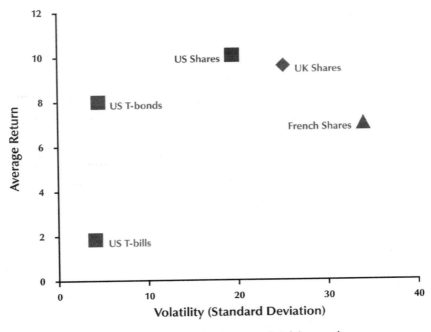

Figure 9.2 A hundred years of risk/reward

option. Their equation uses the standard deviation of the stock price and the risk-free interest rate as the main inputs to the value. Increased volatility, measured as standard deviation of the share price, increases the value of the options. But you can't have your cake and eat it too. Investors expect greater returns to accompany greater volatility. All other things being equal, you would expect a company with greater volatility to be riskier and to have a lower share price. This is the basis behind risk/reward graphs. Figure 9.2 is a chart of the average returns for a few asset classes over the twentieth century, based on a centennial piece in *The Economist*.[4]

What you can see here is a moderate relationship between returns and volatility where investors expect higher returns for higher volatility, but don't always get them. With average US inflation over the same 100 years at 5 percent, you can see that US Treasury Bills would, all things being equal, lose purchasing power. Of course, ideally what you'd like to see is the relationship between investors' perceived volatility, perceived returns, and the overall amount they're prepared to allocate to each asset class at the time they invest. Information of that kind is simply not available and might not be reliable even if you tried to obtain it. Nevertheless, the principles are clear. Investors expect increased returns to compensate them for higher volatility. Conversely, if you can reduce earnings volatility you increase asset values.

REDUCING UNCERTAINTY WITH FISHY MATHS

Volatility takes you back to those risk/reward evaluations. Rod the fisherman could use option theory to evaluate his plans for reducing future profit volatility and to work out the value to him of reduced volatility. Managers in all manner of large businesses use this technique. Furthermore, they can estimate how reducing profit volatility might help their share price, either by looking at the sensitivity of share premia from moving to a lower quintile of volatility, or by estimating the transfer of value from option holders to shareholders from reduced volatility in share prices. Naturally, when the managers' plans involve spending money, the expenditure on volatility reduction needs to be contrasted with the value shareholders place on price/earnings ratios. An analogous expenditure decision for Rod is to weigh up the benefits of volatility reduction against the capital expenditure required, in his case the outlay on a cellphone.

Indeed, when you look at volatility and uncertainty, you find options everywhere. Applying option pricing theory to tangible investment decisions is sometimes described as real options analysis. We undertook an interesting study with the Marine Stewardship Council (MSC), which provides an environmental standard and independent certification program for fisheries and others in the supply chain adhering to sustainable fishing and supply practices. The MSC wanted to estimate the value of certification, and therefore provide evidence of the value of its program. To do this, we turned to Black–Scholes and real option analysis.

The societal value of sustainable certification can be assumed to lie in a better supply of fish combined with reducing the societal cost of unused capacity. Less volatile catches mean more sustainable fish stocks—assuming that the nonvolatile catches are greater than zero. If fish stocks are unstable and the volatility of landed fish is very high, then the economy will have too many boats, canneries, refrigeration facilities, and store shelves. In some years, the boats, canneries, refrigeration, shipping, and stocking facilities are largely idle, in other years they are working flat out. However, if fish catches are more stable and the volatility of landed fish is low, the entire supply chain can be optimized.

Brendan May, Chief Executive of the MSC at the time, summed up a wider point about using real option pricing to support the MSC's not-for-profit work:

> businesspeople are used to undertaking cost/benefit analysis to support their decisions and often feel uneasy when not-for-profit organisations advocate solely intangible or qualitative benefits. Of course, some not-for-profit issues are intrinsically qualitative, hard to measure and tricky to express in financial value terms. Our argument is that not-for-profits should nevertheless try their best to provide empirical evidence to back requests to the business world. This sometimes requires real imagination.[5]

Looking at the Alaskan salmon industry's fish-price data over 30 years, a reasonable estimate was that certification for sustainability could be estimated to reduce the hedging costs of sockeye salmon (to use just one species as an example) from 40 cents a pound to 29 cents. *The Economist* reported the findings and conclusions: "the implied saving is more than $1m a year. That is 50 times higher than the cost to the Alaskan Salmon industry of MSC certification—$100,000 every five years."[6]

We believe that the real option pricing technique can be applied by many not-for-profit organizations to support the economic case for their work, not only in other aspects of the sustainability agenda but also in many elements of environmental and social justice work.

On its home turf of corporate finance, option pricing theory has been much maligned in the late twentieth and early twenty-first centuries. Some of the criticism is to be expected; Myron Scholes and Robert Merton, shortly after receiving Nobel prizes in 1997 for their work in this area, presided at board level over the collapsing hedge fund Long-Term Capital Management, which was caught out by overly relying on option pricing. Option pricing theory does not cover all forms of risk and therefore is not the be-all and end-all. In particular, it tends to underestimate the severity and likelihood of extreme events; it was essentially the multiple extreme adverse events of the Asian crisis and the Russian crisis in the late 1990s that finished Long-Term Capital Management.

Still, much of the criticism of the theory is unwarranted. Few finance people deployed option pricing as their sole trading orthodoxy, but many in the finance industry got carried away with derivative products and trading, especially in the early years of the twenty-first century. Even as early as 1994, *Time* described the fast-growing derivatives market as a "fantastic system of side bets." Once a financial product is a derivative of a derivative (or even further removed from the tangible assets from which the product is derived), it becomes nigh-on impossible to work out exactly what the derivative product represents and how it might behave in certain conditions. The explosion in use of credit derivatives and the subsequent banking crisis of the 2000s illustrate this failing, although it was not a failure of option pricing theory itself but rather a systemic failure of the financial system.[7]

DROWNING IN POOLS OF LIQUIDITY

Option pricing theory also assumes that you can transact easily and at the time (or intervals) of your choosing. In the finance world, that assumption does not always hold; indeed, it tends to fall down when you most need to rely on it. Another reason that crises such as the collapse of Long-Term Capital Management and the banking crisis of the early twenty-first century were so extreme was the rapid and sudden disappearance of liquidity.

If you think volatility is a slippery subject, just wait until we've finished dripping the watery concept of liquidity into the discussion. Part of the difficulty in pinning it down is due to sloppy phrasing and some stems from different scales of time or size, but at heart, there is still a lot of mystery about some forms of liquidity. We hope to provide an overview of liquidity and some of the legitimate disagreements about timing and risk, while also relating the ethereal ideas to real commerce.

A basic definition of *liquidity* is the probability that an asset can be converted into an expected amount of value within an expected amount of time. If you know that you can sell your fishing rod for $100 within an hour, you could claim that it is a liquid asset. If you are very uncertain how much your special edition, double-signed copy of *The Price of Fish* is worth, let alone how long it might take to sell it, where, and to whom, then the book is—perish the thought—rather illiquid.

Going back to your fishing rod, and assuming it's rather expensive with graphite parts, it might be a very liquid fishing rod at $100 but very illiquid at $1,000. Of course, if there is a fishing rod exchange, your fishing rod might be more liquid than you think, even when it is out of the water. If every Wednesday there is a great fishing rod exchange market in your home town, you may have greater liquidity if you know a week in advance that you need some cash. If you know you can sell your fishing rod on eBay, you may have greater liquidity still. This is a key function of markets: they help people to be more certain that an asset can be converted into an expected amount of value within an expected amount of time. Markets provide liquidity. Without liquidity, transactions are less efficient because the costs of matching buyers and sellers (search costs) rise and prices may be wrong. Markets increase the probability that people can sell things when they need to at the right price.

Cash is, normally, the most liquid asset because it has the most certainty of value. Liquidity would not be an important issue if the price of a share were constant, which in turn would infer that you could always find a buyer. If a share was known to have a fixed price, the cost of liquidity would simply be the interest-carrying cost less dividends received. Note that cash can be converted into itself. You can swap $20 bills with a friend and both of you have completely changed your physical assets with great ease and great certainty of value. Neither of you lost a penny in this highly liquid asset transfer. Whereas if you swap fishing rods with a friend, particularly a cheapskate who likes to fob you off with a cheap imitation of a high-class rod, at least one of you may feel you lost something in the transfer.

An electronic bank account is a little—only a little—less liquid than cash. An equity share is still less liquid. A house is a bit less liquid: it can be difficult to sell and the value obtained can fluctuate, sometimes markedly. A share in a horse-racing syndicate is still less liquid. Assets that can only be sold after an exhaustive search for a buyer are illiquid. Are hedge funds liquid? Michael Nystrom pointed out that, during the subprime credit crisis:

having money in such a fund can be even less liquid than a house in Detroit. Some hedge funds have suspended redemptions which is akin to saying, "Yes, your money is here and it is (ahem) safe—but you can't have it just now..." When can you have it? Well, that depends. Maybe never?[8]

What is needed may not be cash. A lot of fairy tales have been built around liquidity. In these cases, liquidity is still the probability that an asset can be converted into an expected amount of value within an expected amount of time, but the value needed may be gold, chocolate, enchanted rings, ensorceled shoes, or magic beans.

At a personal level, you can easily understand the importance of liquidity. If you owe money to someone and they choose the time of repayment, it is good to have liquid assets you can change into cash easily and with certainty. If you can't raise money when you need it, despite having a wealth of assets, you have a liquidity crisis. For the sake of liquidity, you're better off with equity shares than shares in a horse-racing syndicate. We have all heard of wealthy people, perhaps with great estates, who have too little ready cash. Naturally, some people try to fill this commercial gap, for example pawnbrokers who make their living by providing liquidity for less liquid assets, at a price.

Traders love to bandy the word liquidity and talk constantly about how liquid or illiquid markets are. To quote the financial economist Maureen O'Hara:

> as a starting point we might agree that liquidity relates to the ability to buy and sell assets easily. Elaborating on this further, a liquid market is one in which buyers and sellers can trade into and out of positions quickly and without having large price effects.[9]

Intriguingly though, when a trader makes money on a deal, he or she picked the right market moment. Obviously, when he or she loses money on a deal, the complaint is that liquidity unfairly dried up.

The key point here is that it is very difficult, if not impossible, to ascertain whether a market has moved against someone or become less liquid. Liquidity is seldom factored into trading models, partly because major players ignore it, and partly because it is very difficult to do. Is its absence a form of friction hampering position adjustment (a transaction cost)? A relationship between the size of a position and the market as a whole (a price cost)? A calculation of the trading volume afforded at particular price levels (bid–offer bands)? A calculation of the volume below which such information does not move price (normal market size)?

TIME, VALUE, PROBABILITY, AND MONEY

Our definition of liquidity—the probability that an asset can be converted into an expected amount of value within an expected amount of time—is a bit messy because you have to think simultaneously about three characteristics of liquidity—probability, value, and time—along with one very basic assumption about liquidity—that you understand money. Let's start with time.

There are two valid meanings of liquidity in the phrase "caught short," one slightly rude, the other having to do with this vital point about not having the necessary money when you need it—timing illiquidity. Businesses, like people, need to keep a close eye on timing liquidity. The more liquid a business, the better able that business is to meet short-term financial obligations. Liquidity ratios are measurements used to estimate the degree of a company's liquidity. Despite the appearance of mathematical certainty, businesses and people suffer liquidity crises often, especially when creditors are knocking at the door and debtors are late with payments. Again, there are some who try to fill this commercial gap, for example banks that provide short-term credit facilities to firms or credit card companies that provide short-term facilities to people. Note that a bank increases its liquidity by shortening the average term of its loans. We don't like timing surprises. Time to "go liquid" is a crucial part of understanding liquidity, but not the entire picture.

Moving on to the value of liquidity, people feel that it's ideal to be able to get a price from a market before they sell. Auctions are markets where, if you are using reserve prices, you would like to know the minimum you will get when you sell, but you remain very happy to get more. You are very disappointed when you expect to sell something for one price, but get much less, or buy something for one price, but pay much more. There are at least two reasons for your disappointment. First, you may have not anticipated the fees and charges in your market. Second, you may not have achieved the price you anticipated. Returning to the idea of selling a house, you can be disappointed if your estate agent's fees seem high or the indicative price you were given turns out to be too high. Lo, Mamaysky, and Wang show that small fixed costs can give rise to large "no-trade" regions, even for professional traders, leading to significant effects on liquidity and asset values. We don't like value surprises.[10]

Let's touch on the third characteristic, probability. Risk is frequently defined as probability times impact. So the risk of not being able to sell something for the value you expect at the time you want can be quantified. If you know you can probably sell your $1,000 fishing rod for $1,000 with, at worst, a 50 percent chance of its selling for $500, your value at risk is, on average, $250. If you know you can probably sell your $1,000 fishing rod in a week with, at worst, a 50 percent chance of selling it in three weeks, your timing at risk is two weeks: a week normally, but another week at risk on average. To combine the value and time into a single liquidity risk measure, you have to know the cost of not having the money during a possible extra week, perhaps a large penalty for missing a payment deadline, then add it to the average value at risk of $250.

The traditional way of adjusting value at risk for the cost of liquidity is to ensure that you choose a horizon for price movements that is at least greater than an orderly liquidation period, ignoring extreme events. You can also try to develop ways of converting timing risk into cost in order to arrive at a single number. But remember all the pitfalls we have discussed in earlier chapters when trying to turn sophisticated probability functions into convenient single numbers! In summary:

timing liquidity + value liquidity + market liquidity
= certainty (value, time)

So how do you evaluate one asset or market as being more liquid than another? Typically, we refer to three indicators of liquid markets: resilience, depth, and tightness. These indicators relate quite closely to the characteristics of liquidity described above: probability, value, and time. *Resilience* is the speed at which prices return to a new equilibrium once the impact of a large trade has dissipated. *Depth* measures the volume of trading needed to affect prices significantly. *Tightness* indicates the cost and speed of turning a position around, the ability to match supply and demand rapidly. Combining all three indicators, you can imagine throwing a rock into a rippling pond and measuring how quickly the pond returns to normal ripples (resilience), whether it is so shallow you see the bottom when the rock's momentum is absorbed (depth), and how easily a small or large rock enters the pond (tightness). You can equally ask: how soon will things return to a "normal fair value," how much does a change in quantity affect price, and how much does a change in timing affect price?

Tightness is typically measured by bid–ask spreads or the speed of order matching; in other words, immediacy. Depth is typically measured by price impact, the amount prices change based on the quantity traded. If a large trade does not have much effect on price, then the market is assumed to have great depth. Resilience is often indicated by volatility or volume traded.

Related to liquidity is "normal distribution size," above which the size of the trade may move prices on its own. This is typically a percentage of the typical volume traded on a typical day, below which it is assumed that there will be no significant price movement due to a single trade. Yet numerous studies on many exchanges have failed to prove conclusively one way or the other that normal market size can be predicted for any particular share, or that trade publication rule exemptions help or hinder efficient markets.

There is much more work to be done on liquidity measurement. Ideally, one could look at the total market, each firm's inventory, and how much each firm wants to buy or sell when and where. Yet it still seems that the best predictor is a trader's nose: traders seem to be able to sense what constitutes a market-moving trade, but agree that it varies substantially from day to day, security to security.

Finally, and rather importantly, we must examine our assumptions about money, monetary policy, and global money supply. Christopher Brown-Humes relates:

> in the early 19th century, the Bank of England's main policy tool was a weather vane. When the wind blew from the East, ships sailed into London and the Bank supplied money so traders could buy the goods being unloaded at the docks. If a westerly wind blew, it would mop up any excess money to stop too much money chasing too few goods, thereby avoiding inflation.[11]

The old gold standard was abandoned, in part, to give governments more ability to manage broad money supply. There is a lovely, apocryphal story about an analyst at the Bank of England who noticed that gilts went illiquid at 11.45am most days. After much deeper analysis, he realized that the illiquidity was due to Sweetings, the renowned fish restaurant in the City of London near St Paul's cathedral, which doesn't allow the booking of tables. If you're not in Sweetings by noon, you won't get a seat. So the gilt markets went illiquid at 11.45am because traders went for some fish and some liquid refreshment.

We can unify these different elements of liquidity using that basic economics tool, the supply and demand model. Supply and demand models are believed to apply under perfect competition, where no single buyer or seller affects prices and prices are known. The law of supply states that the quantity supplied is related to price: the higher the price of the product, the more suppliers will supply. The law of demand states that demand is the opposite of supply: the lower the price of the product, the more consumers will demand. The supply curve slopes upward to the right as quantity increases. The demand curve slopes downward to the right as quantity increases. Taken together, this represents the overall supply and demand model, illustrated in Figure 9.3.

At the intersection of consumer demand and producer supply there should be an equilibrium price. At the intersection, the quantity supplied equals the quantity demanded, equilibrium. If the price for a good is below equilibrium, then consumers demand more of the good than producers are prepared to supply, thus there is a shortage. Either prices rise or consumers consume less, or both. Conversely, if the price for a good is above equilibrium, then consumers demand less of the good than producers produce, thus there is a surplus: either prices fall or producers produce less, or both. The presence of buyers attracts sellers, and the presence of sellers attracts buyers.

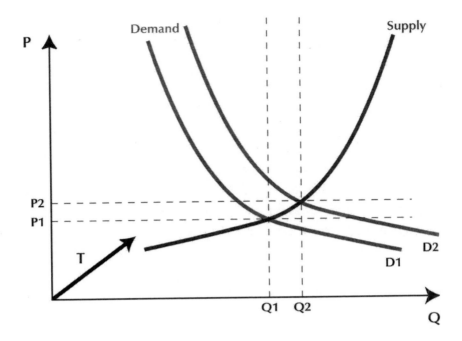

Figure 9.3 Mind your liquidity Ps and Qs

Figure 9.3 shows demand moving from D1 to D2. Demand is increasing. Thus, the price must move from P1 to P2 and the quantity from Q1 to Q2 in order to keep things in equilibrium. Notice that the total market, the square formed by P2 multiplied by Q2, is now larger than P1 multiplied by Q1.

Supply and demand curves are part of an elegant and useful model, but the model must be used with care. In reality there are no equilibria because information is neither perfect nor stable. Traders cycle endlessly between prices rising and quantities rising, then prices falling and quantities falling, only to bring prices up again. In fact, the term disequilibrium might be more accurate because no price ever settles down.

We have to enrich this model by pointing out that liquidity involves both time and quantity, so we have added an orthogonal axis showing time. What makes a liquidity change more special than a normal price movement and return to equilibrium? Let's start with the definition of liquidity. On either the price or the time axis, the problem is that supply and demand curves are not as smooth or as continuous as the model might suggest. In any market, certain size lots emerge as more or less liquid. Who wants a one-bedroom mansion or a twenty-bedroom apartment? Who wants to buy a 5,060-bushel wheat future if the Chicago Board of Trade 5,000-bushel wheat contract is most common?

A market helps to increase the odds that buyers and sellers meet with appropriate quantities at appropriate times. This increases liquidity. Markets typically increase liquidity by publishing prices to attract people, by providing volume and other trading information, and by standardizing contracts, contract sizes, terms, and conditions, all in aid of increasing the odds that a deal can be struck. Markets try to encourage gaps to be filled in the supply and demand curves, to give confidence that the curves are as continuous and known as possible, and that positions won't move too rapidly. Yet more information leads to more spurious movements and people trade on the movements. It is difficult to separate the noise from the information. It is also difficult to distinguish a normal price movement from an abnormal price movement, or a normal transaction time from an abnormal transaction time. Figure 9.4 tries to illustrate the fogginess of liquidity; indeed, it can be helpful to think in terms of clouds rather than curves. Though you try to pin the tail on the supply or demand curve, you are partially clouded. *Liquidity risk* is the likelihood that you are significantly off in your estimation of time or cost; in other words, that you will be surprised.

In order to reduce liquidity risk, traders try to reduce the potential of being surprised by the supply and demand curves not being what they thought. They will spend a lot of time and money trying to ensure that they don't inadvertently fall into a liquidity hole, an area where prices and timing surprise more than normal or typical rules don't seem to apply. Where are some of these holes? Well, one is small-cap stocks. These are equities with

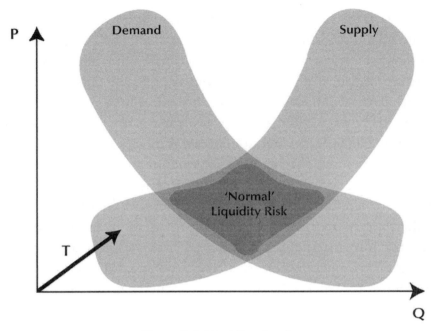

Figure 9.4 Liquidity clouds

small market capitalization, which are typically thinly traded. It takes a very large-value trade to be even a small percentage of a large-cap stock for a well-known large company. A small-value trade may be a very large trade in a small-cap stock. Spreads, the difference between buying and selling prices, may be used as a simple measure of liquidity costs. Less liquid stock should have higher spreads reflecting their increased risk. In short, you can't expect to sell shares in small caps, in any volume, cheaply or quickly, and a small amount of buying or selling can change prices markedly.

LIQUIDITY AND LUCIDITY AMONG THE DARK POOLS

Another set of holes arises from what are called *dark liquidity pools*. These are backwaters, often overlooked pools of capital separate from the main trading markets. They can exist within a large financial institution or among a group of financial institutions trading outside public exchanges. To understand these dark pools, imagine you bump into a friend who wants to buy your house. How do the two of you agree a price? Well, you probably look at estate agents' websites to see what other people are paying. You may well conclude such a sale and gleefully avoid agents' fees. You are both happy, but you have also reduced information for others. Two other friends trying to conclude a similar deal are not aware of the price of your sale. You have removed liquidity from the estate agents and information from the market. A well-functioning market is one that provides efficient price signals through a "price discovery" process, smooths the exchange of ownership, and reduces the risks involved in transferring assets or rewards. In this example, you and your friend have traded "off market" using the price discovery of the estate agents without the transaction costs. If you both had to look at the estate agents' websites before agreeing a price, you were parasitic on the agents' price discovery. If estate agents didn't publish prices and sales, you wouldn't have known a fair price for your transaction.

Large trades contain potentially valuable information about the likely price movements of the instrument being traded. Complete transparency is believed to harm liquidity: market makers will be loath to provide risk capital to support trading if all of their moves must be published in advance. Typical market participant responses to inconvenient or costly regulatory disclosure requirements are to move "off exchange," move "offshore," "cross" trades, create segregated "professional" exchanges, or plead for exemptions.

There is a balancing act for an exchange in ensuring that it is seen to provide the best price, while at the same time ensuring that the incentives to trade off exchange are minimized. This is achieved by sufficiently rewarding principal risk takers to encourage them to take risks in the future. Exchanges teeter on issues of legitimate asymmetric information and the rights and responsibilities of market participants to share information. International competition among exchanges is fierce. International standards and standards bodies affect domestic markets; domestic regulators increasingly find that funds flow globally and regulation seems to need to follow. Previously "mutual" exchanges are increasingly "for profit"; technology has blurred the definition of an exchange, let alone the fact that many firms are systematic internalizers, effectively acting as exchanges for their direct clients.

Regulators have no monopoly on fundamentalist fervor about the importance of publishing information on trades. Different market participants favor different disclosures and academic studies indicate that certain types of disclosure may improve market efficiency while others harm efficiency. There are sensible debates about the amount of post-trade disclosure (how much, how long delayed, how detailed, how anonymous) and pre-trade disclosure (bid/offer, quantities). Regulators and many academics like to promote centralized exchanges that prevent parasitical use of exchange prices by restricting off exchange trades, or protecting exchanges competitively through barriers to entry, or permitting certain monopolistic advantages to exchanges. Naturally, alternative trading systems (ATSs) argue that forcing all trades "on exchange" would raise the cost of trades unnecessarily, and that a large proportion of trades can occur on ATSs without degrading price formation.

LIQUIDITY CRISES AND BLACK HOLES

Over the centuries there has been a constant tickertape of financial crises where, to continue the liquid metaphor, liquidity either evaporates or freezes. Avi Persaud articulates such crises as "liquidity black holes."[12] A physical black hole is a region of space formed from the collapse of a star, where gravity is so strong that nothing, not even light, can escape after falling past the event horizon (the edge of the black hole). A liquidity black hole is a region in finance where liquidity is falling so rapidly that nothing, not even a large financial institution, can escape after prices start to fall. Everything dries up. Persaud says: "a liquidity black hole is where price falls do not bring out buyers, but generate even more sellers." He points out that this definition is easily falsified. Normal price falls do not increase sellers, they increase buyers, while in a liquidity black hole price falls cause an increase in sales flow. People pay close attention to the total volume traded as an indicator of confidence in a market. This is rather strange, as one can easily imagine that confidence in a market should lead to less trading. Perhaps the opposite of Avi's liquidity black hole is the financial analogue of a supernova, a "liquidity white bubble," where price rises do not bring out sellers, but generate even more buyers.

Liquidity black holes bear a strong resemblance to bank runs, where depositors seeking to take their money out of a solvent bank, which they perceive might fail, precipitate a crisis that attracts other depositors to withdraw their funds, which leads to certain failure. William Janeway concludes: "when average opinion comes to believe that average opinion will decide to turn assets into cash, then liquidity may be confidently expected to go to zero."[13] Naturally, the ones who precipitate the crisis have their cash, while the laggards are left penniless. As Brandon Davies points out, in a black hole "he who panics first, panics best," while in a white bubble we say, "he who smugs first, smugs best."

Unable to escape a liquidity black hole, both the supply and demand curves get kinkier, with more holes, the bands of uncertainty for value and price widen markedly, and all these changes accompany a precipitate drop in price. Recall the characteristics of liquidity risk in supply and demand curves:

- Not necessarily smooth.
- Not necessarily continuous.
- Uncertain around value and time.

Just like their physical cousins, black holes and white bubbles are intriguing because past a certain point, the system, in this case the financial system, feeds on itself, drawing on its own energy to keep going to the limit. As asset prices fall, some dealers will suffer losses at close to their loss limits and must sell assets to avoid exceeding them. As asset prices fall further, so other dealers get close to their limits and are induced to sell, creating a downward spiral in asset prices until "offer no bid." Even worse, as share price deflation reprices existing portfolios, so volume selling to realize the price is often based on the price of the extreme one or two latest trades, which in turn become the basis for repricing the portfolio again.

But don't these black holes bottom out eventually, a bit more like hurricanes petering out than black holes gobbling up the universe? Yes, balanced buyers and sellers can return to dramatically lower prices. Mercilessly, many black hole implosions then initiate white bubbles. In a liquidity white bubble, the remaining, successful traders have stock that now rises, attracting other traders, leading to more assets that can be leveraged, leading to more purchases, leading to more value, and so on.

The 1988 Brady Commission's report into the October 1987 collapse of the US stock market attributed the magnitude and swiftness of price declines to portfolio insurance based on dynamic hedging.[14] Funds pursuing such strategies controlled $100bn, only about 3 percent of the market value (pre-crash), but their inability to replicate portfolio rebalancing in times of market distress led to a "buy dear, sell cheap" strategy within the overall system, dragging others with them.

Nevertheless, you can make money in a liquidity crisis, particularly if you have a longer-term view; that is, you are able to buy cheaply and wait. There is almost always a flight to simpler products and a flight to quality, which lets risk takers buy complex products and hold them or disaggregate them and try to match sections of the supply and demand curves.

You can try to distinguish exogenous (outside the system) events from endogenous (inside the system) events, but the system's own reaction affects its environment; feedforward or positive feedback in a cybernetic sense. Liquidity black holes or white bubbles are not just large price falls or rises from the release of new, or even shocking, economic data or firm results; they are unstoppable forces emanating from within the price-setting system itself. The misbehavior of people's perceptions gets locked into a price-setting system that creates, for a time, an unbreakable spiral in one direction. Because of the way markets function, they must exceed (or undershoot) a price before they can go back. They must always oscillate around a price, changing with any new information or preferences. There is no stable optimum.

TRADING ON ICE

There is an old phrase that "liquidity begets liquidity," meaning that once some people start trading, more people will join them. It is often used to explain away monopolistic problems with exchanges. The assumption is that a successful, and beneficial, exchange will inexorably draw all relevant trading to its increasingly liquid market. Most traders claim that more liquid markets are better for everybody than less liquid markets. Not surprisingly, while they last, liquid markets are better for traders. In liquid markets traders can conclude many deals with concomitant commission. In illiquid markets traders have fewer trades and more risk.

However, a number of economists question the notion that liquidity is inherently good or bad. Maureen O'Hara summarizes

Keynes', Tobin's, and Summers' criticisms as "liquidity begets instability." The ability to buy and sell easily might drive short-term markets and exacerbate market changes, perhaps inducing liquidity crises. Bernard Lietaer suggests that only 2 percent of foreign exchange transactions relate to the real economy, while the remaining transactions are purely speculative.[15] That's a heck of a lot of froth.

Persaud and others point out that there are a number of problems with the structure of today's markets that do markedly increase susceptibility to liquidity disruptions:

- *Interlinked global markets*: Liquidity problems now reverberate across markets and borders and there is greater correlation among asset classes.
- *More rigorous and regular benchmarking*: Constant appraisal induces people to track benchmark indices in similar ways and to buy or sell at identical times.
- *Regulatory rationalization*: Common strategies, credit policies, and margin requirements lead to similar sales frenzies to maintain capital adequacy.
- *Information systems commoditization*: Using similar analytics and computer systems increases the likelihood of similar trading strategies and investment approaches.

What might we recommend to make liquidity crises less likely? Perhaps not a lot, as perhaps liquidity black holes are an immutable feature of the universe. As long as there are markets, it is likely that there will be liquidity crises. Yet not all should be defeatism. We subscribe to the ideas put forward by Persaud, Lietaer, and others that increased diversity in financial markets would lower the risk of liquidity black holes. Investors would exhibit a range of behaviors, so sellers are more likely to meet buyers part way and be more patient.

In addition to stressing more work on control and measurement of the money supply, we would summarize our recommendations as follows:

- *Measurement*: A number of fractal measures or biodiversity indices could help investors distinguish a deep and diverse liquidity pool from a deep and homogenous one. If there are better analogies for liquidity in measures such as digital television signal quality or quantum physics, perhaps it is possible to measure choppiness, gaps, and uncertainty better using those measures than some of the more common continuous physical functions.
- *Market structures*: Some adjustments to market structures might reduce the risk of black holes, such as advanced encryption systems for anonymous and confidential trading, including the exchange of inventories and buy/sell intentions. We also wonder about encouraging markets where trade orders are randomized in time and position before being matched.
- *Heterogeneity*: Encouraging the broadest possible range of investors, from individuals, to corporates, investment managers, insurers, share clubs, gamblers, or hedge funds, into multiple markets should reduce liquidity risk.

TRANSACTIONAL SYSTEMS

We have now explored three of our four streams—choice, economics, and systems—and in the process grappled with some of the big questions that underpin our commercial systems. Is measurement unequivocally a good thing, or does excessive reliance on measurement and targets become counterproductive? How does feedforward, or action people take on the basis of their perceptions, affect the behavior of markets? To what extent can we value volatility and control liquidity in commercial systems?

Nevertheless, choice, economics, and systems are not sufficient to make sense of the way the world really works. We still cannot explain the extraordinary diversity of goods and services, let alone the huge discrepancies in price and/or pay rates you sometimes see between seemingly similar commercial propositions. Why do some commercial ideas thrive while others wither and die? What is the role of innovation in real commerce? When is change continuous and when is it dramatically punctuated?

Chapter 10 focuses on commercial diversity and the ways in which value emerges in real commerce. It initiates our evolution stream, blending choice, economics, systems, and evolutionary thinking. Chapters 11 and 12 continue to intertwine all four streams.

10 | IT'S A MAD, BAD, WONDERFUL WORLD: COMMERCIAL DIVERSITY

Some goods and services seem to be ridiculously over-priced, just as some people seem to be ludicrously over-paid. But are we simply failing to recognize true value when we make such an assertion? With commerce varying so much between cultures and over time, can we really know what does and does not represent value? Perhaps the market is the best place to establish value; or could those wicked prices and monster pay packets simply reflect skewed markets due to fads and fashions, or flawed exchange of information between sellers and buyers, or even cheating? In order to explore these questions of real commerce, we consider diverse subjects such as information asymmetry, money, positional goods, and tournaments. In the process, we introduce ideas related to our fourth and final stream, evolution.

INFORMATION ASYMMETRY, SIGNALS, AND SCREENING

In 1970 George Akerlof wrote a paper on the market for "lemons"—bad secondhand cars—for which he shared the 2001 Nobel Prize in economics.[1] His paper described "asymmetrical information," where one party, the seller, knows more than the other party, the buyer. The used-car market is one where quality is variable and guarantees are indefinite. There are serious incentives for a seller to pass off a low-quality product as a higher-quality one. However, buyers take these incentives into consideration and refuse to treat any used car as "above average." Sellers then conclude that they shouldn't sell above-average cars on the used-car market, which in turn lowers the average car quality. Ultimately, there are no cars worth trading. In some ways, markets such as these exhibit a colloquial form of Gresham's Law: the bad drives out the good when things trade at unknown quality. The conclusion is that in situations involving great uncertainty in respect of quality, competitive markets may fail to emerge or fail to persist.

Kenneth Arrow suggests:

> when there is uncertainty, information or knowledge becomes a commodity. Like other commodities, it has a cost of production and a cost of transmission, and so it is naturally not spread out over the entire population but concentrated among those who can profit most from it.[2]

When information is concentrated asymmetrically in favor of sellers, the market is weakened, possibly to the extent that liquidity vanishes. Akerlof looks at several asymmetries in favor of sellers, including the issuing of credit in the developing world and the additional imperfections that arise from poverty and economic underdevelopment. Situations where the buyer has better information than the seller are less common, but include sales of old art pieces without prior professional assessment or consumers buying many forms of insurance, which in turn frequently involves "adverse selection" or "moral hazard."

In 1961, George Stigler preceded Akerlof with "The Economics of Information," an exploration of how information and ignorance interact with markets. He posed a suggestion about "reputation" put to him by Milton Friedman that a department store "may be viewed as an institution which searches for the superior qualities of goods and guarantees that they are good quality."[3] Economists have also spent a lot of time trying to understand signaling and screening. Michael Spence, Joseph Stiglitz, and George Akerlof shared the 2001 Nobel Prize for pioneering work in this area. *Signaling* is about parties with positive information asymmetry conveying meaningful information about the quality of their goods or services. *Screening* is done by parties with negative information asymmetry in order to learn relevant information and to eliminate unacceptable choices.

In one of many papers on screening, Stiglitz looks at credit rationing as a prime example of the market imperfections that arise through information asymmetries and the resultant use of screening by the lender.[4] Another good example of signaling and screening is education. Much higher education might not be strictly necessary for employment, but, as Michael Spence points out, bright prospective workers might wish to signal their willingness and ability to learn, while potential employers, who are on the wrong side of the information asymmetry when hiring, might choose to use the educational record as a way of screening prospective employees. In short, it is worthwhile for the worker and the employer to communicate educational qualifications.[5]

There are five conditions of information asymmetry in favor of the seller that lead to market failure:

- Buyers cannot assess quality before a sale is made.
- Sellers know the quality prior to sale and gain by passing off lower quality as higher.
- Sellers have no credible disclosure technology or method.
- The market lacks effective public quality assurances (by reputation, standards, or regulation).
- The market lacks effective guarantees.

Situations where the seller usually has better information than the buyer are numerous: stockbrokers, theaters, language translators, and health treatments all come to mind as examples of highly variable, quality markets with difficult choices for the buyer. In fact, in most "professional" situations, the seller has information supremacy.

The bottom line is that lemon markets don't collapse if buyers have to go to the market regardless of their reluctance to buy. Company law, articles of incorporation, or taxation requires many companies to purchase audits, however useful or useless such audits might be, or requires pension funds to get actuarial advice, however useful or useless such advice might be. In other lemon markets, huge potential value may keep the market alive, for example you might find a magnificent used car at a very cheap price, particularly if you're better informed than average, perhaps a car mechanic yourself. In some cases, a lemon market might remain liquid because the prices are very low, for example if you can get a used car at a price only slightly above that of its value as scrap metal alone.

SILENT TRADE, INFORMATION, AND COMMUNICATION

Sophisticated information exchange is not a prerequisite for real commerce. Consider, for example, the silent trade, also known as "dumb barter" or "depot trade." For many centuries, sub-Saharan Africa, particularly the western Sahel, was rich in gold and poor in salt. The people of the Sahel needed salt from the desert to flavor and preserve their food. Europeans valued gold. The British called areas southwest of Timbuktu, on the Niger tributaries from Jenne to Ghana, "Guinea," from which the British gold coin takes its name. For well over a millennium, salt was worth its weight in Guinean gold along the transition from Sahara to Savanna, where sub-Saharan Africa starts to turn green.

Herodotus records the silent trade on the west coast of Africa outside the Straits of Gibraltar around 440 BC:

The Carthaginians say also this, namely that there is a place in Libya and men dwelling there, outside the Pillars of Heracles, to whom when they have come and have taken the merchandise forth from their ships, they set it in order along the beach and embark again in their ships, and after that they raise a smoke; and the natives of the country seeing the smoke come to the sea, and then they lay down gold as an equivalent for the merchandise and retire to a distance away from the merchandise. The Carthaginians upon that disembark and examine it, and if the gold is in their opinion sufficient for the value of the merchandise, they take it up and go their way; but if not, they embark again in their ships and sit there; and the others approach and straightway add more gold to the former, until they satisfy them: and they say that neither party wrongs the other; for neither do the Carthaginians lay hands on the gold until it is made equal to the value of their merchandise, nor do the others lay hands on the merchandise until the Carthaginians have taken the gold.[6]

Many commentators remark that dumb barter is a method by which people with no common language can barter goods. Less remarked on is that even if people speak a common language, dumb barter is a way to avoid physical confrontation. Dumb barter requires trust. Indeed, Herodotus' description of the trading he observed is reminiscent of the "platter of seafood" thought experiment we described in the section on trust in Chapter 3.

Bernstein writes of the silent trade:

What must those poor diggers have thought of the funny people from the north country who swapped inestimable salt for stuff whose only role on earth was to give men pride and pleasure by letting them see its lustre?[7]

The practice of silent trade was not restricted to bartering gold for salt. In east African Azania, Cosmas Indicopleustes, a voyaging sixth-century Greek merchant-monk, describes bartering gold for beef.

The silent trade also provides us with an ideal opportunity to introduce some of the principles of information theory. Claude Shannon was a remarkable American electronic engineer and mathematician who, as a telecommunications engineer at Bell Telephone laboratories, was at the heart of the twentieth-century information revolution. His enduring fame emanates from a paper he published in 1948, "A Mathematical Theory of Communication."[8] This is widely held to have initiated information theory. It opens with the statement: "the fundamental problem of communication is that of reproducing at one point, either exactly or approximately, a message selected at another point." The paper is famous because in one step it connected basic ideas such as:

- *Bit*—the fundamental unit of information.
- *Channel capacity and compression*—the measure of the maximum amount of information a channel can carry.
- *Entropy*—the measure of uncertainty as a measure of value, or the idea that the value of a specific bit of information depends on the probability that it will occur.
- *Redundancy*—the degree to which information is not unique in the system.
- *Noise*—any additional signal that interferes with the reception of information.

It is not difficult to grasp information theory. We can illustrate it using a simple communication, the message "Happy Birthday!" to one's mother. You see in Figure 10.1 the seven elements of information theory, as Shannon set them out, going from top left to bottom right.

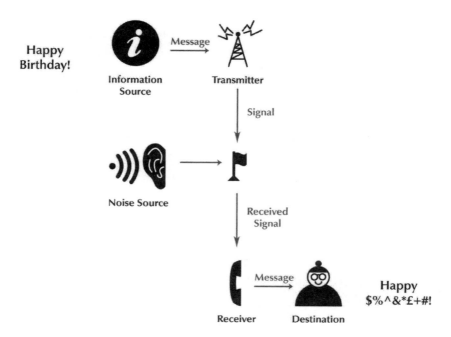

Figure 10.1 Shannon's information theory meets mother's birthday

- ❧ The start is a *source message*, the material that an information source wishes to transmit, such as the words or poetry that you wish to send your mother.
- ❧ This propagates from the *information source*, an entity that is responsible for formulating a particular message from a set of possible messages: your choice of particular birthday message for your mother.
- ❧ The *transmitter* is an entity that changes the signal into a form that can be sent to the receiver, such as your child writing out "Happy Birthday!" on a birthday card or you tapping that message into a computer.
- ❧ The *source signal* and *received signal* represent the form in which the message is physically sent, perhaps a letter or email, along a channel (the medium used to send the signal), such as post or broadband.
- ❧ The *noise source* is anything that introduces something not intended by the information source, perhaps a postal worker

dropping the birthday card in a puddle or a computer transmission error.

- The *receiver* is the opposite of the transmitter, translating the signal into a message that can be processed by the destination, such as your mother's eyes or her computer screen.
- The *destination* is the recipient of the message, your mother.

This sequence of events leads to the transmission of a received message: the combination of the signal and any noise that has been introduced, perhaps a damp, muddy card or a garbled email. Shannon's is clearly a simplifying theory that ignores meaning. A lot of the criticism of it starts by pointing out, rather self-evidently, that communication is not this simple. In fairness, Shannon made no claims that the theory was all-encompassing. He wanted to describe and solve technical problems. Social humans, though, experience multiple levels of communication.

At a technical level, there is the basic pen and paper or bits and bytes. Above that, there is the system of communication, a postal network or a telecommunications infrastructure. Above that, there is a social system fixated on anniversaries of planetary solar alignment and the severing of an umbilical cord. Above that, there is you and your mother's relationship. Above that, there is your mother's sense of humor, which is why it might all go wrong when you make a joke about her age in the poem you found so witty when you composed it.

Information theory notes that common things are generally shorter than less common things, so "dear" is shorter than "birthday." Information theory also notes that redundancy adds robustness to the message, so your mother probably still understands "Happy $%^&*£+#!" You also need robustness at the social level. If you call your mother every day, you'll probably find that she gets over your tasteless poem. If you call her once a year, she may nurse her umbrage at your joke until it grows into a family rift.

Perhaps the most advanced idea that Shannon put forward is that of valuing information. Stephen Littlejohn explains this concept well:

Information is a measure of uncertainty, or entropy, in a situation. The greater the uncertainty, the more the information. When a situation is completely predictable, no information is present. Most people associate information with certainty or knowledge; consequently, this definition from information theory can be confusing. As used by the information theorist, the concept does not refer to a message, facts, or meaning... a situation with which you are completely familiar has no information for you.[9]

University of Toronto economics professor Harold Innis was influential in developing modern theories of communication. He dwelt on the interaction of empires and communication. His theory was that the media people choose will affect the shape and durability of their society. He divided media into two types: "time-binding" and "space-binding." His most famous example is the distinction between time-binding stone and space-binding papyrus:

The concepts of time and space reflect the significance of media to civilization. Media which emphasize time are those which are durable in character such as parchment, clay and stone. The heavy materials are suited to the development of architecture and sculpture. Media which emphasize space are apt to be less durable and light in character such as papyrus and paper. The latter are suited to wide areas in administration and trade. The conquest of Egypt by Rome gave access to supplies of papyrus which became the basis of a large administrative empire.[10]

DOES MONEY MAKE THE WORLD GO ROUND?

Is money no more than information or communication? Innis was an influence on his more famous colleague at the University of Toronto, Marshall McLuhan, of "the medium is the message" fame. Indeed, within a few pages of his timeless quote, McLuhan touches on money as a medium of communication:

> money is a language for translating the work of the farmer into the work of the barber, doctor, engineer, or plumber. As a vast social metaphor, bridge, or translator, money—like writing—speeds up exchange and tightens the bonds of interdependence in any community. It gives great spatial extension and control to political organization, just as writing does or the calendar. It is action at a distance, both in space and in time.[11]

"Money as communication" begs the question of whether money is time-binding or space-binding. Modern definitions tend to state that money is a medium of exchange with two properties: it can be used as a unit of account and as a store of value. To be money, the medium of exchange must be a standard of deferred payment. This is why perishable fish may be a medium of exchange from time to time (consider the trading sardines in Chapter 1), but fish has never really taken off as money.

TURN TO STONE

We can rapidly conclude that money is a medium of exchange that is both time-binding and space-binding. In order to store value (or defer payment), the medium of exchange must span time. To be a useful unit of account, the medium of exchange must span space and communities.

Nonbarter transactions communicate across both time and space. The silent trade is an example of space-binding money: barter using gold and salt as units of account. Our next example illustrates primarily time-binding money, using stones as a store of value.

Yap is one of a small collection of sandy, shale, and coral islands known as the Caroline Islands (or sometimes the Yap Islands) in the Micronesian archipelago of the South Pacific. William Furness provided an enduring account of the Yap currency in his 1910 book *The Island of Stone Money*.[12]

Fei stones are large stone wheels from the size of saucers up to about 8 feet in diameter. They come from limestone quarries on the Palau island of Babelthuap, almost 300 miles away. Limestone is unheard of on the Yap Islands; the fei stones were all transported by canoe. Smaller stones paid for pigs and fish. Apparently the first stones were carved in the shape of fish, but the Yapese soon carved larger, rounded stones in which they punched holes to make them more mobile, though it could take up to 20 men using poles to move a large stone. To keep the stones from jingling in their (nonexistent) pockets, they would leave them standing outside their homes as a sign of wealth. When a big transaction needed to take place, rather rarely as Furness notes, the stone "coin" would often sit placidly by, despite a change of ownership. Indeed, Furness reports an account of

> a family whose wealth was unquestioned, acknowledged by everyone and yet no one, not even the family itself had ever laid eye or hand on this wealth; it consisted of an enormous fei, whereof the size is known only by tradition; for the past two or three generations it had been, and at that very time it was lying at the bottom of the sea.

The stone had sunk a few hundred feet from the coast in a violent storm. As plenty of people had seen it and the owner was deemed blameless for the loss, both the value of the stone and its ownership were recognized by the islanders. Furness again: "The purchasing power of that stone remains, therefore, as valid as if it were leaning visibly against the side of the owner's house." So fei stones silently demonstrate the importance of honesty and trust, as well as the somewhat imaginary nature of all money systems.

The people of Yap also risked inflation and taxation. In the late 1870s, an enterprising Irish-American copra trader, David O'Keefe, on ascertaining the Yapese demand for fei, devised a cunning plan. Cora Lee Gilliland relates:

> [O'Keefe] was paid with copra for transporting [fei] from the quarries to Yap, enabling the Yapese to obtain [fei] with much less risk of life or loss of stone. Captain O'Keefe obtained both power in the islands and wealth in the Hong Kong market through this device.[13]

Some sources suggest that the additional stones that thus flooded the market were inflationary (they certainly tended to be larger, the newer stones reaching diameters of up to 12 feet) and were not valued as highly as older stones, which had been acquired through more toil and risk. Gilliland is less sure. By the time anthropologists started to ascertain the relative values of stones a secondary market had developed: the anthropologists themselves were buying stones for museums. As is so often the case with inflation, the root cause is unclear.

With more certainty we can state that taxation reared its ugly head. The Germans bought Yap from the Spanish in 1898. The Germans wanted to move from coral paths to roads, but the natives weren't particularly keen on the work. One enterprising German went round marking the most valuable fei with a black cross to denote that the government had acquired that fei: a tax. Furness relates: "this instantly worked like a charm; the people, thus dolefully impoverished, turned to and repaired the highways to such good effect from one end of the island to the other, that they are now like park drives." When the government officials erased the crosses, the people rejoiced in their freedom and "rolled in their wealth."

Milton Friedman, always keen on a taxation story, picked up on this incident and related it to an event during the Great Depression. In 1932 the Bank of France feared that the US would break away from the gold standard. It asked the Federal Reserve Bank of New York to convert its dollar assets (held in the US) into gold. It didn't want to bear the shipping costs, however, so it simply asked the Federal Reserve to store the gold on the Bank of France's account. The officials dutifully labeled up the correct number of gold ingots "property of the French," which Friedman points out might as well have been a cross in black paint. Yet this French gold transaction was as real to the nervous American people as the German stone tax was to the Yapese. Headlines fretted about the drain of gold by France, the dollar weakened, the French franc strengthened, and the banking panic of 1933 can at least in part be attributed to the incident. Friedman summarizes: "what both examples—and numerous additional ones that could be listed—illustrate is how important myth (unquestioned belief) is in monetary matters."[14]

In 1931, Keynes poetically and prophetically forecast:

[Gold] no longer passes from hand to hand, and the touch of the metal has been taken away from men's greedy palms. The little household gods, who dwelt in purses and stockings and tin boxes, have been swallowed by a single golden image in each country, which lives underground and is not seen. Gold is out of sight—gone back again into the soil. But when gods are no longer seen in a yellow panoply walking the earth, we begin to rationalize them; and it is not long before there is nothing left.[15]

EARNING CURVE: THE LABOR THEORY OF VALUE

One final point on the Yap people—Furness suggests that although they have not heard of Adam Smith or Ricardo:

> [they] have solved the ultimate problem of Political Economy, and found that labour is the true medium of exchange and the true standard of value. But this medium must be tangible and enduring and as their island yields no metal, they have had recourse to stone; stone on which labour in fetching and fashioning has been expended, and as truly a representation of labour as the mined and minted coins of civilisation.

This point brings us neatly back to the questions we raised at the start of this chapter. Are wicked prices and monster pay packets caused by fads and fashions, or does poor exchange of information between seller and buyer hold the key?

In order to explore the possible iniquities of high prices and excessive pay, you need to appreciate the labor theory of value. Huge pay differences tend to be especially hard to swallow, so we shall examine that aspect first. The star of a top-billing US television series will make at least $1 million per episode, 10 times as much as co-stars and perhaps 30 times as much as supporting cast. The average pay of listed company executive directors in the UK tends to be 30 to 50 times the national average, in sectors such as banking even more.

Adam Smith and David Ricardo also struggled with large earning differentials. They both placed great store in the idea that value was created principally by labor. In *The Wealth of Nations* Smith said:

> the real price of every thing, what every thing really costs to the man who wants to acquire it, is the toil and trouble

of acquiring it. What every thing is really worth to the man who has acquired it, and who wants to dispose of it or exchange it for something else, is the toil and trouble which it can save to himself, and which it can impose upon other people.[16]

This argument leads to two notions of value: value "in use" and value "in exchange." The things that have the greatest value in use often have little or no value in exchange and vice versa. For instance, paper money has little value in use but great value in exchange. Fish retains great value in use but has little value in exchange. Furthermore, value in exchange can vary from gold or diamonds, whose value in exchange in uncertain times depends, to some degree, on the difficulty of counterfeiting them, to paper money, whose value in exchange in certain times, depends, to a great degree, on laws against counterfeiting being enforced.

Early economists also cherished a third idea: "intrinsic value." Early concepts of intrinsic value are wrapped up in the labor theory of value: something ought to be worth the amount of effort it took to produce it. Theory-of-value economists felt that property derives from labor through the act of "mixing" one's labor with items in the common store of goods, which in turn led inexorably to the importance of property rights. Classical economists sought an invariable measure of value and spoke of "real costs" and "absolute values." They began with the assumption that value in exchange was equal to or proportional to labor. As Smith observed, "labour, therefore, is the real measure of the exchangeable value of all commodities."

While this approach is appealing, the problems are many. Is an hour's work just an hour's work, or do we need to distinguish between hard workers and slackers? Clearly, too, we need to distinguish skilled workers from unskilled workers. We should also highlight the fact that some workers work only with their minds, while others, even if they wished to do so, would be considered mentally worthless. And similarly, some workers work only with their hands, while others would be considered manually worthless. Of course, some workers use copious quantities of raw materials, or specialist tools, or power—the means of production—so they need to be distinguished from purely manual or mental laborers. And the means of production, as well as control of natural resources, leads us to consider the role of capital in producing intrinsic value. Finally, time becomes a problem. Some goods and products are perishable, such as a bumper catch of fish. Some labor can be stored almost indefinitely, say stonemasonry. Other goods, such as wine, increase in value over time.

According to Smith, in primitive societies the amount of labor that produced a good determined its exchange value, but in more advanced societies the exchange value included compensation for the owner of the means of production. Today people use discount rates to reflect the risk of holding an asset over time. Smith, Ricardo, and Marx all tried to relate value to labor. Smith understood that profit came when the "labor commanded" for a product—that is, the amount of labor that is purchased by selling the product—exceeded the "labor embodied" in the manufacture of the product. Ricardo more clearly distinguished labor commanded from wages, as did Marx. Marx then examined whether the excess of labor commanded less wages is profit or exploitation.

Smith and the early classical economists understood many of the complexities in the labor theory of value. For them, price and value were related to labor, but were not identical to it. The theory does not deny the role of supply and demand in influencing price, because classical economists saw the value of a commodity as something other than its price. Marx acknowledged that he believed prices were based on labor, but only when supply and demand were in equilibrium:

It suffices to say that if supply and demand equilibrate each other, the market prices of commodities will correspond with their natural prices, that is to say, with their values as determined by the respective quantities of labour required for their production.[17]

Neoclassical economics favors the positivist, nonnormative side of the debate, underpinned by general equilibrium theory in which prices form through supply and demand, taking account of the interaction of preferences, technology, and endowments. Thus, a few fervent neoclassical economists would deny that excessive pay exists; the amount cannot be excessive because by definition it is set by the market. Some ethical economists are bothered because excessive pay seems iniquitous. Rather more economists are bothered because they are sure it would be much better to have economists higher up the earnings lists.

Conveniently, the distinction between value in use and value in exchange points to the observation that increases in the value in exchange of something with a previously low value in use correlate with times of scarcity. The British economist Lionel Robbins famously defined economics as "the science which studies human behaviour as a relationship between ends and scarce means which have alternative uses." Scarcity can be natural or artificial. Somewhat perversely, scarcity can be created, through all manner of exclusionary or exclusivity tactics such as monopolies, seals of approval, royal warrants, branding, or death. Willful destruction can also create scarcity. If you want to be rich, make yourself scarce, or dead; nothing guarantees the value of an artist's extant work more than the certainty that they won't produce any more. Agency problems can also create scarcity. If you have to act through an agent, for example the old stockmarket distinction between broking and jobbing, or the legal distinction between barristers and solicitors, opportunities exist to use scarcity to push up prices.

FADS, FASHIONS, AND LOCALIZED CONFORMITY

Yet scarcity is not always the objective measure that Robbins' definition infers. Indeed, his very use of the word "science" reflects an objective perspective that soon breaks down when observing real commerce. How do you account for fads, fashions, and positional goods within such a science?

In the rich seam of fads and fashions, scarcities, information asymmetries, and externalities do in fact abound. Fads and fashions exemplify commercial diversity, across both space (varying societies) and time (fads and fashions are all transitory to a greater or lesser extent). They allow people to observe the evolution of real commerce while it is happening.

Fads are crazes adopted for brief periods. Fashions are modes of expression where people expect the mode to change more rapidly than the culture, yet they endure longer than fads. Fads are typically ephemeral, frivolous, and of little significance. You know something is a fad when hating it is almost as faddish as loving it, within a short space of time—"I simply hate that new gadget/song/style/celebrity." Fashion too, by definition, must change, but it's more enduring and often becomes synonymous with a period or culture. You know something is a fashion when people find the need to conform quietly despite their dislike, and often don't speak their true thoughts for many years—"You know, I never could stand blue jeans."

Neither fads nor fashions are timeless. Fads are things like hula hoops or cellphone ringtones. Fashions involve larger commercial decisions such as a real Prada bag or a house in a fashionable resort. Commitment matters: peel-off tattoos are a fad; painful tattoos are a fashion. And yes, there is often quite a bit of evolution and competition between the two. In the fashion industry, brand names and logos are well protected, yet designs are not. Smaller, innovative designers often lose their designs to bigger businesses with more resources. Yet the relative freedom that fashion designers have to "take inspiration" from others' designs helps to start new fads and fashions, keeping the industry successful. Stronger intellectual property rights could kill the business.

Fads and fashions can markedly affect the price of fish. Koi, for example, are ornamental varieties of carp, highly prized by collectors for symbolic and decorative reasons. The practice of breeding decorative carp is recorded nearly 2,000 years ago in China and possibly predates those records, but koi took off as a fashion in early twentieth-century Japan. Koi can live for many decades if well looked after. The most fashionable fish have been known to change hands for tens of thousands of dollars each. Price is affected by the amount of selective breeding required for a particular look, the health of the resulting koi, and of course fashion. One variety, known as Ghost koi, proved relatively easy to breed and as a result are a less expensive, popular option; perhaps a fad. Koi carp aficionados will tell you that Ghost koi are not the same species as true koi, as they have been cross-bred with other species. Nonexperts might even mistake a humble young goldfish (neither fashionable nor faddish) for an almost identical-looking young koi carp, as they are subtly different species of carp, but with unsubtly different price tags.

Economists are very interested in how fads and fashions start. Bikhandani, Hirshleifer, and Welch observed: "[o]ne of the most striking regularities of human behavior is localized conformity."[18] They point out that economics dictates you should believe something or follow someone when the benefits of believing or following outweigh the costs, otherwise not:

An informational cascade occurs when it is optimal for an individual, having observed the actions of those ahead of him, to follow the behavior of the preceding individual without regard to his own information.

Localized conformity of behavior and the fragility of mass behaviors can be explained by informational cascades, which can develop where no one questions behaviors. These behaviors may be correct or incorrect. This is another manifestation of heuristics and biases, but in the context of following commercial trends. Donald Cox notes:

> believing a falsehood is not necessarily a dumb or crazy thing to do. It may well be the smart choice. After all, the truth is costly to unearth, so having more of it [truth] means having less widgetry and everything else; if we spent all our time checking facts there'd be no time left to earn a living, go to the beach, sleep.[19]

However, localized conformity can be dangerous. You may find it disturbing to realize that medical doctors follow fads too. Tonsillectomies were a baby-boomer fad; the authors both had tonsils removed after a few childhood colds. The procedure was frightening, mostly useless, and sometimes even fatal. Cox relates informational cascades to another medical fad, the useless treatment of ulcers, until the 1980s, when Warren and Marshall developed their bacterial treatment against the strong tide of received wisdom that ulcers were not caused by bacteria.

Informational cascades only reverse when the benefits of discovering true information start to outweigh the costs, but the cascade itself increases the costs and thereby reduces the likelihood that benefits will exceed them. When asked why he no longer went to a popular Minneapolis restaurant, Yogi Berra famously tried to reverse an informational cascade by exclaiming: "Nobody goes there no more, it's too crowded!"

Fads are typically frivolous: they involve little risk and little reward, but are of uncertain value. You may decide to go to a friend's party wearing something strange and faddish you wouldn't have been seen in a month ago, but laugh it off if everyone starts to make fun of you. However, wearing the wrong fashion to work, even today, can set your career back. This, in a funny way, actually reverses the typical risk/reward tradeoffs. A fad is very uncertain, but involves little risk or reward, while a fashion is rather more certain but involves some genuine risk and reward.

When a herd of investors enter a market together, you have a fad. In the finance literature both a fad and a bubble describe asset prices above what is considered to be the asset class's fundamental market value. But how do you know the fundamental market value? Well, you don't. You just believe that strong shifts are transitory and that you will see "reversion to the mean" in the longer term. There is a strong resonance here with Smith, Ricardo, and Marx seeking intrinsic value. In the long term they expected to see prices reflect the amount of labor in a good.

Brands are an intrinsic part of fads and fashions. In the case of information asymmetry, brands convey information from sellers to buyers—"You don't know how good or bad my product or service is, but at least you know the brand." In the case of fads and fashions, brands communicate two different things. First, the brand exacerbates the localized conformity. We have a "passive consumption culture," we buy something if everyone else has it—"Everyone else has a Prada bag, so unless they're grossly overpriced, I'll just assume they must be good and buy one." Second, the brand is meant to convey something about the user or wearer—"I'm a member of the Prada tribe." Information is being conveyed to the community, which leads us to positional goods.

POSITIONAL GOODS

Fred Hirsch, in *The Social Limits to Growth*, distinguished between material and positional goods.[20] Material goods are traditional, private goods whose production and supply interact with demand under a law of diminishing marginal utility. Consumers derive less utility from each successive unit until they cease to purchase. You can only eat so much food; you can only use so many washing machines. Positional goods possess a relative or social value rather than an absolute one. Examples of positional goods include exclusive real estate, branded education, or trendy restaurant reservations. Satisfaction from a positional good depends on how much you have in relation to everyone else. Material goods can be created with time and effort, while positional goods are more easily redistributed than created. Positional goods are inherently scarce, at least in the short term. In economic terms their supply is inelastic. Supply cannot rise enough to satisfy the demand of everyone who wants a positional good. The supply of beautiful, lonely beaches is at best fixed, or at worst dwindling. Not everyone can have a high-status job. If some people have a better education, then others must have a worse one.

Hirsch explored the allocation of positional goods and pointed out that traditional supply and demand via price are insufficient. He looked at three common methods of allocating positional goods—screening, crowding, and auctioning—and their weaknesses. *Screening*, such as for university entry, encourages elitism. *Crowding*, such as on a popular exotic island, destroys the positional good; while *auctioning* of scarce goods leads to absurd valuations. Hirsch explored well the limits of market economies in improving people's conditions, but failed to provide ways of breaking beyond those limits. He himself favored vague cooperative actions, reducing pay for high-status jobs, and moving positional goods out of the private sector into the public sector.

The ideas behind positional goods are not new. Anthropologists have explored potlatch cultures and Kula rings, while biologists have explained peacock's tails, all in terms of signaling position and fitness. People have made fun of the nouveau riche for centuries: Thorstein Veblen coined the term "conspicuous consumption" in his 1899 book *The Theory of the Leisure Class*. An increase in ownership of positional goods benefits some participants at the expense of others. We can't all be the trendiest, most famous, or live in the best neighborhood. There is even the pseudo-disease "affluenza," negative symptoms arising from being, or desiring to be, relatively wealthy. Some positional goods can't be expanded, for example there may be only one president or prime minister of your country. Other positional goods are rivalrous, for example if you build your beach house near my isolated beach house, the value of my beach house is diminished. Most goods have a positional and a material component. You may want a ticket to a concert, but might also pay vastly more to have a private box so that other people envy you.

Intriguingly, we use resources from the material economy in order to buy the capacity to compete in the positional economy, so that one affects the other, sometimes wastefully. Luxury brands are the positional goods a lot of people like to mock. Perversely, adding to the price of a luxury product increases its positional value. Christian Dior supposedly advised Pierre Cardin not to sell at low prices: "Make it expensive. Talent should be paid for." You may also need to consume more material goods simply to preserve your relative position.

Positional goods help us understand seemingly excessive pricing, but we need to understand one more distinction to comprehend excessive pay: price competition versus tournament competition.

TOURNAMENTS

A tournament is a competition in which contestants play a series of games to decide the winner. A tournament differs from price competition in that there is one winner, not two or more players with more or less profit. The American football coach Vince Lombardi used to say: "Winning isn't everything; it's the only thing." Winning outright changes the nature of competition. The economics are no longer about matching supply and demand at a price; rather, you need to pay the price to win.

Normal commercial operations provide plenty of examples of tournaments, from competitive tendering with its "best and final offer" stage, to bidding for television franchises, spectrum bandwidth, or mineral concessions. There are two major observations on commercial tournaments. The first, which we discussed in Chapter 2, is that winners of commercial competitions frequently gain Pyrrhic victories or reap a winner's curse: winning bidders in auctions tend to overpay. The second is that cost/benefit analysis becomes binary: all or nothing. This binary nature of tournaments explains, to a large degree, the large amounts paid to sports stars in team sports. Being second best in a tournament makes little sense when you could have paid a little more to be champion. But then everybody else pays a little more, and so on. Better just to buy the best players regardless of cost.

The governing bodies of many sports recognized this potential problem as sports started to professionalize in the late nineteenth century. Different sports tried to keep the lid on pay in different ways. Baseball had its infamous "reserve clause agreement," so that no other team could sign a player without the consent of that player's team, which made it nigh-on impossible for baseball players to call the shots over their salaries for the best part of a century. When the agreement fell apart in 1975, players' salaries sky-rocketed. Cricket, rugby, and sailing remained quasi-amateur sports until the second half of the twentieth century and it is only relatively recently that any players have earned sizeable sums from those sports. Soccer has tended to be more like a free market than most other sports, which, together with its huge popularity, makes players' salaries at the elite level of that sport extremely high.

This freer market in sport players doesn't just hike up salary levels due to tournament pricing, it also hikes up the level of thinking behind the value of sportspeople. As journalist and former cricketer Ed Smith suggests when talking about American football, the relaxation of transfer restrictions has led to an unintended consequence of improved price discovery. He uses as his example the subject of Michael Lewis's book (later adapted into an Oscar-winning movie) *The Blind Side*. It is unsurprising that the highest-paid football player tends to be the quarterback, but the second-highest-paid player now tends to be the left tackle, rather than a runner or receiver. Left tackle is a rather anonymous role, so that a comparatively high price tag was quite a surprising outcome to most pundits initially. But as the player whose job it is to protect the most valuable quarterback, left tackle proved to be, in real commercial terms, second only to the quarterback in the pecking order for pay. The free market didn't just deliver higher pay to footballers willy-nilly,

> [it] also discovered that some sportsmen are more essential than received wisdom previously imagined and others more replaceable. The market, once unleashed, cannot be restrained from challenging accepted opinion—what the economist Joseph Schumpeter called the "waves of creative destruction". "Football common sense", the old wisdom of most fans and football insiders, had been quite wrong.[21]

We can now turn to drawing four ideas together—information asymmetry, localized conformity, positional goods, and tournaments—to help understand the real commerce of excessive pay.

We shall look briefly at excessive pay in two areas, professionals and corporate executives. Each of the four ideas adds to pressure for excessive pay:

- *Information asymmetry*: No one knows how good any professional or senior executive will be until after, sometimes well after, they have been commissioned or hired. This leads people to focus on the wrong element of price: not the outcome but some input such as hours worked.

- *Localized conformity*: We tend to follow others in the way we commission and reward professionals and executives. A good example is everyone giving estate agents a commission based on the value of the home sold, when frequently a larger home is easier to sell. Other approaches include the buyer paying the commission, splitting the commission, having staged commissions, or even having sliding commissions downward based on size. Executive pay tends to be regulated by remuneration boards comprising mostly other executives.

- *Positional goods*: The brand of a professional can matter to others. Your private banker on your checkbook or the tour operator you use may be no better than others, but if the brand, and its consequent cost, say something to others, you may find the social cachet worth the additional expense. Having a branded, famous chief executive means that some other firm doesn't have that person.

- *Tournaments*: Sometimes you need to win. If you are about to embark on a major law suit, the name of a major law firm behind you can often bring matters to a speedy, even non-litigious solution. You can't afford to lose. Similarly, you don't know whether a 100,000-person company depends on a charismatic chief executive or not. But do you want to be the board member who tried to find out and failed? Just pay top dollar and sit back comfortably, claiming that you've bought the best you could afford. And at even 1,000 times the average salary in the firm, it's less than a 1-percent-of-the-wage-bill gamble.

Globalization might be increasing the tournament nature of work, as well as the intensity of competition. Gerald Musgrave says:

> it is not just the Olympics where being fourth is not one-fourth as good as getting the gold—think of being fourth behind Microsoft or Google. It is not just generals or lawyers who get paid a lot for participating in fierce competition. No one wants to come in second in a competitive battle that may mean life or financial death.[22]

Yet a global culture weakens the importance of local positional goods. Do your overseas friends care that you live on the locally ritzy avenue in a two-bit town? Perhaps only the highest sky-scraper in Singapore might impress those friends abroad. Do they care that you're a member of some exclusive golf club in Paraguay? That you're professor at some large, but very modern and trendy university whose name they've only just started to recognize? Increasingly the international lingua franca for positional goods is their price. How much did it cost you to send your daughter to that school, get your son that holiday, earn that award, buy that house?

The cost of the positional good helps people to understand its value, and paradoxically now unites the positional good with the material good. Sadly, this approach of bringing everything together under a single measure, money, makes us unidimensional. Instead of celebrating the richness of life and its measures—health, happiness, family, fame, location, intellect, success, influence, beauty—these days it's really money that talks. If we succumb to wealth as the measure, we have truly created a world where only a few can feel relatively superior. This argument uncovers the ultimate paradox of real commerce: wealth itself is a positional good and, like most positional goods, ultimately it is not that satisfying.

STREAM D | Evolution

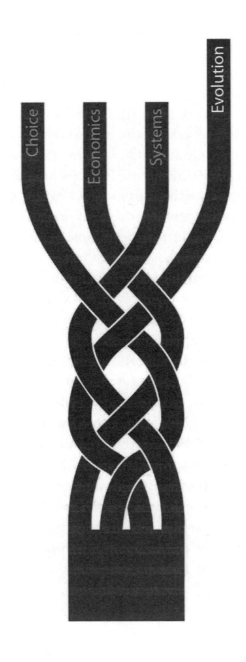

11 | ENCLOSURES OF THE MIND: INNOVATION AND COMPETITIVE SELECTION

We continue to explore the evolution stream by looking at innovation and competitive selection. Competition is essential to markets, but without innovation, we have no new competition. In the words of Michael Porter: "innovation is the central issue in economic prosperity."[1] Research and development expenditure in OECD countries represents between 1 and 3 percent of GDP, well in excess of $500bn per annum when government, major corporate, and smaller organizations' R&D is taken into account. Yet while it is widely recognized that innovation is crucial to economic development and competitive selection, evidence suggests that all too little is known about fostering it.

CREATIVE DESTRUCTION, FAILURE, AND SUCCESS

Joseph Schumpeter gave prominence to ideas of evolutionary economics in 1942 with his concept of *creative destruction*. This means simply that markets create new things through innovation that must displace existing things. To Schumpeter, entrepreneurial innovation sustained long-term economic growth, while simultaneously destroying the value of established companies that enjoyed some degree of monopoly power. Successful innovation erupts from economic systems that are full of birth, struggling, killing, eating, breeding, and dying.

Schumpeter tried to define innovation:

- ❧ "The introduction of a new good—that is one with which consumers are not yet familiar—or of a new quality of a good.
- ❧ The introduction of a new method of production, which need by no means be founded upon a discovery scientifically new, and can also exist in a new way of handling a commodity commercially.
- ❧ The opening of a new market, that is a market into which the particular branch of manufacture of the country in question has not previously entered, whether or not this market has existed before.
- ❧ The conquest of a new source of supply of raw materials or half-manufactured goods, again irrespective of whether this source already exists or whether it has first to be created.
- ❧ The carrying out of the new organization of any industry, like the creation of a monopoly position (for example through trustification) or the breaking up of a monopoly position."[2]

That is a very broad definition; so broad that any commercial change can be described as an innovation.

The OECD attempts in its many comparisons of nations to define and measure innovation. Its standard guideline is the Oslo Manual, which defines innovation as follows:

> technological product and process (TPP) innovations comprise implemented technologically new products and processes and significant technological improvements in products and processes. A TPP innovation has been implemented if it has been introduced on the market (product innovation) or used within a production process (process innovation). TPP innovations involve a series of scientific, technological, organisational, financial and commercial activities. The TPP innovating firm is one that has

implemented technologically new or significantly technologically improved products or processes during the period
under review.[3]

For the OECD, nothing is an innovation until people buy it;
innovation is about making a difference in the marketplace.
However, the OECD definition is, in some ways, even broader
than Schumpeter's. Within it, every novel wrapper for a burger,
every new phone-answering phrase, every inventive internet
click function, and every new fashion accessory can be described
as innovations. Momofuku Ando, the inventor of instant noo-
dles, perhaps becomes as important as Thomas Edison or Jonas
Salk.

How do we distinguish invention from innovation? Perhaps
invention is having a great idea that might be practical, while
innovation is introducing it to the world. Albert Einstein
pointed out, "innovation is not the product of logical thought,
although the result is tied to logical structure." Furthermore, if
many people can immediately find innovative uses of a new
product or process, how innovative are they? In *Outside
Innovation*, Patricia Seybold suggests that, in effect, we are all
innovators.[4] Indeed, user innovation is increasingly recognized
as a key source of economic transformation. Products and services are often used differently from the ways their designers
anticipate.

The definitional problem is deep—and circular. New inventions that are not commercialized are not innovation. If a new
invention is commercialized, but unsuccessfully, it isn't a lasting
innovation. If one company is superior to its competitors, that's
because it is innovative. If a company fails, that's because it
wasn't innovative enough. Yet the survival of European and
Japanese behemoths is attributed to their size rather than their
capacity for innovation, so are those businesses' absorption
strategies innovative? Even worse is the notion of "disruptive

technology": technological innovation that overturns the dominant technology or product in the market, for example steamships for sailing ships or microcomputers for mainframes. Of course this disruption is unpredictable, but there are still sailing ships and mainframes, so when is evolution truly disrupted?

Innovation has become synonymous with success, leading to even more confusion. This conflation is especially surprising as it has long been recognized that failure is an important part of learning and innovating. Woody Allen famously quipped: "If you're not failing every now and again, it's a sign you're not doing anything very innovative." More subtly, we rather like Herman Melville's observation:

> he who has never failed somewhere, that man can not be great. Failure is the true test of greatness. And if it be said, that continual success is a proof that a man wisely knows his powers—it is only to be added, that, in that case, he knows them to be small.[5]

Innovation is simultaneously noble failure and unexpected success. This paradox reminds us of thinker Arthur Koestler's closed belief systems. *Closed systems* have three main peculiarities. First, they claim to represent a truth of universal validity that explains everything. Second, such systems cannot be refuted by the evidence, because all potentially damaging data are automatically processed and reinterpreted to make them fit the expected pattern. Third, criticism is invalidated by shifting the argument to the motivation of the critic. Koestler provides an example of a closed system from the orthodox Freudian school of psychoanalysis:

> if you argued that for such and such reasons you doubted the existence of the so-called castration complex, the Freudian's prompt answer was that your argument

betrayed an unconscious resistance indicating that you yourself have a castration complex; you were caught in a vicious circle.[6]

Innovation can fulfill the first peculiarity of a closed system: it can be used to explain everything about economic change. Superior performance is due to superior innovation, while failure is due to inferior innovation. Innovation fulfills the second peculiarity of a closed system: it cannot be refuted by the evidence. All change is innovation and all nonchange is a failure to achieve true innovation. To meet the third peculiarity of a closed system, we invalidate criticism by shifting the argument to the motivation of the critic. If your great efforts at innovation had no great result, perhaps you didn't really believe in radical innovation or didn't really innovate properly. The solution? More and/or better-focused innovation.

People struggle to define innovation, so they wind up mimicking Justice Byron White on pornography: "We know it when we see it." And clearly, given the focus on innovation by governments, the media, and businesses, people want more of it. In many ways, innovation has hallmarks of religious fervor. If your faith in innovation is strong enough, you will prevail. Of course, as Coco Chanel complained, innovation isn't everything: "Innovation! One cannot be forever innovating. I want to create classics."

GENES OR GENIUS?

There are numerous comparisons to be made between commerce and evolution. Darwin's evolutionary theories apply in many circumstances where there are individuals in a population, offspring who inherit a mix of characteristics, a randomization of characteristics, and the demise of those members of the population who are least fit to survive.

The idea of evolving business strategies is appealing both as a means of generating novel ideas and as a means of optimization. Koestler again: "the emergence of biological novelties and the creation of mental novelties are processes which show certain analogies."

The term *genetic algorithm* is a description for many automated problem-solving approaches that attempt to develop methods that "evolve" from partial solutions toward a satisficing answer. Genetic algorithms use biological evolution as a metaphor for their approach. They evolve a population by assessing individuals' fitness for a task or function. Successful organisms survive to become parents of the next generation using breeding processes that promote crossover, and possibly mutation. The algorithmic cycle can be summarized as:

1 Create initial population with characteristics.
2 Evaluate each individual for "fitness."
3 Select parents.
4 Breed new individuals and incorporate mutation.
5 Replace some or all of the parents with new individuals.
6 If end condition not satisfied, then repeat from Step 2, else quit.

Dawkins in *The Selfish Gene*[7] and many other writers describe applications for genetic algorithms ranging from automated musical scores to designing buildings to finance. For instance, in developing an ideal lifting crane for a particular problem (load, center of gravity), a genetic algorithm might start with an initial set of parameters for cranes (wood:steel, long-arm:medium-arm:short-arm, steam:electric) that will be combined in an initial round to create new combinations. At the end of the round the cranes are evaluated according to a fitness algorithm based on their ability to solve the problem; the most successful cranes pass on more of their characteristics to the next set of combinations in the next round of simulation. Over many rounds, genetic algorithms can evolve to reasonable solutions, for example an acceptable crane specification for the problem at hand. However, "reasonable" solutions may be local optima and not the desired solutions at all. The comparison between genetic algorithms and evolution in nature is, in this regard, fairly direct.

The attraction of genetic algorithms lies in the recognition that complex organisms can arise not from chance or design, but from the accumulation of small changes that assure survival of the fittest. As Koestler says:

> the evolution of life is a game played according to fixed rules which limit its possibilities but leave sufficient scope for a limitless number of variations. The rules are inherent in the basic structure of living matter; the variations derive from adaptive strategies.

On the other hand, the degree of fitness varies. Genetic algorithm techniques might produce an "ideal" result, but only for a particular time or a particular use. Yet if we could apply genetic algorithms to modeling the evolution of firms, then we would gain valuable insights.

Darwin acknowledged in his notebooks that his thoughts on biological evolution were influenced by the economic thinking of his day, not least the work of Thomas Malthus.[8] A business analogy for biological evolution, linking Darwin and Schumpeter, seems straightforward: death is bankruptcy; survival is based on profit; the next generation are spinoffs, mergers, or derivative organizations. Real-world data is readily available for simulation, such as corporate accounts. However, what constitutes the corporate genome? Profit and loss would only evolve to show a trite result that high revenues and low costs were desirable. Balance sheets and cashflow would likewise produce banal results linking fitness with assets and cash. One attractive proposition is that the corporate genomes might be the set of risks and rewards that businesses accept. While attractive, this is problematic. There is a paucity of data even for a single company on what constitutes the set of risks and rewards. For instance, a reward might be the flexibility and commitment gained from hiring solely graduates (a policy pursued quite strongly by many firms); the consequent risk might be graduates' relative inexperience or higher likelihood of departing. Most risks and rewards are subjective assessments or perceptions, not *ab initio* facts. Comparing risks and rewards between firms quantitatively seems next to impossible.

Analogies between biological evolution and business can be problematic in other ways. In the case of species evolution, we know that there is randomness due to mutations of the genome. While serious biological debate continues on the subject of punctuated or gradual mutation, we can posit that the equivalent random element for business is innovation. But what is the source or font of innovation?

We like Richard Dawkins' concept of memes or replicators:

Examples of memes are tunes, ideas, catch-phrases, clothes fashions, ways of making pots or of building arches. Just as genes propagate themselves in the gene pool by leaping from body to body via sperms or eggs, so memes propagate themselves in the same pool by leaping from brain to brain.[9]

You can imagine memes as seeds of ideas showering down on the earth, randomly distributed. Great ideas might be expected in small countries and large, roughly on a per capita basis. More ideas might be expected in large organizations than small, because there are more people. The organization's job must be to nurture those people: to treat ideas like seeds that need the right soil, the right nutrients, the right sunlight, and the right water to grow.

Still, there is a significant risk of taking biological analogies too far, as Kast and Rosenzweig warn:

> Social organizations are not natural like mechanical or biological systems; they are contrived. They have structure, but the structure of events rather than of physical components, and it cannot be separated from the processes of the system. The fact that social organizations are contrived by human beings suggests that they can be established for an infinite variety of objectives and do not follow the same life-cycle pattern of birth, maturity, and death as biological systems.[10]

CENTRALLY PLANNED EVOLUTION?

So where do you find fountains of innovation and progress? There are a number of views on where these sources might be discovered, yet attempts to engineer fountains of innovation have almost always petered out. Consider the statistics of new technology commercialization by structured organizations. It takes about 100 research ideas to generate about 10 development projects, of which two will usually make it through to commercialization. Only one will actually make money when launched. In the US and the UK alike, around half of the private sector's development money is spent on projects that never reach the market. Governments' R&D track record is even worse. At the same time, investors value intangible assets such as talent more and more.

Governments have always liked controlling births and deaths, or at least running the registries of births and deaths. They are even more keen on claiming credit for turning showers of ideas into economic improvement. Somewhat problematically, in a world where being the global leader increasingly matters for many activities, each nation retreats from the (perhaps obvious) conclusion that it can only be technologically excellent within smaller and smaller ranges of activities. People lament declines in their nation's gross patent applications or other broad measures purporting to show technological virility. Globalization of technology leaves them feeling behind and "somebody has to do something."

It is no surprise, therefore, that since the Second World War, we have become more and more convinced that government should play a direct role in innovation. Every few years, any government worth its salt (and indeed any government worth less than that) launches yet another innovation initiative with much fanfare and pompous speechifying. However, instead of focusing on the general condition of the soil for new ideas, governments tend to try to grab the innovation just as it germinates and incubate it in a separated, intensive hothouse where direct credit can be claimed.

We haven't mentioned fish in this chapter yet, but we can now dispel a few red herrings about financing innovation.

RED HERRING 1: R&D NEEDS GOVERNMENT SUBSIDY

Ronald Reagan famously said: "Government's view of the economy could be summed up in a few short phrases: If it moves, tax it. If it keeps moving, regulate it. And if it stops moving, subsidize it." One should smirk (or cry) at this phrase in the context of R&D; clearly governments and voters already presume it needs subsidizing, so it must have stopped moving.

Michael Porter has been influential in directing government attention to regional innovation clusters driving national innovation systems, particularly in his 1990 book *The Competitive Advantage of Nations*, where he introduced the notion of an interlinked "diamond" cluster consisting of demand conditions, factor conditions, firm rivalry, and supporting industries.

Unfortunately, the implication of diamond clusters rather unglamorously directs government to getting the conditions right, making sure the soil for innovation is fertile. If governments had focused on the soil conditions we would never have had various US, Australian, or European innovation initiatives such as the UK's Alvey or Foresight, or the EU's Esprit or Framework Programmes for Research and Technological Development. The UK has fervently funded electronics and aerospace since the war, to the point that there is no global UK electronics firm and merely one sort-of aerospace firm that is, in truth, really just a military contractor with most of its earnings coming from only three governments.

In 1982 the Japanese Ministry of International Trade and Industry made computing its priority. Europeans, and to a lesser degree Americans, were unnerved. The Japanese were spending $1bn (when that was a lot of money) on their Fifth Generation Computer project. This aimed to create an "epoch-making computer" with supercomputer-like performance and usable artificial intelligence capabilities. All that money and more disappeared into what is widely regarded as a failure. Where is the Japanese Google or Microsoft? It is amusing, and saddening, to work out that government-funded research efforts tend to result in the demise of the industry concerned, whether it is Asian, European, or American.

Nevertheless, in the spirit of scientific analysis, let us try to progress from anecdotes about frustrated nationals or failed programs to looking at actual research. Terence Kealey conducted extensive statistical research into the economic laws of scientific research. He set out three economic laws of funding civil R&D:

1   "The percentage of national GDP spent increases with national GDP per capita;

2   Public and private funding displace each other;
3   Public funds displace more than they do themselves provide."[11]

With or without a grounding in statistics, common sense goes a long way to explaining Kealey's premise. Imagine two shipbuilding firms, Pollock and Hoki. Hoki wins a government R&D project for something big and novel for ships, say actually building boats from the same indestructible material used to make the black boxes for aircraft. Pollock, believing it can't compete, abandons boat parts and moves into airships. Yet Hoki might well be "all at sea" to a greater extent than Pollock. Of course the government oversight committee restricts it to researching things they all agree on, rather than innovative ideas. Hoki's R&D slows down as it awaits oversight from government committees, cashflow problems emerge as government funds arrive late with huge bureaucratic overheads, and, when all is finished, its intellectual property leaks out through committee members and the government publishing a number of trade secrets for public relations purposes. So the whole process costs more, takes longer, and results in a single, weakened, government-subsidized shipbuilding firm instead of two vibrant competitors, plus a corporate culture at Hoki where political lobbying skills matter as much as, or perhaps even more than, technological capability.

Government and professional commentators are also particularly bad at spotting winners. William Sherden, in his delightful 1998 book *The Fortune Sellers*, tears apart any structured ability of government or private "futurologists" to spot winners in science or technology.[12] We have a particular soft spot for a certain blue-blooded consultancy's brazen approach. The consultancy walks into every industry analysis with a predicted number. If there are 50 major players in the industry, it predicts that in 10 years there will be only 20; if there are 10 major players, it predicts that in five years there will be only 5;

if there are 5 major players, it predicts that in three years there will be only 3. Almost inevitably, these predicted numbers support the idea of national or regional champions. Strangely, as governments and investment managers amalgamate firms toward these mesmerizing numerological simplicities, managers are powerless to resist these predictions. Such consultancy prophecies tend to become self-fulfilling. Meanwhile, innovation is driven out of these industries while the consolidation proceeds. The winners are those firms who ignore the fateful numbers and continue to innovate and transform themselves, though *post facto* the consultancy can always claim that they differentiated or specialized to the point that they were no longer in the industry in question.

Ashby's Law of Requisite Variety is also relevant to this analysis.[13] Originally from cybernetics, this states that the amount of appropriate selection that can be performed is limited by the amount of information available, and that for appropriate regulation the variety in the regulator must be equal to or greater than the variety in the system being regulated. Or, the greater the variety within a system, the more regulation will reduce its variety. Significant government direction of R&D inevitably reduces the essential variety behind true innovation; thus, as innovation is about variety, government direction of R&D is necessarily counterproductive—inferior to no direction at all.

So can large private-sector firms do better than governments? All large corporations would like to be called innovative, reasoning that, as Steve Jobs said, "innovation distinguishes between a leader and a follower." It is easy to find articles stating that the job of organizations is to innovate. There are two religious sects for corporate leaders, both stark and unforgiving: top-down versus bottom-up. In the top-down sect, policy and planning lead to innovations. In the bottom-up sect, of wild markets and innovation, you have no idea from where the next big idea will come. Sadly, large numbers of stories show that large companies are not that good at "hard," measurable innovation of the top-down variety. But bottom-up innovation means that corporate headquarters has no idea where the next big idea will emerge so that it can justify being a large corporate, a very uncomfortable situation. Naturally, large corporations want to buy innovation consultancy snake oil.

One of our colleagues, Stephen Martin, tells a story of a former boss, Frank Lynn. Frank was part of a thinktank put together by Jimmy Carter to answer the question: "If the USA is so good at inventing new things, how come we don't launch that many new products?" Frank concluded that by the time a company has grown enough to invest in R&D, its channels to market have matured to the point where they are no longer suitable for launching and selling the output of R&D. Furthermore, neither state-funded research nor government aid helps innovation for either large or small firms.

That leads neatly to our second red herring which, like the third, is about organizational scale and comes from the paper "Jumbo Bonsai Meets Pocket Battleship."[14]

RED HERRING 2: LARGE ORGANIZATIONS NEED TO BE MORE INNOVATIVE

"Innovation culture" dominated the R&D management literature in the 1980s at, for instance, 3M, DuPont, and GE. Unfortunately, by 2000, a more common comment was: "Who needs a research lab?" In Peter Drucker's words:

> this explains why, increasingly, development and growth of a business is taking place not inside the corporation itself but through partnerships, joint ventures, alliances, minority participation and know-how agreements with institutions in different industries and with different technologies.[15]

There is also little correlation between R&D and sales growth. We particularly like this marketing blurb for the book *Weird Ideas That Work*, which points out why innovation is subversion in large firms:

> There are massive rewards for original thinking, but an innovative company is—and has to be—a pretty weird place. Convinced that their ideas will work, creative people deceive their managers and disobey direct orders. They are sneaky, vindictive and misguided to the point of lunacy. They try ridiculous things and dismiss the advice of experts. Not only are true creatives messy and noisy, they're almost always wrong. And that's if you're doing it right.[16]

No wonder these unruly, disobedient innovators find few corporate homes. Large organizations don't need innovation, they need to be able to absorb smaller, innovative organizations, either directly or indirectly through alliances or purchasing. Oil, pharmaceutical, computers, and global mining are four examples of industries where larger firms are working hard at absorbing smaller, more innovative firms rather than being innovative themselves. This makes sense. Large firms cannot be innovative because their existence requires structure and process, but they can identify smaller firms with valuable technologies or techniques. The pharmaceutical industry consists of a few mega-corporations feeding off smaller innovators. There are over 3,000 biotechnology firms when two decades ago there were virtually none.

On the other hand, no wonder corporate lawyers burgeon in growing technical industries. It's one thing to defend intellectual property grown in-house: keep it a secret. However, when you pay hard cash for intellectual property, it requires sophisticated teams of bright lawyers to protect it.

RED HERRING 3: SMALL COMPANIES NEED TO BE MORE VIRTUAL AND MORE NETWORKED

Supposedly, according to *The Economist*:

> the fundamental building blocks of the economy will one day be "virtual firms", ever-changing networks of subcontractors and freelancers, managed by a core of people with a good idea… [h]owever… organising costs (which technology tends to lower) determine the size of the firm. So, the real-time enterprise might end up being larger than its less nimble predecessors.[17]

This leads back to the most fertile ground for innovation memes being the allotments of sole entrepreneurs or very small teams who organize, manage, and assume the risks of a business or enterprise. However, even though the large corporate track record is 2 out of 100, small entrepreneurs almost certainly have worse odds; probably more like 0.5 to 1 percent. *The Economist* also notes:

> Of 1,091 Canadian inventions surveyed in 2003 by Thomas Astebro, of the University of Toronto, only 75 reached the market. Six of these earned returns above 1,400%, but 45 lost money. A rational manager will balk at such odds. But the entrepreneur answers to his own dreams and demons.[18]

Worse, much research has shown that successful entrepreneurs vary so wildly, from the meek to the wild, from the octogenarian to the child, that it is hard to distinguish entrepreneurs in advance from the general population. The memes fall randomly on different people in different fields, all networked into their industries in vastly differing ways.

So if governments cannot directly fund innovation and large firms are bad at it, and random entrepreneurs are the only salvation, how can policy makers increase innovation? The key policies are to increase sensible risk taking through better information, lower costs of failure, and greater rewards; and to make the ground more fertile by getting the basic commercial environment right: even-handed legal systems, strong antimonopoly conditions, robust consumer protection law, a continuous flow of ideas, sound information provision, solid infrastructure, reliable education, and open markets (in trade, people, and capital).

TAX SQUEEZE SPINS

It might sound simplistic, but investors invest to make money, not to innovate. They look on the investment proposition in straightforward risk/reward terms. The taxation level is a crucial element in risk/reward calculations.

It is at this point that we must raise a depressing fact. Over the years, a number of European trade and industry officials have wondered why Europeans develop fewer entrepreneurial businesses. A colleague of ours, Dr. Kevin Parker, trains scientific entrepreneurs. He estimates that the budding North American technology entrepreneur has a 1 in 30 chance of actually making the leap. His estimate for the UK is that 1 in 150 will do so.

There are certainly at least two contrary effects at work: better lifetime security in large organizations and risk-money displacement. Most rational Europeans should stay in jobs with large private or public organizations until they are eligible for pensions. Why take risks with long-term family incomes? Likewise, European tax rates are typically at an effective 50 to 60 percent level for most middle-income families when all taxes are taken into account. After paying more tax, making extra pension provisions because you can't rely on the state, buying private health insurance to queue jump the poor public health system, and paying extra for your children's education to give them an edge in a weak school system, it's little surprise that you don't fund your brother or sister-in-law starting up a new business in his or her attic. The US, by comparison, until recently had an effective 35 to 40 percent tax level when all taxes were taken into account. It's no surprise that Americans historically could take more entrepreneurial risks. They could afford to lose more and they stood to gain more from success.

High rates of taxation lead to tax squeeze spins. The answer is lower tax rates. But of course, it garners more votes to pledge more money to government R&D, to spend more money on innovation-awareness campaigns, to subsidize private-sector R&D, and to try to develop more networks of business and academia. All of this effort costs money and increases tax rates, making the tax squeeze spin even worse. European government policy makers don't like the truth, that less innovation policy and less tax would probably make Europe far more innovative.

MAINTAINING OUR STANDARDS

Government also has a potential role in standards for innovation. Peter Swann elegantly describes the difficult balancing act and the paradox of standards.[19] Standards, and pseudo-standards such as patents, encourage more rapid functionality development, but at what cost and what missed opportunities? Standardization too early leaves the innovation space unexplored. Standardization too late leads to much wasted effort filling the space. With a de facto standard that approaches a monopoly, large areas of the innovation space are unexplored. Greater confidence in a standard or de facto standard by consumers and producers may lead to rapid advances; or monopoly rents and the greater critical mass of sup-

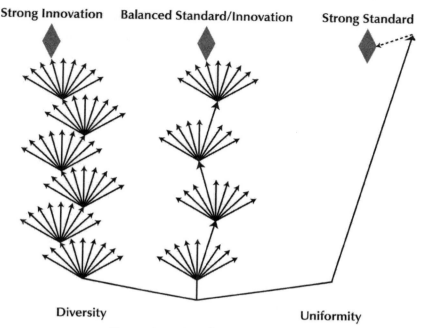

Strong Innovation   **Balanced Standard/Innovation**   **Strong Standard**

Diversity   **Uniformity**

Figure 11.1 Standard innovation

porting items around the standard may hinder development. Figure 11.1 is an illustration.

Standards really matter on the battlegrounds of commercial generals. If your standard is widely accepted, you can make a lot of money. For example, Dolby is a dominant standard for audio noise reduction owned by Dolby Laboratories. A standard can also be a process, for instance the Professional Association of Diving Instructors (PADI) has a cash-generating licensed standard for training and certification. Giving your standard away may make commercial sense. If you have invested significant monies in research and development for one standard, it will harm your competitors if their competing standards are not adopted. If you sell services or products based on other standards, you have a major job managing your relationships. A typical consumer electronics company, take Apple, lists on its website over 100 of its own trade and service marks, plus those of dozens of other companies.

Competition in standard adoption is often called "standards wars" and is common. Edison fought the introduction of George Westinghouse's alternating current, preferring his own direct current standard. As Bill Bryson relates well in *Made in America*, Edison even tried to popularize the verb for electrical execution as "to Westinghouse" and voluntarily electrocuted a condemned prisoner for the state of New York using alternating current in order to popularize the dangers of AC.[20] Standards wars have been especially visible to consumers of electrical products over the past century. Anyone still owning an LP record player, an eight-track tape player, or a videodisc player has experienced such problems.

U-matic is the name of a videocassette format developed by Sony in 1969. It was one of the first to contain the videotape inside a cassette, rather than being open reel. Sony made a lot of money from U-matic. Then in 1975, it introduced Betamax, technically superior to VHS, a consortium standard. Sony's proprietary strategy clearly backfired when Matsushita, the parent of JVC, chose VHS over Betamax in order to avoid a U-matic rerun where Sony dominated. VHS's defeat of Betamax became a classic marketing case study, where a proprietary technology format is conquered by a format allowing multiple, competing, licensed manufacturers. By 1984, 40 major companies complied with the VHS format in comparison to Betamax's 12. Sony admitted defeat in 1988 when it began producing VHS recorders.

Standards evolve and the standards competition takes familiar forms. Proponents claim that Betamax was superior, yet home users appeared to like the fact that VHS could record for longer, about the length of a feature film. Nevertheless, there are morals to learn about "early lock-in to bad standards" and "angry orphans," or "enraged-by-pace-of-change consumers."

Independence matters, but it is hard to ensure. Economic literature is replete with articles on the subject of *regulatory capture*, the concept that some producers in certain sectors lobby so skillfully that they persuade certifiers to interpret standards in the interest of the producers. Examples include airlines, transport companies, or telcos that lobby to restrict competition based on excessive safety requirements or restrictive standards. Likewise, the agricultural industry in many countries seems to be able to get regulators to prefer its interests over those of consumers based on notions of safety when keeping out imports, or public confidence when trying to sell substandard product.

These days, the classic standards approaches are contrasted with the increasingly popular "open standards" of information technology. In its European Interoperability Framework for pan-European eGovernment Services, the European Union set out the following criteria for openness:

- "The standard is adopted and will be maintained by a not-for-profit organisation, and its ongoing development occurs on the basis of an open decision-making procedure available to all interested parties (consensus or majority decision, etc.).
- The standard has been published and the standard specification document is available either freely or at a nominal charge. It must be permissible to all to copy, distribute and use it for no fee or at a nominal fee.
- The intellectual property—i.e. patents possibly present—of (parts of) the standard is made irrevocably available on a royalty-free basis.
- There are no constraints on the re-use of the standard."[21]

BIODIVERSITY

Early in the twentieth century, Schumpeter argued that innovation and technological change come from entrepreneurs, or wild spirits. He created the German phrase *Unternehmergeist*, meaning entrepreneurial spirit. But later, he indicated that in the US it is big companies, with the resources and capital to invest in research and development, that are the real movers. Society needs both big and small. An innovation economy needs biological diversity.

So in a world where we must expect the unexpected, predict the unpredictable, and think the unthinkable, one of the most important unknown variables about innovation is: What are the unknown variables? What policies can society develop within all this uncertainty?

Well, the first thing to acknowledge is that those who consider the abolition of intellectual property rights have a point. There probably exists a moral right not to have someone claim your work as their own, but beyond that, all the legal rights appear to be grounded in the need for a utilitarian system for society, based on the premise that intellectual property rights help society develop more innovations than it would without them. Some people invoke the idea of only protecting "revolutionary patents" for pioneer inventions, outstanding innovations distinguished from the mundane. Jeff Bezos of Amazon, despite vigorously protecting his shareholders' interests with patent defenses of processes such as 1-Click, proposes that the lifespan of software patents should be shortened from 17 years to between 3 and 5 years. "At Internet speed," he says, "you don't need 17 years." Other people believe that establishing intellectual property exchanges will help provide liquidity to the innovation system. However, we believe that a simple rewiring of the core market for creating intellectual rights might make a huge difference.

For instance, trademarks and patents are markets limited by rationing based on trademark and patent office resources. There is little redress if a patent or trademark is poorly awarded. There is a fixed cost to enter the commons, but little return to the public based on what people take from the commons. Copyright is a confused market with no barriers to entry. One approach we suggest would be to introduce the concept of a market agreed between the state and individuals.

Let's call this a controlled options market for intellectual rights. All three basic rights—patents, copyrights, and trademarks—would follow a similar regime (something new for copyright in modern times). The two basic steps to get this to work would be:

- Issue at auction a strict number of tradable options to file patents, copyrights, and trademarks each year, for different durations.
- Set a requirement for patent, copyright, and trademark offices to indemnify prior art and other safeguards by quoting a price for the indemnity (insurance) and publish the amount of the indemnity and the amount paid by the applicant.

This approach would allow dynamic pricing of the value of these monopolies on the traded option market: How much do people and companies wish to pay to gain a monopoly? If the price is very high, crowding out smaller players, then we may wish to have a societal debate as to how much protection, how much resource, how many instruments we wish to issue. If the price is very low, then we get a better flavor of what matters and can trim resources. We can see clearly if these offices are effective, based on what people are prepared to pay to have access. The option means that the patent, copyright, and trademark offices have orderly queues, while the indemnity means that the degree of risk of sloppy work is clear and they still have to keep up standards of acceptability. If the indemnity is reinsured, then we have even better market indicators of risk. If we accept the concept of competing offices sharing a registration database (somewhat similar to the international patent office situation today), then, for example, Patent Office A can be contrasted with Patent Office B on economy and efficiency measures as well.

But perhaps the biggest innovation policy is simply the notion of diversity. Increased innovation means assuming increased risk in pursuit of higher reward. If evolution applies to markets, then, like other ecosystems, governments should pursue policies that encourage biodiversity. Biodiversity means encouraging competition, so that one type of firm does not unnaturally predominate. It requires aggressive antimonopoly enforcement. It means not leaping in too early with standards and regulations, and, when we do, making sure that they are founded within standards markets. Biodiversity means lowering risk and increasing reward for entrepreneurs, such as reducing the stigma and effects of bankruptcy. It probably means lower tax rates so that more rewards can be kept. Improved biodiversity also means improved infrastructure quality, perhaps through universally better education.

12 | IS THE PARTY OVER?
SAVE THE WORLD

Is sustainable commerce a realistic global aim? Can economies grow for ever or are there limits to growth? Will developing economies save the world, or destroy it? How should humanity go about trying to tackle the world's wicked problems? Are there grounds for us to sustain the hope that humanity will come to terms with the challenges it faces, or is our own species destined to encounter the extinction element essential to evolution? Such questions will probably never have permanent answers, but we should never stop asking them.

GROW YOUR OWN

Since the time of Malthus, the debate has been between those who believe that humankind can cope with growth and those who, like Malthus, predict that population growth will lead to severe resource scarcity and, ultimately, a world in which people wouldn't want to live. The absurdity of some optimistic growth equations is lampooned in an adage that used to do the rounds of Economics departments: "Assuming constant returns to scale and infinite sunshine, then with fixed inputs of a flowerpot and soil, and variable inputs of seeds, fertilizer, and water, one farmer could feed the world from a flowerpot."

This witticism illustrates the law of diminishing marginal returns. In real life, adding more and more seed, fertilizer, and water to fixed inputs of soil results in decreasing returns to scale. There is a famous fable about the creator of chess, whose emperor was so pleased with the game that he asked the inventor to name his gift. The wise inventor asks the emperor to give him wheat for 64 days, representing the 64 squares of the chessboard, starting with one grain of wheat to be placed on the first square on the first day, simply doubling the number of grains placed each day for the 64 days. The emperor agrees, unaware of the power of numbers. By day 32, the ration is nearly 4.3 billion grains of wheat, about 100,000 kilos worth. By day 64, the ration would be far greater than the quantity of wheat in the whole world. That's exponential growth for you.

You might think that doubling the ration each day is a silly example. But even more recognizable examples of exponential growth generate big numbers. If you place £1 in a savings account and leave it there earning a fixed rate of compound interest for 50 years, you would end up with £11.46 if the interest rate was 5%, £74.36 if the rate was 9%, or £117.39 if the rate was 10%. Economist Kenneth Boulding draws the obvious real-world conclusion: "anyone who believes exponential growth can go on forever in a finite world is either a madman or an economist." We discussed the worrying linkage between compound interest and economic growth in Chapter 4. A compound, risk-free return on money can only come as a result of wealth transfer from "have-nots" to "haves" or from perpetual growth. The linkage between economic growth and environmental sustainability is similarly daunting, given the finite resources available on earth. In short, environmental sustainability is a tough equation.

TRY TO I-PAT YOURSELVES ON THE BACK

We'd like to introduce you to one simplifying equation that helped structure many of our thoughts on sustainability, I-PAT:

$$I = P \times A \times T$$

Human Impact (I) on the environment equals the product of:
    population (P);
    affluence (A);
    technology (T).[1]

The I-PAT equation has its origins in a 1970s debate among the ecologists Paul Ehrlich, John Holdren, and Barry Commoner. Their arguments were whether population growth or post-Second World War production technologies were more responsible for environmental degradation. Ultimately, various academics have used the resulting equation as their jumping-off point for musing on environmental futures.

In essence, as population and affluence grow, the environment will increasingly degrade. Commoner pointed out the importance of technology: technological growth can both increase and decrease impact. I-PAT forms the accepted core for a great deal of work, including that of the Intergovernmental Panel on Climate Change (IPCC).[2]

POPULATION

Let's start examining I-PAT with the term P, population. Martha Campbell claims, with some justification, that "the population–environment connection has become a taboo subject... too sensitive."[3]

Today's world population is estimated at around 7 billion people; 2,000 years ago there were only about 170 million people on the planet. It took millennia for the population to reach 1 billion, around the year 1800. Having spent most of the past two millennia growing across the planet, population growth in the last century has been made possible by medical advances and the green revolution. So it took 123 years to double to 2 billion, 33 years to get to 3 billion, and we've been adding about 1 billion people just over every dozen years since 1960. Exponential growth of a single species clashes with the boundaries of the biosystem.

Two points are often made about demographic forecasts. One is that among the many forecasting professions, demographers are considered to be the most accurate. The second is that demographers are frequently wrong. Demographic predictions combined with productivity predictions lead to bigger errors. The predictions that have failed to arrive range from Malthus in the late 1700s to the Club of Rome's Limits to Growth in the late 1960s and early 1970s, though the Club's prediction of scarce nonrenewable agriculture pressure is starting to look prescient.

In 2003 the United Nations Population Division ran some forecasts to the year 2300 using different total fertility rates; illustrated in Figure 12.1. Today's global total fertility rate is 2.3. A fertility rate of 2.0 or lower implies a shrinking population. The UN estimates that population will peak at 9.2 billion in 2075, based on the critical assumption of a world total fertility rate of 2.0 by about 2050. More optimistically, with a fertility rate of 1.8 the world population in 2300 would be about 2.3 billion. However, with a total fertility rate of 2.4, the world population would be about 36.4 billion in 2300. A bright or bleak future depends on a sensitive 0.6 difference in the fertility rate.

Nevertheless, there are two rays of light. The first is that the total fertility rate does seem to be dropping. UN forecasts before 2000 were for 12 billion in 2050 rather than 9.2 billion in 2075. The second glimmer is Warren Thompson's 1929 theory of demographic transition to explain the inverse correlation found between wealth and fertility within and between nations. He postulated four economic stages running from preindustrial to developing to developed to mature, accompanied by population growth rates of subsistence, growing rapidly, stationary, and declining. Some economists even propose a fifth, postindustrial, service-based economy with more rapidly declining populations. At the World Population Conference in Bucharest in 1974, Karan

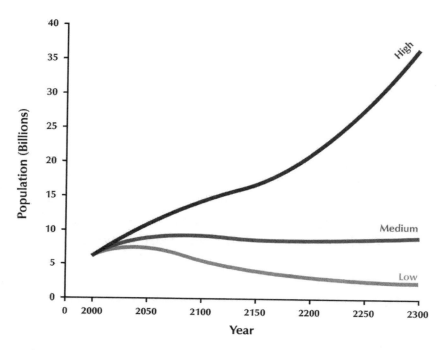

Figure 12.1 Benign future or bleak future?

Singh, a former minister of population in India, summarized the demographic–economic transition: "development is the best contraceptive."

The revised UN forecasts for 2050, which assume that total fertility rates will drop a little, project the global population increasing by about 50 percent between 2000 and 2050. Returning to the I-PAT equation, our environmental impact in 2050 is thus very likely to be 50 percent worse than it was in 2000 due to population growth. Let's now turn to the second term in the equation.

AFFLUENCE

Affluence has rocketed. In 1950 there were 50 million automobiles in the world. Today there are approximately 1 billion.

Enormous consumption differences exist between various parts of the world when measured in terms of GDP per capita or the number of automobiles per person. Goldman Sachs coined the term BRIC economies, for Brazil, Russia, India, and China. Currently the GDP of the BRIC's combined economies are around 15 to 20 percent of the G6 combined economies (France, Germany, Italy, Japan, UK, and US). The world's average person is at roughly Chinese levels of consumption. To get an idea of the potential impact of increased affluence, if the average number of flights per person in the UK in 2010 was emulated by China in 2020, the implication is a tenfold increase in global air traffic during that decade. Likewise, global automobile numbers might double.[4]

Studies by the Millennium Ecosystem Assessment and by the United Nations Environment Programme raise concerns over the depletion of natural capital, with more than half of the "ecosystems services" provided by nature being used unsustainably. WWF and Bioregional, in their One Planet program, have come up with an evocative way of measuring increased affluence. Instead of asking whether the glass is half full or half empty, they wonder: "How large is the glass?" They argue that humanity effectively exhausted the planet's environmental capacity to support current human lifestyles at around the 5 billion person mark, in about 1985. If everyone on the planet today lived at European levels of consumption, humanity would need three planet earths. If everyone lived at US levels of consumption, that number would increase to five.[5] Obviously, it's easiest to blame the rise of the East or the South for the planet's future problems, but something like a quarter of China's carbon emissions are, according to the Tyndall Centre for Climate Change Research, produced for export to the West. At the moment, it's affluent Westerners who are unsustainable.

Again, there are a couple of rays of hope. Simon Kuznets, a Nobel Prize-winning econometrist, came up with an inverted U-shaped curve to explain why, as GDP per capita rises, inequality increases. However, after a particular point of industrialization and urbanization, economies become knowledge economies of increasing equality. Kuznets' original curve is subject to some debate, but there is a widely touted environmental variant. This is also an inverted U-shape where, as GDP per capita increases, environmental pollution increases. However, after a particular point of wealth or standard of living, people start to care about the environment and things get cleaner. There is some empirical evidence for direct pollutants decreasing with increasing wealth, but the evidence is weak or inconclusive for biodiversity, natural resource depletion, or carbon emissions. A bit like applauding a drop in the total fertility rate while population continues to rise, we see the rate of impact decreasing, but environmental impact continues to rise. After a point, the rate of energy intensity per additional unit of GDP drops, but this may be due to people above certain levels of affluence valuing items that have less energy intensity, for example services such as massages or information or games. The ratio of energy per additional unit of GDP has fallen in most developed countries, but total energy use is still rising.

A second, exceedingly small ray of hope is that the numbers are wrong. Much of the economic analysis depends on national accounts. There has been justifiable criticism for decades that national accounts do not take account of resource depletion, as Hermann Daly warned the World Bank in his departure speech: "stop counting the consumption of natural capital as income."[6] National accounts depend on GDP; Paul Ekins points out that you can measure biophysical throughput, production, economic welfare, and environmental growth, but GDP is only a poor proxy for the first three.[7] It does not take account of the social costs of maintaining environmental quality. On the one hand, dealing with natural disasters increases GDP. On the other hand, many activities that reduce harmful consumption also reduce

GDP, such as local electricity production and consumption, voluntary work, or open software movements. If you had a well-maintained environment and a lot of people living sustainably off the land, you might also reduce GDP markedly. This points to future analytical problems in measuring changes in affluence using GDP or similar measures.

Returning to the I-PAT equation, if you base the affluence factor on everyone reaching European standards of living by 2050, increased affluence worsens the environmental impact by 300 percent between 2000 and 2050. Combined with projected population growth of 150 percent, you should expect environmental impact to be 450 percent worse in 2050 than in 2000. If you had used US figures for target affluence, then the impact would have been 750 percent worse. If you imagine that the Kuznets curve idea is correct, then you could introduce another, positive affluence term where a large proportion of humanity chooses to sacrifice consumer affluence for a better environment. It's a delightful idea, but we don't believe that there is yet evidence to suggest that people will make such choices in large numbers.

TECHNOLOGY

Turning to the third term in the I-PAT equation, technology is ambivalent. Technology is in some ways a factor for environmental good and in other ways a factor for environmental bad. It is difficult to measure technology's impact on the environment, so the surrogate used is normally something to do with energy intensity per unit of affluence. Affluence based on GDP per capita is a bit unsteady; well, so is energy intensity. The I-PAT population and affluence factors are easier to research than the technology factor. As expressed in the equation T is the "residual" term, representing everything that has an impact on the environment that is not population or affluence.

Technology has enabled population growth and increased affluence in the past 500 years. Actually, the aberration is more specific: people in Northern Europe and North America have spent the past 500 years increasing affluence because they haven't had to pay all the environmental costs of doing so. Yesterday's unpaid costs include deforestation, whaling, and river pollution. Today's hot cost debate is carbon emissions from fossil fuels. But carbon is only one part of environmental damage. There are numerous other externalities for which we should account, such as mineral extraction limits, biodiversity losses, or even noise pollution. Much environmental impact could be internalized to the economy; in other words, charged for. It is a reasonable assumption that in future, as we get more crowded, many more environmental impacts will be internalized into commerce. Most long-term investment analysts believe that the argument for inevitable internalization is compelling, thus they spend increasing time on environmental, social, and governance analysis. Many investment analysts contend that I-PAT implies long-term investment strategies based on increasing value for natural resources and increasing value for firms that improve resource utilization.

If technology has created some of these problems, perhaps it can solve them. Many scientists and inventors hope to find a "silver bullet" technology that will eliminate or scrub carbon dioxide emissions, or clean polluted seas, or remediate polluted land, or generate energy without environmental impact. There are technologies of which we are unsure—ranging from synthetic biology, to nuclear fusion and fission, to geoengineering, to carbon capture and sequestration—that might have the power to do enormous good. In *Whole Earth Discipline*, ecologist Stewart Brand asserts, contrary to a typical ecologist's agenda: "[C]ities are green. Nuclear power is green. Genetic engineering is green. Geoengineering is probably necessary."[8] Equally, technologies exist, such as nuclear weapons or tar sand exploitation, that might have seriously detrimental effects on the environment. Many environmentalists decry a reliance on future technological improvement or "techno-fixes." For them, controlling population and reducing consumption take precedence over waiting for technology to cure things. For some it is an article of faith or ethics that behavior must change so that we take responsibility for our actions as well as relying on improved technology. Others rightly question whether techno-fixes already exist or will be invented in time.

Returning to the I-PAT equation, we suggest that the jury is out on technology, so we might as well start thinking more deeply about the potential impact.

IMPACT

How can we define and measure impact? It has many dimensions. To quote a Forum for the Future paper for the London Accord:

> while climate change is understandably the overriding concern at present, we are in danger of making investments in unsustainable and commercially unviable options if we focus only on the immediate impact on carbon and fail to recognise the wider sustainability of the abatement measures being proposed.[9]

By focusing on one dimension, such as climate change for biofuels, other sustainability problems pop up, such as the loss of food production. Forum for the Future recommends a balanced assessment of natural, human, social, manufactured, and financial capital.

A general definition of sustainability might be the capacity to maintain a certain process or state indefinitely. However, this would imply no change and no expectation of change. And if there is one constant missing from most I-PAT discussions, it is the scale of change needed for sustainability. The seventh of the eight UN Millennium Development Goals is "Ensure Environmental Sustainability." If humanity wants to live sustainably, then impact must ultimately be zero. Think about this for a moment: sustainability on geological timescales. We couldn't mine anything or dispose of anything unless it was on geological time. We're talking about millimeters per year of landfill: just enough permitted waste per annum that over a few million years the landfill returns under pressure to rock we can mine for the minerals and metals we failed to recycle. There is no point in talking about stabilizing carbon emissions. If we started today we would have to eliminate them and accept that we might be allowed to emit miniscule amounts again in a couple of hundred years or so, when the historical CO_2 of the industrial revolution starts to be reabsorbed.

So let's try to roll back impact to the three-planet level. If we take the agreed minimum 450 percent impact from population and European-level affluence we arrived at earlier and invert it, Europeans need to reduce their impact to less than 22 percent of today's impact by 2050. We could easily argue for an even greater reduction than that. Still, at a 78 percent reduction, without major technological change, that's your car being replaced every 25 years rather than every 5 or a 50-year landfill lasting two-and-a-half centuries. It's one boiled kettle for every five today, one room lit out of five, one car journey for every five, one airflight for every five. Social persuasion won't be sufficient, not even close. But major price changes might be enough (of course, price changes *and* persuasion would be better).

A 78 percent reduction may seem absurd. To bring UK CO_2 emissions per capita into line with global emissions per capita, people in the UK would need to reduce emissions from a bit over 10 tonnes per person to 1 tonne per person, a 90 percent reduction. Numerous economists anticipate the long-term price of carbon rising markedly, with sums bandied about of €40/tonne, €100/tonne, and even €200/tonne, at which point you're talking €7,200 per family of four per year, if the family wishes to emit carbon at today's levels. Some people talk about spending $10 trillion upgrading global electricity infrastructure over the next 30 years.

The foreword to the 1987 Brundtland Commission Report is frequently quoted when referring to society's changing expectations: "[W]hat is needed now is a new era of economic growth that is forceful and at the same time socially and environmentally sustainable."[10] The report provides a working definition of sustainable development as "development that meets the needs of the present without compromising the ability of future generations to meet their own needs." This definition permits us to take future capabilities into account. Humanity has to use its own judgment, for better or for worse, to anticipate what future generations need and what they will be able to do.

We don't have trouble with this definition, but we do have trouble trusting humanity to exercise that judgment wisely. Humanity has a terrible record on intergenerational transfer. We need look no further than the immense underfunding of pensions. That's just money. But future generations will need to trust the current generation on carbon emissions, clean-up costs, future homes, and nuclear power. We don't really know what burdens we're imposing on its descendants. People have a terrible record predicting either technology or economic growth over long periods. In short, we don't know what future generations will need nor of what they might be capable, and the current generation cannot trust itself to make good decisions on their behalf.

GLOBAL RISKS

There are a tremendous number of global risks, among them malaria, corruption, armed conflict, governance, pandemics, and climate change. There are many scarcity issues: water, cropland, living space, and fish. There are also many quality of life issues, such as obesity, longevity, genetic modification, access to medicine, and employment opportunities. The world is in need of a bit of saving. But what can humanity actually do about these risks?

Global risks are events or circumstances that are beyond any particular party's capacity to control, that may have an adverse impact on many different parties across geographic borders, industries, and/or sectors. Given that financial markets are increasingly interconnected and are more frequently the mechanism by which global risks and rewards are transmitted, such as micro-finance, internalization of carbon emissions, or motivations for drug companies to research tropical diseases, the robustness and resilience of financial markets themselves constitute a global risk.

Global risks are persistent. For instance, most modern people believe that slavery has been eradicated. Given that Britain abolished the slave trade in 1807 as well as slavery throughout the British colonies in 1833, and the US went for abolition following its Civil War, it is hard to believe that slavery persists. Yet Anti-Slavery International soldiers on as the world's oldest international human rights organization, with roots back to 1787. People are still bought and sold like objects, forced to work for little or no pay at the mercy of their "employers." Bonded laborers often take, or are tricked into taking, loans. To repay the debt, they work constantly and, while sometimes receiving basic food and shelter as "payment" for their work, may never pay off a loan that can be passed down for generations. Controlled by an employer, treated as a commodity, and with restrictions on their movements, slaves are found in the developing and developed world alike. Despite bans in the 1948 Universal Declaration of Human Rights and the 1956 UN Supplementary Convention on the Abolition of Slavery, the Slave Trade and Institutions and Practices Similar to Slavery, women from Eastern Europe are bonded into prostitution, children are trafficked between West African countries, and men are forced to work as slaves on Brazilian agricultural estates. Early and forced marriages of women and girls can force them into lives of servitude. The International Labour Organization estimates that child labor affects the health and welfare of 126 million children worldwide.

Commercial enterprises strive to create value for shareholders and other stakeholders, and have mechanisms that allow them both to respond to their existing environment and to anticipate change. Enterprises specifically work to reduce risk. They attempt to lessen the likelihood of adverse events or the impact on the enterprise if the risk materializes. Their risk-management systems focus on competitive advantage for the individual enterprise. However abstract they may be, global risks affect enterprises, even those not apparently involved, in different ways—disruption to a distribution channel, impairment of facilities, network interruption, reputation harm, higher commodity costs, and more—that are concrete enough to warrant management attention, but still beyond any particular enterprise's capacity to control. Some of the risks have their origins in business activity, such as accounting misconduct, but entail a broader threat to society. Others, such as poverty and disease, pose a more tangible threat to society, but can in part be mitigated by businesses through economic development, and particular products and services.

Global risks characteristically rate as low probability and high impact to the enterprise, rendering them too complex and uncertain for any single entity working in isolation to manage. Because organizations have a bias toward assigning the greatest importance to those risks that are within their control, enterprise risk systems classify global risks as "beyond the organization's control." Not protecting your building against flooding is negligent, while not helping to prevent New York flooding isn't negligent, and sea-level rises are definitely somebody else's problem. Local efforts are displaced by apparent action, however feeble, from a central or higher authority. But external global risks are not necessarily beyond society's collective capacity to manage, just beyond the scope of a single enterprise.

Companies pay attention to global risks because, if left unmanaged, a global risk can render daily risk-management efforts meaningless. The level of concern about a global risk is driven by management perception of what is most likely to affect the business. An oil-price spike, for example, is of significant concern to a transportation company, slightly less to a food manufacturer vulnerable largely to the indirect commodity price impact, and still less to a services company that transfers its costs to its clients. The problem is trying to figure out what an individual enterprise can do. Companies struggle with global risks because the ownership, complexity, scale, and degree of uncertainty are so great:

- *Complexity*: No part of the problem can be isolated and solved; solutions that work are, of necessity, holistic. Asset values affect economic returns, which affect investment decisions, which affect politics, which affect communities, which affect compliance, which affect asset values, and so on. Solutions to global risks are likely to involve mechanisms, such as markets, that are not predictable. It is hard to anticipate the causal interactions of forces. Complex behavior, within broad conceptual predictions, tends to emerge rather than being directed.
- *Scale*: The effort involved in managing a global risk is beyond the capacity of any single firm, region, nation, or

trade group. Heal and Kunreuther, in "You Can Only Die Once," point to the threat of systematic underinvestment in risk management where "the incentive to invest in protection approaches zero as the number of unprotected agents increases."[11]

- *Uncertainty*: The degree of uncertainty grows with the number of unknown quantities, difficulties with measurement, and problems with prediction. How do you model decisions under uncertainty? What can your firm really do about global warming that might make a cost-beneficial difference? Multiple actors and political tensions mean that putting values on outcomes is inherently controversial. Should your firm value, for example, alleviating third-world hunger ahead of preventing bird flu?

WICKED PROBLEMS

Fritz Zwicky, C West Churchman, and others contributed to the development of a term introduced in the 1970s by Horst Rittel and Melvin Webber, wicked problems. Rittel explored ill-defined design and planning problems, which he termed "wicked." These are not the comparatively tame problems most decision theorists study, for example chess, game theory, or puzzle solving. The real world is messy, circular, and aggressive.

With wicked problems you don't understand the problem until you have developed a solution. Indeed, there is no definitive statement of "the problem." It is ill structured, an evolving set of interlocking issues and constraints. Since there is no definitive problem, there is also no definitive solution. The problem-solving process ends when you run out of resources. Solutions to wicked problems are not right or wrong, simply better, worse, good enough, or not good enough. Every solution to a wicked problem is a "one-shot operation" and every attempt has consequences.

As Rittel says: "one cannot build a freeway to see how it works."[12] The Catch-22 of wicked problems is that you can't learn about the problem without trying solutions, but every solution you try is expensive and has lasting unintended consequences that are likely to spawn new wicked problems.

Wicked problems are not only about global risks. Building a new power station or train system or computer program can be a wicked problem. Wherever the problem affects the solution and vice versa, where solutions are enmeshed in society and everyone cares, you probably have a wicked problem. Certainly most global risks—with long timescales, distant countries, and, when it grabs their attention, everyone wanting to do something immediately—qualify as wicked problems.

A few single approaches to solving global risk problems can be ruled out. Let's start with government on its own. For many wicked problems, dinner-party answers start with the phrase: "Somebody ought to..." Of course, what people really mean by "somebody" is an omniscient, omnipotent being who will come down and make everyone else act properly, pay to fix things, and avoid all future problems. In the financial markets, everyone awaits the coming of new super-regulators who won't make the mistakes of those who came before them. Sadly, neither that government nor that regulator exists. Less flippantly, Muhammad Yunus, founder of Grameen Bank and winner of the 2006 Nobel Peace Prize, says:

Governments can do much to address social problems. They are large and powerful, with access to almost every corner of society, and through taxes they can mobilize vast resources... So it is tempting to simply dump our world's social problems into the lap of government and say, "Here, fix this." But if this approach were effective, the problems would have been solved long ago... governments can be inefficient, slow, prone to corruption, bureaucratic and self-perpetuating. These are all side effects of the advantages governments possess: Their vast size, power, and reach almost inevitably make them unwieldy as well as attractive to those who want to use them to amass power and wealth for themselves.[13]

Consider governments in the context of climate change. According to the UNFCCC (United Nations Framework Convention on Climate Change), 86 percent of capital investment against climate change will come from the private sector. The comedian Jay Leno once quipped: "According to a new UN report, the global warming outlook is much worse than originally predicted. Which is pretty bad when they originally predicted it would destroy the planet." Government alone doesn't work, but neither does commerce. The UN and national governments won't solve climate change, yet the private sector needs governments, and perhaps NGOs, to create rules that favor climate change solutions, such as effective costs for carbon emissions. We often wonder when we look at the increasing scale of the global NGO sector, are NGOs a sign of dysfunctional governments or a recognition that global risks need highly variegated responses?

Consider also governments' role in the crisis of fish stocks. A 2009 World Bank study concluded that the global recorded landed catch of about 160 million tonnes is subsidized to the tune of about $10bn per annum. If overfished stocks were allowed to recover, a sustainable catch of around 80 million tonnes could be taken with about half the present fishing effort for a genuine additional annual profit of about $50bn on a global fish-food market of $400bn. The reason that fishing continues at that inefficient, less profitable level can be summarized in one word: subsidies. Taking into account additional losses to recreational fishing and marine tourism, the study estimates the lost economic benefits over three decades as at least $2 trillion.[14] In addition, experts believe that there will be many examples of fisheries collapsing in the coming decades; indeed, some anticipate a widespread collapse of commercial fisheries by the middle of the twenty-first century. In *The End of the Line*, Charles Clover suggests that, unless there is concerted and sensible action on a global scale, humans might soon be eating jellyfish as the only remaining commercially viable source of food protein from the sea.[15] In this instance, governments seem to be exacerbating the problem, not alleviating it.

Aid alone also doesn't work. Our memories of development aid are long, but the relief seems short. Paul Collier, in his book *The Bottom Billion*, summarizes:

> The story so far: a group of countries with nearly a billion people living in them have been caught in one or another of four traps [conflict, overabundance of natural resources, landlocked, or poor governance]. As a result, while the rest of the developing world has been growing at an unprecedented rate, they have stagnated or even declined. From time to time they have broken free of the traps, but the global economy is now making it much harder for them to follow the path taken by the more successful majority. As a result, even when free of the traps they sit in limbo, growing so slowly that they risk falling back into the traps before they can reach a level of income that ensures safety.[16]

Globalization alone won't work. For about 1 billion people, globalization has been good. For about 4 billion people, it is helping improve things. But for the bottom billion people, export diversification is harder, because China and India are displacing comparative advantage opportunities, "capital flight has become easier," and "emigration has become more attractive." Collier emphasizes that external interventions, aid and military, can help and can work, but that donors need to be more limited, and much sharper in their interventions.

Another truism is that solutions to wicked problems do not work as "top-down," imposed solutions. Yet neither are wicked solutions just about commerce; any more than today's problems are all caused by poor government. Indeed, excessive trust in the private sector or markets to solve wicked problems can lead to complacency. We cannot simply sit back and wait for the invisible hand to arrive and for the free market to save the day. Economist Jeffrey Sachs also explored the market price of fish in his 2008 book, *Common Wealth*:

> Two subtle issues are at work in this example. The first is that the market price of a species will generally not reflect the species' societal value as part of Earth's biodiversity. Market prices do not reflect the value that society puts on avoiding the extinction of other species, only on the direct consumption value of those species (for food, aphrodisiacs, pets, hunting trophies, or ornaments). Second, the rate of interest diminishes the incentive for the resource owner to harvest the resource at a sustainable rate. If the value of the resource is likely to grow more slowly than the market rate of interest, the blaring market signal is to deplete the resource now and pocket the money!... As expected from the theory, slower-growing animals and plants are especially endangered today. Consider as an example one major category: slow-growing megafish. Their slow growth makes them a "poor investment" even in managed fisheries, and their large size makes them an easy prey.[17]

Making markets work in such circumstances means finding ways of giving future generations a voice in today's prices. Two methods are worth mentioning. The first is valuing existence against extinction, an extension of option pricing from Chapter 9. For example, a lot of research is under way to value biodiversity and ecosystem services. A central theoretical question relating to the measurability of biodiversity lies in the extent to which it is possible to develop a unit of measure, in the same fashion as carbon emissions have been established as the unit of measurement for climate change impact assessments. A number of potential biodiversity metrics conflict, for example estimating genetic diversity is not the same as estimating species diversity, which in turn may have little to do with total biomass. Simpler measures may well consist of measuring the acreage of land set aside or square kilometers of conservation areas.

A second method is to find ways of involving more guarantors of future performance. Within the financial services community, three broad categories can be distinguished: investors, those who directly own assets; traders, those who make money from helping others buy and sell; and guarantors, those who guarantee or underwrite events, for instance insurers. One can insure that a natural resource is returned in a condition comparable to when it began to be exploited. For example, an insurer can underwrite that a group of fishermen will return a fishing resource after many years capable of yielding similar amounts of fish in the future. In most of these cases, the guarantor tries to turn preventing a one-off event, in this case a fishery collapse, into a series of annual payments that make such an event uneconomic.

We often contend that something isn't a risk if no one is prepared to pay to avoid it or its effects. Take a frivolous example, the risk that the sky might turn from blue to purple. Assume that if the sky turns purple there are no physical dangers, just a color change. Assume too that one could make a payment to reduce the chance of the sky turning purple. If no one wants to pay, then we would call the sky color change an event, not a risk. On the other hand, perhaps people are prepared to pay to avoid having to adjust to new color schemes or to keep cultural continuity with old masters' paintings. Then the sky color change is a risk.

You may find it frivolous that people will spend money to avoid something that has no negative effects, but if they are prepared to pay to avoid it, it is a material risk. And that is why developing ways for us to pay to avoid risks is probably the biggest step in moving toward solutions for global risks.

One of the big problems with global risks is determining how much it matters to act *now*. Global solutions are plagued by the tension between the room for action versus the degree of uncertainty. This is why things are frequently left so late. If you wait, you may find new ways of solving problems, but the problem also grows in scale. Actions are of two types: resilient or robust.

Communities potentially exposed to hazards can adapt, resist, or change to maintain an acceptable level of functioning and structure. That's *resilience*. Despite variations in starting assumptions or parameters, resilient systems, communities, or societies still function in the presence of partial failures or other adverse, invalid, or abnormal conditions. Resilient actions get by; resilient systems perform within the range of historical volatility.

Robust actions, on the other hand, try to solve the problem or handle a previously unreasonable scale; robust systems handle step changes in volatility. Much of the difficulty with global problems is people getting used to them. A resilient approach to famine is to establish a reasonable disaster-relief program: let's just get by for now. A robust approach to famine is to overhaul everything from agriculture to transportation to markets to governance to try to prevent famine from happening: let's solve it once and for all. In some cases, robust approaches aren't attempted because of lack of confidence. In others, robust approaches are overdone, for instance seeking a silver bullet technology such as nuclear fusion for many years. In some cases, robust approaches have achieved wonders, such as the eradication of smallpox. But solving global, wicked problems via robust approaches involves a lot of different activities by a lot of different agents. Neither governments, nor enterprises, nor not-for-profit organizations can solve such problems without collaborating with each other.

REAL COMMERCE

We have now explored four streams of thinking: choice, economics, systems, and evolution. We believe that all four of these streams need to be included and integrated in order to understand the price of fish—in order to make sense of the way the world really works.

We want to acknowledge two other words that help to explain the integration of knowledge that we seek. They might seem archaic, but we believe they are useful for our purposes and in any case overdue for revival. The first is *consilience*, which means the unity of knowledge, or, more literally, the leaping together of knowledge. The idea originates in ancient Greece, although the English term is usually attributed to the nineteenth-century thinker William Whewell, who sought to describe a synthesis of inductive reasoning from several disciplines. The humanist biologist Edward Wilson revived the term in the late twentieth century in his book of the same name. Consilience is the best we can find to describe, in one word, the integration and fusion of knowledge we envisage when we describe the blending of our four streams into real commerce.

The second word is *catallactics*. The Austrian economist Ludwig von Mises used this regularly, as did his one-time protégé, Friederich von Hayek. In the 1940s, Hayek said that catallactics "was derived from the Greek verb *katallatein* (or *katallasein*) which meant, significantly, not only 'to exchange' but also 'to admit into the community' and 'to change from enemy into friend.'" Indeed, Hayek even suggests that someone who studies exchange or commerce might be called a catallactist rather than an economist. There is a rich point here: we assert that real commerce, combining the several disciplines that affect the price of fish, is more akin to catallactics, as Hayek defines it, than to economics as normally defined. Communities matter.

Chapter 13 explores ways in which real commerce, by seeking consilience and catallactics, might help humanity to manage wicked problems and give us sustainable hope for the future.

13 | SUSTAINABLE HOPES: A REAL COMMERCIAL BREAK

Consilience, the "jumping together" of ideas, emerges in many areas where people struggle to move forward. More complimentary terms for the same concept include "multi-discipline" or "unifying."[1] There are numerous examples of consilience helping matters advance. Uniting biologists with chemists, engineers, and materials scientists has led to biomimetics, where designers try to mimic natural designs. Biomimetics has led to buildings with cooling systems based on termite mounds, adhesive tools based on lizard feet, and self-cleaning surfaces based on lotus plants. Cellphone technology has transformed many fields, from scientists acquiring soil imagery samples to the geolocation of buying opportunities. There are numerous examples of consilient innovation in finance, ranging from cellphone currencies across Africa, to microfinance where small amounts are lent on a community basis, to microinsurance where crop insurance is entwined with a bag of seed and making a cellphone call to activate the insurance at the time of planting. Many of these innovations move from the harsh environments of their birth to developed countries—think of the emergent peer-to-peer lending as first-world microfinance.

One good example of consilience is the use of transferable fish quotas. A regulator sets a species-specific total allowable catch, typically by weight for a given time period. Quota shares are allocated and can be bought, sold, and leased. Transferable quotas can be allocated to individuals or communities. This is a good example of consilience about choice, deciding how to help people choose sustainable fishing; economics, using markets to allocate scarce resources; systems, thinking holistically about the environment and society; and evolution, from the science of complex biosystems to the evolving technologies of fishing that make it increasingly efficient. The first country to adopt transferable quotas as a national policy was New Zealand in 1986. Based on its success, transferable quotas have spread globally and it is estimated that about 10 percent of the annual marine harvest is now managed by transferable quotas.

The idea we proposed in Chapter 11 of rationing the allocation of intellectual property rights through tradable options is conceptually similar to transferable fish quotas. It is also another good example of consilience, using all four of our streams.

Furthermore, in some work we did for the UK government, we proposed an extension whereby the quota, the right to fish, was distinguished from the activation, actually using the quota. To use a fishing quota triggered the need for an activation certificate, and an activation certificate was only valid with an insurance guarantee that the user would not harm the underlying fishing resource, else the insurer would have to pay to return the resource to its former condition. It would be possible to own a transferable fish quota without fishing, for example an NGO trying to buy breathing space for fish. Those who overfished would be subject to commercial costs for their recklessness. The fishing community would be brought to the fore.

Catallactics, studying community exchange scientifically, helps us to understand that sterile market transactions are the rarity, not the norm. On examining transferable quotas, we are struck by the intense amount of community involvement. Many of the success stories involve people following, consciously or unconsciously, Nobel Prize winner Elinor Ostrom's principles on which we touched in Chapter 5. Fish quotas arouse strong emotions, from Iceland and the Faroe Islands to Australia and New Zealand. Where they work well, the amount of community involvement is intense. The community as a whole often has an input into setting the total allowable catch, distributes some of the quotas, frequently helps people to exchange quotas to those who can best use them, helps police the system, resolves disputes, and fights off daft central government edicts. Transferable fish quotas are one example of real commerce in action: improved community exchange based on a consilience of streams of thinking.

STREAMS OF CRITIQUE

Community markets are a good thing and also a good example of consilience and catallactics in action, but such markets are not sufficiently good to address all wicked problems. Former World Bank vice-president Jean-François Rischard cautions: "if we leave all problem-solving to the market, emerging social problems [such as job security] will be left unattended."[2] Markets are self-organizing, information-processing systems that direct societies. Markets can and do help to set goals through prices. Information efficiency should mean that prices aren't predictable, but that they help to communicate values through society and therefore direct commercial efforts. The goals may be odd, but markets set them. However, markets are hardly infallible; we need no further proof than to look at various manias and panics such as tulip bulbs or credit crunches. Good markets should provide information that permits improved decision making about risk: "the reason free markets work is because they allow people to be lucky, thanks to aggressive trial and error, not by giving rewards or 'incentives' for skill."[3] Answers to wicked problems are going to be messy. No one tool will do the job.

Taking our four streams of thinking in turn, we know that each one has far to travel. On *choice*, developments in the field include an increasingly better understanding of how the brain works when we decide things, often based on direct neural imaging. At a macro level, new types of analyses are being used on all forms of information, ranging from phone calls to online auctions to micro-employment websites. These analyses are giving us new insights into group decisions. We have recognized in several earlier chapters that the "rational man" assumption is at best incomplete and sometimes simply wrong. People's motives are complex. Self-interest is not always the primary motive; people are prepared to act in economically nonselfish ways. It is possible that emerging from the study of choice may be new ways to organize work and even democracy itself.

There are many valid criticisms of *economics*, intensified by financial crises of the 2000s. Some critics point out that macroeconomists seem to use theory to generate seemingly opposed policy measures, most notably quantitative easing versus fiscal tightening. Without doubt macroeconomics has room to develop, but equally, a more developed macroeconomics could help the world to develop. Others critique an overly mathematical bias and the need for more empirical work. Some point out that key elements of finance, not least of which are money and the banking systems, are exogenous to mainstream economics; that is, they are not part of the theory. Keynes points out that "money plays a part of its own and affects motives and decisions"[4] without being part of economics. This criticism points to a shortfall, but one that should be recognized as complex and worthy of study, not a fatal flaw.

Critics of current *systems* thinking often maintain that we will be unable to handle future severe restrictions on per capita resources. They contend that our systems cannot handle a low- or no-growth or steady-state world; that built into our basic systems is an inability to function without growth. These critics want to move beyond "capitalism," or, predicting collapse, to start designing a postcapitalist society. Capitalism is a Marxian strand of political and economic thought, and is a fairly narrow view of a messy world. We have emphasized a much wider view of political

292

economy in this book, starting with incorporating Adam Smith's views on open markets[5] through to modern thoughts on public choice theory and the consilience of all four streams of thinking.

In *The End of the Line*, Charles Clover points out that the history of fish is more akin to mining than harvesting. We find a new source of fish and we mine it until it runs out. Many natural resources, such as most fish stocks, have been "external" to the world economy, taken as free, and are thus rapidly exhausted. Many "free" or "commons" resources are being rapidly internalized as we reach the limits of growth. As land runs out and has to be reused, the historical underpricing of land ceases. As fish run out and have to be sustainably fished, the historical underpricing of fish ceases. This is not a failure of the systems. On the contrary, as prices are increasingly internalized, our systems have more opportunities to make a positive difference. We see nothing contradictory about a sustainable world and the continuation of most current systems for the allocation of resources. We agree that humanity's realization that free exploitation of the commons has ended will force adjustments to current behavior. Our contention is that, while current behavior must change, open market systems should be able to respond to those changes.

Finally, *evolution* itself will evolve. We are still in the early stages of applying evolutionary thinking in areas outside biology. While there are some successes, such as applications of genetic algorithms in computing, evolutionary thinking has untapped potential for helping us improve innovation processes or develop new organizational structures. Muhammad Yunus wonders about the structure of government, private-sector firms, and NGOs:

> things are going wrong not because of "market failures". The problem is much deeper than that. Mainstream free-market theory suffers from a "conceptualization" failure, a failure to capture the essence of what it is to be human.[6]

Yunus proposes a new type of entity: a social business. Social businesses would be nonloss, nondividend businesses that might pay investors back their loans, but that is it: "Rather than being passed on to investors, the surplus generated by the business is reinvested in the business." The principal financial problems today for such organizations are difficulties with tax and obtaining debt. We do agree with Yunus that society could make it easier to set up such businesses, but what he proposes does not strike us as novel. There have been many mutual businesses, many businesses that reinvest profits in their community; take the cooperative movement for a start. However, novel or not, real commerce does anticipate the evolution of new forms of catallactics based on the consilience of thinking well beyond today's dominant government-versus-markets spectrum.

Historical exploitation does not prove that we cannot make things work—necessity is the mother of invention. Humankind can trade anything that it values. Looking to the future, historian Malcolm Cooper, in *In Search of the Eternal Coin*, sees long-term value enshrined in three components: land, energy, and knowledge. He sees land and resources constricting rapidly with population growth, energy generation transforming itself and our ideas of scarcity, and knowledge being the hoped-for long-term driver of future wealth and prosperity.[7] Humankind is likely to value many new goods and services and knowledge in many new ways. As we internalize more and more resources into our systems due to scarcity, real commerce becomes more important rather than less.

REAL COMMERCE: COLLABORATIVE SPACE

Our focus on the "price of fish" highlights the fact that, after millennia of buying and selling fish, governments and markets still do not know their true value. Price is not the same thing as value. Over the long term, value should be the same as a price that leads to proper decisions about consumption, exploitation, and investment, without extinguishing the resource. The many jokes about accountants knowing the price of everything and the value of nothing touch on an uncomfortable truth. There are many mechanisms for organizing the price, and few seem to work well. These mechanisms include markets, the state, and community allocation. We need to seek more earnestly how to establish a price that equals value over the long term using the best mechanisms we can. When the price is the same as the value, there are opportunities for sustainable financing. So far, price has not equaled value for fish. This is the biggest, wicked decision-making problem of all: knowing how to set a price that equals the value.

Individual people can make big intellectual differences; think Aristotle, Newton, Einstein. The problems of resource scarcity outlined in this book will benefit from intellectual insights, but will equally need implementation around the globe. In commerce, individuals improve the world collaboratively, as groups. We need to exchange and work with others to make a difference. Individuals matter, however, because organized as families, companies, institutions, or communities, we make bigger differences.

As important as the organization of human behavior is the organization of human thought. This book attempts to show the value in uniting four streams of thinking—a consilience—so that future decisions about commerce are shaped by a wider array of human thoughts than any single discipline. We are what we decide to be, but these wicked problems of resource scarcity should not, and will not, be decided solely through choice, economics, systems, or evolution, nor indeed through any one theory or discipline.

If we were shaping our decisions about commerce using a combination of choice, economics, systems, and evolution, could we hope for a sustainable world? Let's take fish again.

There are numerous horror stories of depleted fish stocks, and the global situation does look grave. But equally there is evidence of success; there are examples where people have reacted to crises and restored hopes for sustainability. At any point in time there are success stories. In Chesapeake Bay, steep declines in the number of striped bass in the 1970s led to programs that stopped overfishing and resulted in their return. There are rising hopes for the return of oyster stocks to the bay as well. As we write, fishermen and scientists are praising the success of Alaskan halibut, Canadian sablefish, US hake, Bering Sea pollock, and New Zealand and Australian rock lobster fisheries management, among others. It seems that people can make a difference.

People have made a difference using a variety of mechanisms. From choice, they have looked at why fishermen get up in the morning, at how they decide where to fish, at how their customers choose what to buy, at why society values fish so much. From economics, people have looked at markets, labor productivity, agents' honesty, antimonopoly structures, property rights, freedom of trade, capital formation, and property transfer. From systems, they have examined the role of fishing communities in democracies, the roles of regulation and cheating, and the use of technology from fishfinders to modern engines and boats. From evolution, they have looked at the development of fishing stocks in complex biosystems and the development of markets in complex societal relationships.

COLLABORATE OR COLLAPSE

A few years ago we worked on an approach to solving wicked problems that was called "collaborate or collapse."[8] What we were trying to do was to help people map out the universe of possible solutions to wicked problems. We have tested this and used it on several occasions. We'd like to share a little of it as an example of how real commerce thinking might help you to make a difference.

What is a collaborative response? It is one that not only yields general social benefits, but also bestows commercial rewards commensurate with the level of investment. Collaboration requires a concerted effort to align interests, incentives, and institutions. We have to recognize "everything, everywhere at all times": ownership, enforcement, multiple players, multiple player interactions. Solving a global risk is neither the responsibility of public institutions alone nor a burden that public institutions can fairly impose on private institutions. A truly collaborative approach would engage various institutions in dialogue, recognizing not only mutual duties but also unique capabilities at four levels of organization:

- *Single entity*—a family, company, government department, NGO, or other legal entity working on its own.
- *Multi-entity directed*—a collaborative effort led by a single organization, typically operating in a hierarchical manner: top-down to a plan.
- *Multi-entity emergent*—a self-organizing network structure, such as markets or commons-based peer production.
- *Collaborative risk–reward*—an integrated approach among many actors to address risk, adopting multiple interacting and reinforcing strategies and tools, while providing just rewards to participating enterprises: a rich system of many entities at all three previous levels acting in concert.

There are diverse mechanisms available for dealing with global risks and wicked problems. Take malaria: there is malaria@home/malariacontrol.net conducting stochastic modeling of clinical epidemiology via a network computing grid, the Gates Foundation's work, pharmaceutical R&D, antimalarial drugs, direct aid for the afflicted, distribution of mosquito nets, education in affected areas, spraying mosquitoes, draining mosquito breeding areas, or raising funds, to name but a few. Complex global risks imply messy, diverse solutions, with no silver bullet.

In the collaborate or collapse approach we group mechanisms into four general methods:

- *Knowledge*—sharing information and knowledge or conducting research with other entities about the severity, likelihood, and effectiveness of responses.
- *Markets*—market mechanisms pricing risk and reward improvement, possibly through a mixture of supporting economic methods, including, in many cases, direct financial support.
- *Standards*—standards and the audit of standards helping to set goals, share knowledge, improve the effectiveness of market forces, and provide signals from consumers to producers.
- *Policies*—guidelines, legislation, supervision, regulation, and enforcement to underpin solutions.

Methods vary widely, even for similar problems. To take two examples, governments simply banned chlorofluorocarbons (CFCs) to protect the ozone layer, and this policy method worked. In contrast, for sulphur dioxide (SO_2) the US government supported a traded market for emissions, and this market method achieved in months what most believed would have taken regulatory years.

Desirable outcomes to global risks are illustrated in Figure 13.1 and include the following:

- *Expand frontiers* to solve or mitigate a global risk, e.g., developing new drugs that might cure and/or prevent disease,

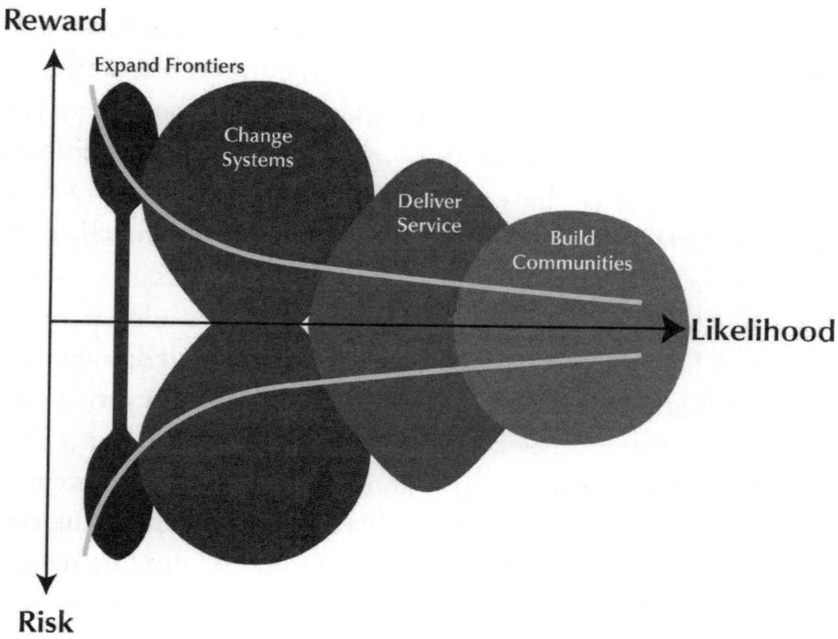

Figure 13.1 Risk/reward desirable outcomes

finding technologies that provide renewable energy, or adapting irrigation techniques to help meet the needs of farmers in barren places.

- *Change systems* to reprioritize a global risk, to develop markets, or to release resources, e.g., the introduction of cap-and-trade carbon markets, or adaptation of government policies on child labor to harmonize divergent home and host country standards.

- *Deliver service* to address immediate needs, e.g., providing care for children in war-torn places, or providing care for the elderly in HIV/AIDS-stricken regions.

- *Build communities* to help people deal with global risks through communitarian activity, e.g., voluntary carbon emission reductions, or enlisting corporate participation in terrorism reduction while creating new commercial opportunities for the provision of security measures.

Activities involved in expanding frontiers, such as finding a cure for a killer disease, are high reward or high risk. The activities either spend lots of money to cure the disease or they spend lots of money but fail. Middling outcomes are unlikely and this type of activity is often best analyzed financially as an option. Activities involved in changing systems are also relatively high risk and/or high reward. Service delivery involves lower-risk, lower-reward activities than expanding frontiers and changing systems. This kind of response is most amenable to cost/benefit analysis. It is very difficult to define objectives and prove outcomes from community building. Volunteers and members are often a mixture of supporters and beneficiaries, with some individuals being both supporters and beneficiaries. Communitarian activities therefore tend to be relatively low risk and low reward and can to some extent be evaluated simply by seeing whether people want to invest their time or pay membership dues.

Let's return to fish as an example of how the combination of methods and outcomes can be used to map global risks. It has become clearer and clearer over time that fisheries' policy problems are particularly exacerbated by two characteristics common to natural resource management:

- *Degrees of uncertainty*: In fisheries, uncertainty stems from a large number of unknown quantities, difficulties with measurement, and poor tools. For instance, which fish eat what, when, and where? What is the investment profile of a fisherman? Can we estimate predicted environmental changes? How do we model decisions under uncertainty?
- *Complexity and the holistic nature of managing sustainable stocks*: No part of the problem can be isolated and solved in isolation. Stocks affect economic returns affect investments affect votes affect communities affect compliance affect stocks.

In short, sustaining the supply of edible fish is a wicked problem that presents global risks. Table 13.1 sets out a selection of possible solutions, contrasting various outcomes with generic methods and providing 16 intersections.

You can see the wide range of responses that might be available to help prevent fishery collapse and move toward sustainable fishing. We have discussed the Marine Stewardship Council several times in this book. It is located primarily in the box where "change systems" intersects with "markets." The MSC tries to

Table 13.1 The price of sustainable fish

METHOD/ OUTCOME	KNOWLEDGE	STANDARDS	MARKETS	POLICIES
EXPAND FRONTIERS	Fisheries research	Commercial R&D, fish futures	Standards research, laboratory skills	Laws of the sea, conservation zones
CHANGE SYSTEMS	Train fishermen in sustainability	Individually tradable quotas, microfinance, new insurance products	Accreditation and certification, e.g., consumer labeling of sustainable fish	Eliminating subsidies and guarding assets, e.g., activation certificates
DELIVER SERVICE	Open-source software and data	Online fish markets, fishermen's mutuals and co-ops	ISO9000, industry/food/ safety standards	Certification requirements for government contracts
BUILD COMMUNITY	Benchmarking and shared facilities	Industry and community guarantee schemes	Voluntary labeling	Government communication projects, e.g., academics and business

harness consumer preference for sustainable seafood products through a branded certification program. If you look at the "change systems" intersection with sharing "knowledge," the Southern African Sustainable Seafood Initiative (SASSI), for example, successfully uses texting technology to help preserve the country's many fish species. Its FishMS service informs users buying fish about which species are in plentiful supply, endangered, or illegal to buy. We won't expand on the many interactions of scale, global and local, inshore or pelagic for a problem such as fishery devastation—it's a multilevel, messy, wicked problem—but the matrix starts to provide a conceptual structure for organizing our thoughts.

As a better illustration of how such a matrix might be useful, we could distinguish between trivia games and games of knowledge. In a trivia game, you know the facts, or you don't. In a game of knowledge, you can reason toward an answer. If the facts spoke for themselves, we wouldn't need reasoning. Our matrix implies that if you comprehend the four streams, and have an understanding of sharing knowledge, markets, standards, and policies, you can seek successful outcomes. Intelligence is the ability to envision the effects of our actions. Each intersection should challenge you to consider a possible mechanism to address a wicked problem. You may not know everything that is known, but you can reason toward answers.

RISKY PRECAUTIONS

Humankind faces some big decisions about future scarcity, or one big indecision. Ultimately, we are deciding on our own probability of extinction. Sustainability does not equal eternal existence. We have to accept risk. We can choose to operate in such a way that the probability of going extinct is something like a 1 in 100-year, 1 in 100,000-year, or 1 in 1,000,000-year chance of collapse, but we are making that choice. Setting the risk of collapse is not easy. Who is really comfortable with measures such as a 1 in 2,000,000-year chance of collapse or its tiny probability of 0.00005 percent? At these extremes we have to use models for which the data is extremely incomplete.

Even if the past were a good guide to the future, our history of the past 2,000 years is patchy, let alone the 20,000,000 years we might want as data to feed a 2,000,000-year estimation model. As humankind has grown increasingly able in the last century to devastate the planet, our social discount rates have not kept pace. As we discussed in Chapter 4, when people attempt to estimate utility discount rates (also known as the pure rate time preference), they often arrive at an estimate of around 1.5 percent. Because the average annual death rate for adults is about 1.5 percent, this is not a surprising number, but it does not bode well for our commitment to investments beyond one generation. Surely we can benefit from the accumulation of skills and knowledge across the generations? As the nineteenth-century historian and poet Thomas Babington Macaulay said: "every generation enjoys the use of a vast hoard bequeathed to it by antiquity, and transmits that hoard, augmented by fresh acquisitions, to future ages."[9] Our generation is building an information infrastructure that might underpin our sustainable hopes for very many generations.

Computer scientist Jaron Lanier explains why we tend to feel queasy about the future:

We have an extraordinary amount of what you could call karma in this generation, because this generation is creating the computer network and the infrastructure of computer software that will be running for a thousand years. I call it the Karma Vertigo Effect because when you realize how much karma we have in this generation, you get vertigo![10]

An attack of Karma Vertigo might prevent us from taking action. So might a German concept now widely promoted as a means of dealing with risk: *Vorsorgeprinzip*, or the precautionary principle. This is a moral or political principle most often applied in the context of the environment or human health, where the consequences of acting on complex systems may be unpredictable. The precautionary principle embodies the idea that if the consequences of an action are unknown, but are judged to have potential for major or irreversible negative consequences, then it is better for society to avoid that action. In the absence of a scientific consensus that harm would not ensue, the burden of proof falls on those who would advocate taking the action.

This principle creates problems in both assessing harm and proving that harm will not emerge. At one extreme, it excludes cost/benefit analysis. A deeper problem is discerning action and inaction. In many circumstances where doing nothing results in harm, the precautionary principle contradicts itself. Is banning mercury in thermometers, freon in refrigeration, or even carbon dioxide exhaust from automobile engines and power plants, removing a risk or taking an action? The precautionary principle raises awareness of ethical responsibilities toward maintaining the integrity of natural systems, and the fallibility of human understanding. In subtly different guises, it is included in the United Nations' 1982 World Charter for Nature, the 1987 Montreal Protocol, the 1992 Rio Declaration on Environment & Development, and the Maastricht Treaty. Karma Vertigo and the precautionary principle raise age-old conundra between "doing something rather than nothing" and "damned if you do, damned if you don't."

When discussing the prospects for solving global, wicked problems, we admit to sitting somewhere on the fence. Our glass is both half full and half empty when we contemplate the future. We do not slavishly subscribe to the precautionary principle, which tends to make people afraid to do anything; nor do we wish to succumb to Karma Vertigo and analysis paralysis. We believe that humanity must take action to find solutions to accelerate the pace of commercial evolution of its own volition, otherwise biological evolution will force outcomes upon us.

REAL COMMERCE AND TIME: IMPERTINENT QUESTIONS AND PERTINENT ANSWERS

So what are the longer-term solutions? More permanent and pertinent solutions demand impertinent questions. The renowned anthropologist Claude Lévi-Strauss studied people. He once concluded: "the learned man is not the man who provides the correct responses, rather he is the man who poses the right questions." In similar vein, the Polish-British scientist Jacob Bronowski believed that good questions were at the heart of science: "that is the essence of science: ask an impertinent question, and you are on the way to a pertinent answer."

In 1993, MIT Professor Danny Hillis posed a cool, impertinent question: "Why can't we build a clock that will last 10,000 years?" In his own words:

When I was a child, people used to talk about what would happen by the year 2000. Now, thirty years later, they still talk about what will happen by the year 2000. The future has been shrinking by one year per year for my entire life. I think it is time for us to start a long-term project that gets people thinking past the mental barrier of the Millennium. I would like to propose a large (think Stonehenge) mechanical clock, powered by seasonal temperature changes. It ticks once a year, bongs once a century, and the cuckoo comes out every millennium.

Hillis's question provides a counterpoint to today's "faster, cheaper" mindset by promoting "slower, better" thinking. This echoes Brian Eno's thought, "I want to be in a Big Here and a Long Now." These questions spawned the Long Now Foundation in 1996, which is building Hillis's clock. The purpose of the Clock of the Long Now is to construct a timepiece that will operate with minimal human intervention for ten millennia, constructed of durable materials, powered by renewable sources, easy to repair, and made of largely valueless materials in case knowledge of the clock is lost, while simultaneously reducing its attraction to looters. The Science Museum in London has displayed a prototype clock since 1999. And just to remind us what 10,000 years means, they've added a digit to every year, so this book was first published in 02011. The Long Now has brought together and motivated people ranging from technology billionaires to the speculative fiction author Neal Stephenson, whose bestselling book *Anathem* was inspired by the project. The Foundation has spawned and nurtured several other projects trying to preserve languages, develop long-term software and media, or bet on long-term events.[11] Warren Buffett placed a $1 million Long Bet: "Over a ten-year period commencing on January 1, 2008, and ending on December 31, 2017, the S&P 500 will outperform a portfolio of funds of hedge funds, when performance is measured on a basis net of fees, costs and expenses." Meanwhile, the Foundation has bought land in the US and is installing the giant, $100 million or so clock in a cavern there.

We don't claim to be as good at asking cool, impertinent questions as Danny Hillis, but we can suggest some quite difficult questions about real commerce and time. "If resource scarcity was wholly built into commerce, would people then act sustainably?" "What would it mean to move from economics focused on scarcity to economics of abundance?" "Can a 20 year old responsibly enter into a financial structure for his or her retirement?" This last question, for example, raises a host of related issues. It draws in actuaries, accountants, life insurance, savings, investments, security, fraud, risk, returns, and firm defaults. An average 20 year old today should, under reasonable actuarial expectations, live to 95. Most 20 year olds with whom we talk assume that they'll live to 120, so the question implies a financial structure that should last 75 to 100 years. Truthfully, we do not know how 20 year olds can responsibly enter into a financial structure for their retirement, but we do know that the question matters.

In 2007, we began using the term *long finance*, in recognition of related thinking in the Long Now Institute, leading to a series of projects that now form the basis of an already substantial initiative. Established by Z/Yen Group in conjunction with Gresham College, long finance aims to improve society's understanding and use of finance over the long term, in contrast to the short-termism that defines today's financial and economic views. It seeks to expand frontiers, change systems, deliver services, and build a community. "When would we know that our financial system is working?" is the core long finance question that tends to generate frustratingly short-term comments and nonanswers from the financial community.

Some answers to these large-scale questions might be decidedly small scale and short term. Studies by Sendhil Mullainathan and others looking at ways of resolving debt traps among small-scale fruit, vegetable, and flower sellers in Chennai reveal intriguing insights into economic behavior in conditions of extreme scarcity and stress (where people tend to make especially poor and extremely short-term decisions). These studies point at ways to alleviate those debt traps through radical but relatively low-cost changes to the structure of local microfinance networks.[12] Such novel and practical solutions echo ideas such as development economist E F Schumacher's "smallness within bigness"[13] that captured imaginations many decades ago. Today's technology may allow us to deploy efficient large-scale solutions based on small-scale activities.

THE REALITY OF REAL COMMERCE

Can we highlight a core theory for you to take away from this book? A simple pendular theory, one that rocks back and forth around one theme, does seem appropriate. Consilience involves bringing together many approaches to thinking about decisions. Catallactics involves making communities work locally, globally, and transglobally. Yet our core theme has been first to try to measure what concerns us. You could argue that we haven't seen any problem that we haven't first tried to measure for a solution. The pendular element is that we need to balance the over-specificity of applying some of the scientific measurement ideas involved in consilience with the looser measurement of the relationships in real communities. Real commerce is about finding ways to set measures that balance the specificity of scientific disciplines with getting communities to work together across space and time.

A good example of the sort of reform that real commerce implies is confidence accounting, where we would prefer that people use ranges rather than discrete values in evaluating financial performance. Confidence accounting would permit the deployment of a wider range of disciplines in commerce, and help financial accounting engage with the wider community. Our pendular theory is that overprecise measurement is bad, while no measurement is worse. Real commerce is about getting measurement closer to the commercial realities of exchange among people.

Many sustainability issues arise because society's core risk/reward transfer system, finance, isn't yet capable of handling long-term risk/reward transfers expressed in simple questions, such as: "How do we fund tomorrow's fish?" The financial industry's answer to the relationship between long-term value and today's decisions has been present value accounting. It is a perfectly sensible concept, yet it has horrific unintentional consequences in long-term projects such as funding sustainable fisheries for slow-growth species of fish.

Some answers might reveal themselves to be evolutionary, or a boring slog of regulatory reform, or a concession that there are no answers. Some answers might be revolutionary: new currency structures, being clearer about utility or narrow banking, introducing policy performance bonds, or enabling pension indemnity assurance. For example, one revolutionary answer to retirement structures might be direct personal retirement cohorts: as you enter work you are chosen to join an impartially selected group of 600 people distributed around the globe who, under the management of a central coordinator, are responsible directly for each other's retirement. The central coordinator directs your retirement cohort to save and sets out the long-term transfers of risk and reward. However, the central coordinator never controls your money, which is quite possibly held in some safe haven and governed by special laws. The cohort is your most important social network, because it, not the state, is responsible for financial security in your retirement.

There are even larger questions. How do we build an equitable, global commercial system across space? How do we fairly transact with future generations, yet unborn, on very long-term sustainability across time? Can real commerce help us measure happiness? Global and local solutions are needed, top-down and bottom-up. As the essayist Wendell Berry states:

[a] good community, as we know, insures itself by trust, by good faith and good will, and by mutual help. A good community, in other words, is a good local economy.

Globally and locally, we need to trade sardines in ways that mean people always have sardines to eat, not just are able to finance them. We believe that real commerce, applying analysis based on choice, economics, systems, and evolution, then implementing solutions sharing knowledge, markets, standards, and policies, may provide long-term answers to such questions.

Commercial transactions and money are inextricably linked to trust in the community. Antiseptic, neutral exchanges of currency don't exist. Each transaction with another person links us a little more to the other person's societal mores, them to ours, and both of us to the future. Without aspirations, our communities have no future, and our coins no value. Long finance seeks to balance trust across space and time. This leads to our long finance koan: "If you have some trust, I shall give you trust. If you have no trust, I shall take it away from you."

Academics have tended to emphasize specialism: knowing more and more about less and less. Perhaps thinkers should emphasize eclecticism, knowing less and less about more and more. Real commerce catallactists should stress the eclectic consilience of choice, economics, systems, and evolution, which jointly challenge the conventional price of fish.

We intend to keep asking uncomfortable, impertinent questions in search of pertinent and permanent answers. We expect you to ask equally uncomfortable and impertinent questions too. After reading this book, we hope you have a better sense of the way the world really works and a better understanding of how to make it a better place.

ACKNOWLEDGMENTS

Anything that might be wrong with the book is entirely down to the authors, but everything that is right with the book owes a great deal to the following people for their kind help, encouragement, and inspiration at various stages of this endeavor:

John Abbink, Giles Abbott, John Adams, Stephen Aguilar-Millan, Ian Angell, Gerald Ashley, John Aubert, Gerald Avison, Will Ayliffe, Liz Bailey, Robert Barnes, Stephen Barry, Charles Bartlett, David Benson, Adrian Berendt, David Birch, Andrew Black, David Blood, Stewart Brand, Nicholas Brealey, Saxon Brettell, Angela Broad, Roberto Buiza, Tomas Carruthers, Alice Chapple, Charles Clover, Pilar Connell, Linda Cook, Malcolm Cooper, Nick Danev, Brandon Davies, Becky Dawson, Dionisis Demetis, Gabriel Didham, Tony Dillof, Mark Duff, Yvonne Duff, Pat Dunphey, Penny Duquenoy, Dudley Edmunds, Paul Ekins, Patrick Ellum, Bill Emmott, Brian Eno, Alexander Evans, Doyne Farmer, Dimitris Fatouros, Michael Feeney, Mark Field, Barry Fineberg, David Fishman, Leonore Fishman, Les Fishman, Ashley Fletcher, Roderick Floud, Alexandra Flynn, Alan Freeland, Bob Giffords, Nick Goddard, Charles Goldfinger, Monique Gore, Charlotte Graham, Axel Grißmer, Loyd Grossman, John Gummer, Chiara von Gunten, Michael Hager, Stephen Haggard, Matthew Haigh, Christopher Hall, Trent Hardman, Bob Harvey, Margaret Heffernan, Niels Heidtmann, Andrew Hilton, Hamilton Hinds, Paul Hirst, Jez Horne, Jonathan Howitt, David Hurst, Neil Infield, Faisal Islam, Lawrence Jackson, Richard Jennings, Haydn Jones, Mike Jones, William Joseph, Con Keating, Laurence Kelly, Alexander Knapp, Sabine Kurjo-McNeill, Sophie Lambin, Peter Lawrence, Matthew Leitch, David Lewis, Bernard Lietaer, Jamie Lindsay, Bruce Lloyd, John Lloyd, Charles Lucas-Clements, Brit Lundell, Maureen Lundell, Nick Mabey, Kelly Mainelli, Maxine Mainelli, Mike Mainelli, Nicholas Mainelli, Xenia Mainelli, Andrew Malecki, Patrick Mallet, Michael Marchant, Sheri Markose, Stephen Martin, Mike Mason, Brendan May, Callum McCarthy, Eoin

McCarthy, Charlie McCreevy, Alastair McIntosh, Doug McWilliams, Christopher Michaelson, Simon Mills, Clive Moffatt, Ben Morris, Robert Muetzelfeldt, Jobst Münderlein, T John Murray, Charles Nall, Richard D North, Ken O'Brien, Mary O'Callaghan, Adam Ognall, David Omand, Jan-Peter Onstwedder, Fred O'Regan, Olivia O'Sullivan, Kevin Parker, Robert Pay, Avi Persaud, Ole Peters, Sanet Philips, John Plender, Richard Poulden, Dave Prentis, Christopher Prior-Willeard, David Pullinger, Stephen Pumphrey, Willie Purves, John Random, Camilla Ritchie, Stephanie Rochford, Simon Rogerson, Joshua Ronen, Alexander Rose, Robert Rowell, Philip Sadler, Nigel Salter, Svetlana Savelyeva, Mark Schaffer, Marc Schlossman, Bobbie Scully, Richard Sealy, Werner Seifert, Paul Sizeland, Andrew Smith, Ed Smith, Keith Smith, Mike Smith, Michael Snyder, Michael Spackman, Neal Stephenson, David Steven, Rupert Stubbs, Doug Sunshine, Richard Susskind, Stewart Sutherland, Kate Taylor, Raj Thamotheram, Arunan Thaya-Paran, Ian Theodoresen, Alison Thomas, Pete Tiarks, Charles Vermont, David Vermont, Eli Wallitt, Aidan Ward, Stephen Wells, Geoffrey West, Margaret Wheeler, Sam Whimster, John White, Carlota Wigglesworth, Jack Wigglesworth, Justin Wilson, Nigel Wilson, Shaun Woodward, George Wyner, Mark Yeandle, and Patrick Young.

We would particularly like to thank our colleagues at Z/Yen Group and our friends at Gresham College for all their support and assistance. In turn, we would like to thank Gresham College's sponsors, the City of London Corporation and the Worshipful Company of Mercers. We would also like to thank the sponsors of the Mercers' Memorial School Professor of Commerce Chair, the Old Mercers' Club, and the Mercers' School Memorial Trust.

Particular thanks to our long-suffering partners, Elisabeth Mainelli and Janie Wormleighton, for putting up with two bears with sore heads during the many late nights, early mornings, and weekend widow incidents that led to the production of this book. As we solemnly promised the last time, "never again, until the next time."

NOTES

CHAPTER 1

1 Seth A Klarman (1991) *Margin of Safety: Risk-Averse Value Investing Strategies for the Thoughtful Investor*, Harper Collins (in turn attributed to Sequoia Fund, Inc., annual report for 1986).

2 Horst W J Rittel & Melvin M Webber (1973) *Dilemmas in a General Theory of Planning*, Policy Sciences 4, Elsevier, pp 155–69, www.metu.edu.tr/~baykan/arch467/Rittel+Webber+Dilemmas.pdf.

CHAPTER 2

1 Reid Hastie & Robyn M Dawes (2001) *Rational Choice in an Uncertain World: The Psychology of Judgement and Decision Making*, Sage.

2 Herbert Simon (1957) *Models of Man*, John Wiley.

3 Gary Becker (1976) *The Economic Approach to Human Behavior*, University of Chicago Press.

4 Daniel Kahneman & Amos Tversky (1979) Prospect Theory: An Analysis of Decision Under Risk, *Econometrica* 47(2): 263–91.

5 Max Bazerman (1986) *Judgment in Managerial Decision Making*, John Wiley.

6 Richard H Thaler & Eric J Johnson (1990) Gambling with the House Money and Trying to Break Even: The Effects of Prior Outcomes on Risky Choice, *Management Science* 36(6): 643–60.

7 Peter L Bernstein (1996) *Against the Gods: The Remarkable Story of Risk*, John Wiley.

8 Shiv Mathur (1988) How Firms Compete: A New Classification of Generic Strategies, *Journal of General Management* 14(1): 30–57.

9 Chris Anderson (2006) *The Long Tail: Why the Future of Business Is Selling Less of More*, Hyperion.

10 Barry Schwartz (2004) *The Paradox of Choice*, HarperCollins.

11 Amos Tversky & Eldar Shafir (1992) Choice Under Conflict: The Dynamics of Deferred Decision, *Psychological Science* 3: 358–61.

12 Herbert Simon (1947) *Administrative Behaviour*, Macmillan.

13 Richard H Thaler (1994) *The Winner's Curse: Paradoxes and Anomalies of Economic Life*, Princeton University Press.

14 Ian Harris, Michael Mainelli, & Haydn Jones (2008) Caveat Emptor, Caveat Venditor: Buyers and Sellers Beware the Tender Trap, *Journal of Strategic Change* 17(1/2): 1–9.

15 Richard H Thaler & Cass R Sunstein (2008) *Nudge: Improving Decisions about Health, Wealth and Happiness*, Yale University Press.

16 Richard H Thaler (2008) Libertarian Paternalism: Why It Is Impossible

Not to Nudge, Edge Masterclass Class One,
http://www.edge.org/3rd_culture/thaler_sendhil08/class1.html.

CHAPTER 3

1   Paul J Zak, Angela A Stanton, & Sheila Ahmadi (2007) Oxytocin
    Increases Generosity in Humans, Plosone.org,
    http://www.plosone.org/article/info:doi%2F10.1371%2Fjournal.pone.
    001128.
2   Albert Carr (1968) Is Business Bluffing Ethical?, *Harvard Business
    Review* Jan/Feb.
3   Robert Axelrod (1984) *The Evolution of Cooperation*, Basic Books.
4   Adam Smith (1759) *The Theory of Moral Sentiments*, A Millar (ed.),
    http://www.econlib.org/library/Smith/smMS.html.
5   James Surowiecki (2004) *The Wisdom of Crowds*, Doubleday.
6   Eric Uslaner (2005) The Bulging Pocket and the Rule of Law:
    Corruption, Inequality, and Trust, Göteborg University,
    http://www.bsos.umd.edu/gvpt/uslaner/uslanerbulgingpocketgoteborg.pdf.
7   Dan Ariely (2008) *Predictably Irrational: The Hidden Forces That Shape
    Our Decisions*, HarperCollins.
8   Melissa Bateson, Daniel Nettle, & Gilbert Roberts (2006) Cues of Being
    Watched Enhance Cooperation in a Real-World Setting, *Biology Letters*,
    http://www.ncbi.nlm.nih.gov/pmc/articles/PMC1686213/.
9   Avi Persaud & John Plender (2007) *Ethics and Finance*, Longtail
    Publishing.

CHAPTER 4

1   George Loewenstein & Richard H Thaler (1989) Anomalies:
    Intertemporal Choice, *Journal of Economic Perspectives* 3(4): 181–93;
    George Loewenstein & Drazen Prelec (1989) Anomalies: Intertemporal
    Choice: Evidence and an Interpretation, Russell Sage Foundation work-
    ing paper.
2   George Loewenstein (1988) Frames of Mind in Intertemporal Choice,
    Management Science 34(2): 200–14.
3   The term "discount rate" is sometimes used to mean annual effective
    rate of interest. This approach takes into account that deposits are often
    placed for over a year. In such a case, the nominal value of the deposit
    plus interest after one year is the stated face value of the financial instru-
    ment. Using this definition of discount rate, you get an idea of the pres-
    ent value of future cash. For example, if a bank offers you an interest rate
    of 25 percent and you place $8 in the account, you expect to retrieve $10
    next year. The bank might describe that instrument as a $10 bill with a

discount rate of 20 percent; that is, it will cost you $8 to buy that instrument, which is 20 percent less than the nominal value of the instrument in one year's time. Treasury Bills are usually described in this way. It can be confusing that the same term is used to mean two subtly different things. We suggest for the purposes of reading this book that you park this alternative definition of discount rate and concentrate on the definition we have set out in the main text.

4 Bernard Lietaer (2001) *The Future of Money*, Century.

5 Thomas H. Greco, Jr. (2009) *The End of Money and the Future of Civilisation*, Floris Books.

6 Richard H Thaler & H M Shefrin, An Economic Theory of Self-Control, *Journal of Political Economy* 89(2): 392–406.

7 Deborah M Weiss (1991) Paternalistic Pension Policy: Psychological Evidence and Economic Theory, *University of Chicago Law Review* 58, http://works.bepress.com/deborah_weiss/5/.

8 Brigitte C Madrian & Dennis F O'Shea (2001) The Power of Suggestion: Inertia in 401(K) Participation and Savings Behaviour, *Quarterly Journal of Economics* 116.

9 Richard H Thaler & Shlomo Benartzi (2004) Save More Tomorrow: Using Behavioural Economics to Increase Employee Saving, *Journal of Political Economy* 112.

10 Irving Fisher (1930) *The Theory of Interest*, Macmillan.

11 Sendhil Mullainathan & Elizabeth Koshy (2008) The Psychology of Debt, CAB/CMF Conference on Microfinance, http://www.ifmr.ac.in/cmf/research/dt/CAB_CMF_Conference_Jan2008.pdf.

12 Sendhil Mullainathan (2008) The Psychology of Scarcity (Class 3) and The Irony of Poverty (Class 5), Edge Master Class, http://www.edge.org/ 3rd_culture/thaler_sendhil08/class3.html; http://www.edge.org/3rd_culture/thaler_sendhil08/class5.html.

13 Jerry A Hausman (1979) Individual Discount Rates and the Purchase and Utilization of Energy-Using Durables, *Bell Journal of Economics* 10: 33–54.

14 HM Treasury (2003) *Green Book*, http://www.hm-treasury.gov.uk/d/green_book_complete.pdf.

CHAPTER 5

1 Skilled political philosophers can justify either extreme of the government versus market debate. Interested readers are welcome to refer to John Rawls' classic defense of principles underlying distributive justice, a social contract, and a government role of significant scale, or to Robert Nozick's equally classic book on political philosophy, which only grudgingly permits a minimal role for governments centered around

enforcement of market contracts and protecting citizens from the monopoly of force. John Rawls (1971) *A Theory of Justice*, The Belknap Press of Harvard University Press; Robert Nozick (1974) *Anarchy, State and Utopia*, Blackwell.

2   C Northcote Parkinson (1958) *Parkinson's Law: The Pursuit of Progress*, John Murray, http://www.economist.com/businessfinance/management/displaystory.cfm?story_id=14116121.

3   H R Bowen (1943) The Interpretation of Voting in the Allocation of Economic Resources, *Quarterly Journal of Economics* 58: 27–48; Kenneth J Arrow (1963) *Social Choice and Individual Values*, Yale University Press.

4   John Maynard Keynes (1936) *The General Theory of Employment, Interest and Money*, Macmillan, http://www.scribd.com/doc/11392072/The-General-Theory-of-Employment-Interest-and-Money.

5   Paul Starr (1988) The Meaning of Privatization, *Yale Law and Policy Review* 6: 6–41, http://www.princeton.edu/~starr/meaning.html.

6   Joseph E Stiglitz (2005) The Ethical Economist, review of *The Moral Consequences of Economic Growth* by Benjamin M. Friedman, Knopf, 2005, *Foreign Affairs* Nov/Dec, http://www.foreignaffairs.org/20051101fareviewessay84612/joseph-e-stiglitz/the-ethical-economist.html.

7   Alexander Hamilton, John Jay, & James Madison (1788) *The Federalist Papers*, http://www.gutenberg.org/etext/18.

8   Herman E Daly & John B Cobb, Jr. (1989) *For the Common Good*, Beacon Press.

9   Arian Ward (2000) Getting Strategic Value from Constellations of Communities, *Strategy and Leadership Magazine* 28(2): 4–9.

10 Garrett Hardin (1968) The Tragedy of the Commons, *Science* 162: 1243–8, http://www.garretthardinsociety.org/articles/art_tragedy_of_the_commons.html.

11 Elinor Ostrom (1990) *Governing the Commons: The Evolution of Institutions for Collective Action*, Cambridge University Press.

12 Robert Putnam (2000) *Bowling Alone*, Simon & Schuster.

CHAPTER 6

1   Ori Brafman & Rod Beckstrom (2006) *The Starfish and the Spider: The Unstoppable Power of Leaderless Organizations*, Portfolio Hardcover.

2   InnoCentive, www.innocentive.com.

3   Kiva, www.kiva.org; Zopa, www.zopa.com; Prosper, www.prosper.com.

4   Jagdish Bhagwati (2004) *In Defense of Globalization*, Oxford University Press.

Notes

5   The Economist (2003) The Case for Capital Controls, *The Economist* May.

6   John Plender (2003) *Going off the Rails: Global Capital and the Crisis of Legitimacy*, John Wiley.

7   Manuel Castells (1996) *The Rise of the Network Society: The Information Age*, Economy, Society and Culture Volume One, Blackwell.

8   International Monetary Fund, Globalization, http://www.imf.org/external/np/exr/ib/2000/041200.htm.

9   John Kenneth Galbraith (1958) *The Affluent Society*, Hamish Hamilton.

10 Joseph Stiglitz (2002) *Globalization and Its Discontents*, Penguin.

11 World Conservation Union (2006) The Future of Sustainability: Re-thinking Environment and Development in the Twenty-first Century, 2006, http://cmsdata.iucn.org/downloads/iucn_future_of_sustanability.pdf.

12 Mark Granovetter (1973) The Strength of Weak Ties, *American Journal of Sociology* 78(6): 1360–80, http://www.stanford.edu/dept/soc/people/mgranovetter/documents/granstrengthweakties.pdf.

13 Malcolm Gladwell (2000) *The Tipping Point: How Little Things Can Make a Big Difference*, Little Brown.

14 Karl Polanyi (1957) *The Great Transformation*, Beacon Press.

15 Michael Wolff (1998) *Burn Rate: How I Survived the Gold Rush Years on the Internet*, Weidenfeld & Nicholson.

16 Yochai Benkler (2006) *The Wealth of Networks: How Social Production Transforms Markets and Freedom*, Yale University Press.

17 Robert Jensen (2007) The Digital Provide: Information (Technology), Market Performance, and Welfare in the South Indian Fisheries Sector, *Quarterly Journal of Economics* 122(3): 879–924, http://www.mitpressjournals.org/doi/pdf/10.1162/qjec.122.3.879?cookieSet=1.

18 Leonard Waverman, Meloria Meschi, & Melvyn Fuss (2005) The Impact of Telecoms on Economic Growth in Developing Countries, Vodafone Policy Paper Series 2, http://web.si.umich.edu/tprc/papers/2005/450/L%20Waverman-%20Telecoms%20Growth%20in%20Dev.%20Countries.pdf.

19 Reuters (2008) Bahaba Fish Story, Anglers Let Big Cash Bonanza Get Away, Reuters, 25 April, http://www.reuters.com/article/oddlyEnoughNews/idUSHAR55771320080425.

20 David Boyle (1999) *Funny Money: In Search of Alternative Cash*, HarperCollins.

21 Schumacher Society, www.smallisbeautiful.org; New Economics Institute, http://neweconomicsinstitute.org.

22 Bernard Lietaer (2001) *The Future of Money*, Century.

23 Ian Angell (2000) *The New Barbarian Manifesto: How to Survive the Information Age*, Kogan Page.

CHAPTER 7

1　http://www.america.gov/publications/books/the-constitution.html.
2　Warren E Buffett (1996) An Owner's Manual for Berkshire's Class A and Class B Shareholders, Berkshire Hathaway, June.
3　Michael E McIntyre (2000) Audit, Education, and Goodhart's Law, Or, Taking Rigidity Seriously, http://www.atm.damtp.cam.ac.uk/mcintyre/papers/LHCE/dilnot-analysis.html.
4　Robert Mundell (1998) *Uses and Abuses of Gresham's Law in the History of Money*, Columbia University, http://www.columbia.edu/~ram15/grash.html.
5　Bank of England, Inflation Report Fan Charts, published quarterly, http://www.bankofengland.co.uk/publications/inflationreport/irfanch.htm.
6　Thomas L. Griffiths & Joshua B. Tenenbaum (2006) Optimal Predictions in Everyday Cognition, *Psychological Science* 17(9), http://web.mit.edu/cocosci/Papers/Griffiths-Tenenbaum-PsychSci06.pdf.
7　Thomas H Davenport & Jeanne G Harris (2007) *Competing on Analytics: The New Science of Winning*, Harvard Business School Press.
8　Jeffrey Zaslow (2002) If TiVo Thinks You Are Gay, Here's How to Set It Straight, *Wall Street Journal* 26 November, http://www.mail-archive.com/eristocracy@merrymeet.com/msg00148.html.
9　Dan Schafer (2006) Statistical Literacy for Efficient Citizenship, http://www.statlit.org/pdf/2006SchaferBlog0927.pdf.
10　University of Iowa, Electronic Markets, http://www.biz.uiowa.edu/iem/.
11　Roman Frydman & Michael Goldberg (2007) *Imperfect Knowledge Economics: Exchange Rates and Risk*, Princeton University Press.

CHAPTER 8

1　Gwilym M Jenkins (1969) The Systems Approach, *Journal of Systems Engineering* 1(1).
2　Edgar E Peters (1991) *Chaos and Order in the Capital Markets: A New View of Cycles, Prices, and Market Volatility*, John Wiley.
3　Benoît B Mandelbrot (1977) *The Fractal Geometry of Nature*, W H Freeman.
4　Benoît B Mandelbrot & Richard L Hudson (2004) *The (Mis)behaviour of Markets: A Fractal View of Risk, Ruin and Reward*, Profile.
5　Paul de Grauwe & Kris Vansenten (1990) Deterministic Chaos in the Foreign Exchange Market, Center for Economic Policy Research, Discussion Paper No. 370, January.
6　David Deutsch (1997) *The Fabric of Reality*, Penguin.
7　Albert Einstein (1941) Science, Philosophy and Religion, A Symposium, New York, http://www.update.uu.se/~fbendz/library/ae_scire.htm.

8   Ikujiro Nonaka (2001) *Managing Industrial Knowledge: Creation, Transfer and Utilization: New Perspectives on Knowledge-based Firms*, Sage.

9   Bryan Bennett & Negley Harte (eds) (1997) *The Crabtree Orations 1954–1994*, Crabtree Foundation.

10 William A Sherden (1998) *The Fortune Sellers*, John Wiley.

11 John Allen Paulos (1991) *Beyond Numeracy*, Penguin.

12 Karl R Popper (1957) *The Poverty of Historicism*, Beacon Press.

13 John Maynard Keynes (1936) *General Theory of Employment, Interest and Money*, Palgrave Macmillan.

14 James Surowiecki (2004) *The Wisdom of Crowds: Why the Many Are Smarter than the Few*, Little, Brown.

15 Moisés Naim (2005) Dangerously Unique, *Foreign Policy*, http://www.freemarketfoundation.com/ShowArticle.asp?ArticleType= Issue&ArticleId=2064.

CHAPTER 9

1   Robert Jensen (2007) The Digital Provide: Information (Technology), Market Performance, and Welfare in the South Indian Fisheries Sector, *Quarterly Journal of Economics* 122(3): 879–924, http://www.mit-pressjournals.org/doi/pdf/10.1162/qjec.122.3.879?cookieSet=1.

2   Peter L Bernstein (1996) *Against the Gods: The Remarkable Story of Risk*, John Wiley.

3   Fisher Black & Myron Scholes (1973) The Pricing of Options and Corporate Liabilities, *Journal of Political Economy* 81(3): 637–54.

4   The Economist (1999) The Foresight Saga, *The Economist*, 16 December, http://www.economist.com/displaystory.cfm?story_id=268876.

5   Ian Harris, Michael Mainelli, & Mary O'Callaghan (2002) Evidence of Worth in Not-for-Profit Sector Organizations, *Journal of Strategic Change* 11(8): 399–410, http://www.zyen.com/index.php/knowledge/ index.php?option=com_content&view=article&id=135.

6   The Economist (2001) Fishy Maths, *The Economist*, 18 August, http://www.economist.com/businessfinance/displaystory.cfm?story_id =E1_SPJGPT.

7   Michael Mainelli & Bob Giffords (2009) The Road to Long Finance, Centre for the Study of Financial Innovation, http://www.longfinance.net/LongFinance/Road%20to%20Long%20 Finance.pdf.

8   Michael A. Nystrom (2007) Global Liquidity Defined, BullNotBull.com, 3 August, http://www.financialsense.com/fsu/editori-als/nystrom/2007/ 0803.html.

9   Maureen O'Hara (2004) Liquidity and Financial Market Stability,

National Bank of Belgium Working Paper No. 55, May,
http://www.bnb.be/doc/ts/publications/WP/WP55En.pdf.

10 Andrew W Lo, Harry Mamaysky, & Jiang Wang (2001) Asset Prices and Trading
Volume under Fixed Transactions Costs, EFA 2001 Barcelona Meetings; Yale
ICF Working Paper, http://ideas.repec.org/p/ysm/somwrk/ysm188.html.

11 Christopher Brown-Humes (2007) Room for Manoeuvre, *Securities &
Investment Review*, Securities & Investment Institute, July.

12 Avinash Persaud (2002) Liqudity Black Holes, World Institute for
Development Economics Research, Discussion Paper 2002/31, March,
http://www.wider.unu.edu/stc/repec/pdfs/rp2002/dp2002-31.pdf.

13 William H Janeway (2006) Risk versus Uncertainty: Frank Knight's
"Brute" Facts of Economic Life, Social Science Research Council,
http://privatizationofrisk.ssrc.org/Janeway/.

14 Mark Carlson (2007) A Brief History of the 1987 Stock Market Crash
with a Discussion of the Federal Reserve Response, Federal Reserve
Board, 2007-13,
http://www.federalreserve.gov/Pubs/Feds/2007/200713/200713pap.pdf.

15 Bernard Lietaer (2001) *The Future of Money: Creating New Wealth, Work
and a Wiser World*, Century.

CHAPTER 10

1 George A Akerlof (1970) The Market for "Lemons": Quality
Uncertainty and the Market Mechanism, *Quarterly Journal of Economics*
84(3): 488–500.

2 Kenneth J Arrow (1963) Uncertainty and the Welfare Economics of
Health Care, *American Economic Review* 53(5): 941–73,
http://www.uofaweb.ualberta.ca/economics/pdfs/Econ699A2-F07-
RuseskiJ-Uncertainty-&-Welfare-Econ-of-Med-Care.pdf.

3 George J Stigler (1961) The Economics of Information, *Journal of
Political Economy* 69(3): 213–25,
http://zaphod.mindlab.umd.edu/docSeminar/pdfs/1829263.pdf.

4 Joseph Stiglitz & Andrew Weiss (1981) Credit Rationing in Markets
with Imperfect Information, *American Economic Review* 71(3): 393–410,
http://qed.econ.queensu.ca/pub/faculty/lloyd-ellis/econ835/readings/stiglitz.pdf.

5 Michael Spence (1973) Job Market Signaling, *Quarterly Journal of
Economics* 87(3): 355–74.

6 George Campbell Macaulay (trans.) *The History of Herodotus*, Volume I,
Book IV, Section 196, http://www.gutenberg.org/etext/2707.

7 Peter L Bernstein (2000) *The Power of Gold: The History of an
Obsession*, John Wiley.

8 Claude E Shannon (1948) A Mathematical Theory of Communication,
Bell System Technical Journal 27: 379–423, 623–56, http://cm.bell-
labs.com/cm/ms/what/shannonday/shannon1948.pdf.

Notes

9 Stephen W Littlejohn (1983) *Theories of Human Communication*, Wadsworth.

10 Harold Innis (1950) *Empire and Communications*, Oxford University Press.

11 Marshall McLuhan (1964) *Understanding Media: The Extension of Man*, Gingko Press.

12 William Henry Furness (1910) *The Island of Stone Money: Uap and the Carolines*, J B Lippincott, http://www.ethnomath.org/resources/furness1910.pdf.

13 Cora Lee C Gilliland (1975) *The Stone Money of Yap: A Numismatic Survey*, Smithsonian Institution Press.

14 Milton Friedman (1991) The Island of Stone Money, The Hoover Institution, Working Papers in Economics E-91-3, http://hoohila.stanford.edu/workingpapers/getWorkingPaper.php?filename=E-91-3.pdf.

15 John Maynard Keynes (1931) *Essays in Persuasion*, Macmillan.

16 Adam Smith (1776) *An Inquiry into the Nature and Causes of the Wealth of Nations*, http://www.bibliomania.com/2/1/65/112/frameset.html.

17 Karl Marx (1865) *Value, Price and Profit*, http://www.marxists.org/archive/marx/works/1865/value-price-profit/index.htm.

18 Sushil Bikhandani, David Hirshleifer, & Ivo Welch (1992) A Theory of Fads, Fashion, Custom, and Cultural Change as Informational Cascades, *Journal of Political Economy* 100(5): 992–1026.

19 Donald Cox (2003) The Economics of "Believe It or Not," 4 August, http://www.econlib.org/library/Columns/y2003/Coxbelieve.html.

20 Fred Hirsch (1976) *The Social Limits to Growth*, Harvard University Press.

21 Ed Smith (2008) *What Sport Tells Us about Life: Bradman's Average, Zidane's Kiss and Other Sporting Lessons*, Viking.

22 Gerald R Musgrave (2006) John Bogle's Views on Executive Compensation, *Business Economics* April, http://findarticles.com/p/articles/mi_m1094/is_2_41/ai_n16675914.

CHAPTER 11

1 Michael E Porter (1990) *The Competitive Advantage of Nations*, Free Press.

2 Joseph A Schumpeter (1912) *The Theory of Economic Development*, Social Science Classics Series.

3 OECD (2005) Oslo Manual: Proposed Guidelines for Collecting and Interpreting Technological Innovation Data, http://www.oecd.org/dataoecd/35/61/2367580.pdf.

4 Patricia B. Seybold (2006) *Outside Innovation: How Your Customers Will Co-Design Your Company's Future*, HarperCollins.

5 Herman Melville (1850) *Hawthorne and His Mosses*, Literary World.

6 Arthur Koestler (1967) *The Ghost in the Machine*, Penguin.

7 Richard Dawkins (1976) *The Selfish Gene*, Oxford University Press.

8 Alain Marciano (2006) Economists on Darwin's Theory of Social Evolution and Human Behaviour, Max Plank Institute of Economics, http://ssrn.com/abstract=673061.

9 Richard Dawkins (1976) *The Selfish Gene*, Oxford University Press.

10 Fremont E Kast & James E Rosenzweig (1981) *The Modern View: A Systems Approach in Systems Behaviour*, Open Systems Group.

11 Terence Kealey (1996) *The Economic Laws of Scientific Research*, Macmillan.

12 William A Sherden (1998) *The Fortune Sellers*, John Wiley.

13 William Ross Ashby (1983) Self-Regulation and Requisite Variety, in Fred Emery (ed.), *Systems Thinking*, Penguin.

14 Michael Mainelli & Stephen Pumphrey (2002) Optimising Risk/Reward in High Ratio Relationships: Jumbo Bonsai Meets Pocket Battleship, *Journal of Change Management* 2(3), 7–20.

15 Peter Drucker (2001) A Survey of the Near Future, *The Economist* November.

16 Robert I Sutton (2001) *Weird Ideas That Work: 11½ Ways for Promoting, Managing and Sustaining Innovation*, Free Press.

17 The Economist (2002) Re-engineering in Real Time, *The Economist* January.

18 The Economist (2006) Searching for the Invisible Man, *The Economist* March.

19 G M P Swann (2000) The Economics of Standardisation: Final Report for Standards and Technical Regulations Directorate, Department of Trade and Industry, London, http://www.dti.gov.uk/files/file11312.pdf.

20 Bill Bryson (1998) *Made in America*, Black Swan.

21 European Interoperability Framework for pan-European eGovernment Services, Version 1.0, 2004, http://www.apdip.net/projects/gif/country/EU-GIF.pdf.

CHAPTER 12

1 Paul R Ehrlich & John P Holdren (1971) Impact of Population Growth, *Science* 171: 1212–17; Barry Commoner (1972) The Environmental Cost of Economic Growth, *Population, Resources and the Environment*, Government Printing Office, pp. 339–63.

2 IPCC (2001) *Special Report on Emissions Scenarios: A Special Report of Working Group III of the Intergovernmental Panel on Climate Change*, Cambridge University Press, http://www.grida.no/publications/other/ipcc_sr/?src=/climate/ipcc/emission/050.htm.

Notes

3   Martha M Campbell (2005) Why the Silence on Population?, Keynote Address to Population and Sustainability Network: Population Increase: A Universal Threat? What Is the Role of Europe?, London School of Hygiene and Tropical Medicine, 13 October, http://www.populationand-sustainability.org/download.php?id=8.

4   Bruce Lloyd (2008) *What Do We Really Mean by "Sustainable"?*, World Future Society, http://www.wfs.org/lloyd08.htm.

5   One Planet Living, http://www.oneplanetliving.org/index.html.

6   Herman Daly (1994) World Bank Departure Speech, 14 January, http://www.whirledbank.org/ourwords/daly.html.

7   Paul Ekins (2000) *Economic Growth and Environmental Sustainability: The Prospects for Green Growth*, Routledge.

8   Stewart Brand (2009) *Whole Earth Discipline*, Viking Books; summary taken from Rethinking Green, The Long Now Foundation via ForaTV, http://fora.tv/2009/10/09/Stewart_Brand_Rethinking_Green.

9   Forum for the Future (Alice Chapple and others) (2007) Investments to Combat Climate Change: Exploring the Sustainable Solutions, The London Accord, Chapter D3, City of London Corporation, November, http://www.london-accord.co.uk/images/reports/pdf/d3.pdf.

10 Gro Harlem Brundtland (Chair) (1987) *Our Common Future: Report of the Brundtland Commission*, Oxford University Press, http://www.worldinbalance.net/pdf/1987-brundtland.pdf.

11 G Heal & H Kunreuther (2002) You Can Only Die Once: Public–Private Partnerships for Managing the Risks of Extreme Events, white paper for conference on Risk Management Strategies in an Uncertain World, Palisades, New York, http://www2.gsb.columbia.edu/faculty/gheal/General%20Interest%20Papers/onlydieonce.pdf.

12 Horst W J Rittel & Melvin M Webber (1973) *Dilemmas in a General Theory of Planning*, Policy Sciences 4, Elsevier, pp 155–69, http://www.uctc.net/mwebber/Rittel+Webber+Dilemmas+General_Theory_of_Planning.pdf.

13 Muhammad Yunus (2007) *Creating a World without Poverty: Social Business and the Future of Capitalism*, PublicAffairs.

14 World Bank and Food & Agriculture Organization (2009) The Sunken Billions: The Economic Justification for Fisheries Reform, http://siteresources.worldbank.org/EXTARD/Resources/336681-1224775570533/SunkenBillionsFinal.pdf.

15 Charles Clover (2004) *The End of the Line: How Overfishing Is Changing the World and What We Eat*, Ebury Press.

16 Paul Collier (2007) *The Bottom Billion: Why the Poorest Countries Are Failing and What Can Be Done about It*, Oxford University Press.

17 Jeffrey Sachs (2008) *Common Wealth: Economics for a Crowded Planet*, Allen Lane.

CHAPTER 13

1 Edward Wilson (1998) *Consilience*, Alfred A. Knopf.

2 Jean-François Rischard (2002) *High Noon: Twenty Global Problems, Twenty Years to Solve Them*, Basic Books.

3 Nassim Nicholas Taleb (2007) *The Black Swan: The Impact of the Highly Improbable*, Allen Lane.

4 John Smithin (2009) *Money, Enterprise and Income Distribution*, Routledge.

5 Adam Smith (1776) *An Inquiry into the Nature and Causes of the Wealth of Nations*, http://www.bibliomania.com/2/1/65/112/frameset.html.

6 Muhammad Yunus (2007) *Creating a World without Poverty: Social Business and the Future of Capitalism*, PublicAffairs.

7 Malcolm Cooper (2010) *In Search of the Eternal Coin: A Long Finance View of History*, Long Finance.

8 PricewaterhouseCoopers (2007) Global Risk, Reward, Business and Society: Collaborate or Collapse? Briefing Paper, PricewaterhouseCoopers.

9 Thomas Babington Macaulay (1825) Essay on Milton, *Edinburgh Review*, http://www.gutenberg.org/ebooks/2332.

10 John Brockman (1996) *Digerati: Encounters with the Cyber Elite*, HardWired Books, http://www.edge.org/documents/digerati/Lanier.html.

11 The Long Now, www.longnow.org.

12 Sendhil Mullainathan & Elizabeth Koshy (2008) The Psychology of Debt, CAB/CMF Conference on Microfinance, http://www.ifmr.ac.in/cmf/research/dt/CAB_CMF_Conference_Jan2008.pdf; Sendhil Mullainathan (2008) The Psychology of Scarcity (Class 3) and The Irony of Poverty (Class 5), Edge Master Class, http://www.edge.org/ 3rd_culture/thaler_sendhil08/class3.html; http://www.edge.org/3rd_culture/thaler_sendhil08/class5.html.

13 Ernst Friedrich Schumacher (1973) *Small Is Beautiful*, Blond & Briggs.

INDEX

Index